DOCUMENTS OF BLACK CONNECTICUT

FIVE BLACK LIVES

FIVE BLACK LIVES

THE AUTOBIOGRAPHIES OF

Venture Smith • James Mars • William Grimes

The Rev. G. W. Offley • James L. Smith

Introduction by

ARNA BONTEMPS

Wesleyan University Press

MIDDLETOWN, CONNECTICUT

ISBN : 0-8195-4036-6
Library of Congress Catalog Card Number : 74-108647
Manufactured in the United States of America
First edition

CONTENTS

INTRODUCTION

SOME slave narratives resemble novels, some favor short stories, some remind us of the as-told-to or ghost-written accounts of personal experiences or adventures found in so many books and magazines today. Some slave narratives, on the other hand, are recognizable autobiographies of survivors of the "peculiar institution," written in their own hands after the individuals had found places of refuge and/or homes in the land of promise, so to speak. The narratives included in the present collection are of this kind.

They are, so far as I am aware, with one notable exception, the only autobiographies of ex-slaves living in Connecticut and recalling their deliverance in the years between 1729 and 1870 to be found in the libraries or other public collections in the state. For reasons related to other publishing plans the J. W. C. Pennington narrative, the exception, is not included.

Copies of the original editions of all these printed autobiographies of the former slaves are, of course, rare today. One such copy, as it happens, was reposing quietly in one of the libraries at Yale University when the present publication was first planned. The other four were found in the collection of the Connecticut Historical Society. All are authentic copies. All are intrinsically priceless in view of everything that has happened in the century and more since they were published, in view of the literature which, directly or indirectly, their fevered accounts influenced.

These memoirs of deliverance from captivity and bondage have turned out to be more durable than anyone anticipated, however. Extremely popular during the antislavery campaign, their appeal seemed only slightly diminished in the decades immediately following. Then it was that efforts to distort or even erase from memory the black experience became vigorous.

Charles E. Tuttle, a dealer in old books, has told how as a boy he had noticed that copies of these memoirs of ex-slaves were gradually becoming scarce. By the time of the Harlem Renaissance of the 1920's, when requests for them suddenly increased in number, copies were definitely hard to find. This aroused two zealous collectors, one black, Arthur Schomburg, and one white, Arthur Spingarn, and Tuttle set out to assist them in a search. In the end the two collectors became friendly rivals and raced each other back and forth across the country and across the Atlantic to see what they could find in out-of-the-way places. Eventually both planted the seeds of special collections that now bear their names.

Even so, it took another half-century for their zeal to trickle down to a public large enough to warrant the reissue of the more significant of these memoirs. Tuttle, Schomburg, and Spingarn have accounted in different ways for the fire that ignited their similar quests, but somehow each seemed to sense a relevance in these memoirs that he could not bring himself to dismiss. Today those voices out of bondage seem to transmit what is now meant by "soul."

More scholarly interest may be attracted by the range of black experience in the South and in the North as recorded in these writings. Venture Smith, for example, goes to a magistrate and complains and gets a hearing after being mistreated by his owner. James L. Smith, on the other hand, tells how he was beaten almost at will by his master. One of the narrators is restless and never quite able to settle down to anything. Another plants himself in Norwich and remains. If there was any one life style resulting from the transition from bondage to freedom, these personal histories do not seem to show it.

What does come clear is a universal human need, a will to freedom.

—ARNA BONTEMPS

New Haven, Connecticut
April 1971

A NARRATIVE

—OF THE—

LIFE AND ADVENTURES

—OF—

VENTURE

A NATIVE OF AFRICA,

But Resident Above Sixty Years in the United States of America.

RELATED BY HIMSELF.

New London: Printed in 1798. Reprinted A. D. 1835, and Published by a Descendant of Venture.

Revised and Republished with Traditions by H. M. SELDEN, Haddam, Conn., 1896.

MIDDLETOWN, CONN. :
J. S. STEWART, PRINTER AND BOOKBINDER.
1897.

Publisher's Note: As is apparent from the preceding title page, the text of Venture Smith's autobiography is reproduced here not from the edition of 1798, but from the reprinting of 1896. The special value of this later edition lies in its additional materials (pages 26-34 herein), which set forth further facts about and impressions of Venture and his family, drawn from the memories of neighbors who had known him in his old age and from a still lively oral tradition.

PREFACE.

THE following account of the life of VENTURE is a relation of simple facts, in which nothing is added in substance to what he related himself. Many other interesting and curious passages of his life might have been inserted, but on account of the bulk to which they must necessarily have swelled this narrative, they were omitted. If any should suspect the truth of what is here related, they are referred to people now living who are acquainted with most of the facts mentioned in the narrative.

The reader is here presented with an account, not of a renowned politician or warrior, but of an untutored slave, brought into this Christian country at eight years of age, wholly destitute of all education but what he received in common with domesticated animals, enjoying no advantages that could lead him to suppose himself superior to the beasts, his fellow-servants. And, if he shall derive no other advantage from perusing this narrative, he may experience those sensations of shame and indignation that will prove him to be not wholly destitute of every noble and generous feeling.

The subject of the following pages, had he received only a common education, might have been a man of high respectability and usefulness; and had his education been suited to his genius, he might have been an ornament and an honor to human nature. It may, perhaps, not be unpleasing to see the efforts of a great mind wholly uncultivated, enfeebled and depressed by slavery, and struggling under every disadvantage. The reader may here see a Franklin and a Washington, in a state of nature, or, rather, in a state of slavery. Destitute as he is of all education, and broken by hardships and infirmities of age, he still exhibits striking traces of native ingenuity and good sense.

This narrative exhibits a pattern of honesty, prudence and industry to people of his own color; and perhaps some white people would not find themselves degraded by imitating such an example.

The following account is published in compliance with the earnest desire of the subject of it, and likewise a number of respectable persons who are acquainted with him.

NARRATIVE OF LIFE OF VENTURE.

CHAPTER 1.

CONTAINING AN ACCOUNT OF HIS LIFE, FROM HIS BIRTH TO THE TIME OF HIS LEAVING HIS NATIVE COUNTRY.

I WAS born at Dukandarra, in Guinea, about the year 1729. My father's name was Saungm Furro, Prince of the tribe of Dukandarra. My father had three wives. Polygamy was not uncommon in that country, especially among the rich, as every man was allowed to keep as many wives as he could maintain. By his first wife he had three children. The eldest of them was myself, named by my father, Broteer. The other two were named Cundazo and Soozaduka. My father had two children by his second wife, and one by his third. I descended from a very large, tall and stout race of beings, much larger than the generality of people in other parts of the globe, being commonly considerable above six feet in height, and every way well proportioned.

The first thing worthy of notice which I remember, was a contention between my father and mother, on account of my father marrying his third wife without the consent of his first and eldest, which was contrary to the custom generally observed among my countrymen. In consequence of this rupture, my mother left her husband and country, and travelled away with her three children to the eastward. I was then five years old. She took not the least sustenance along with her, to support either herself or children. I was able to travel along by her side; the other two of her offspring she carried, one on her back, the other, being a sucking child, in her arms. When we became hungry, our mother used to set us down on the ground and gather some of the fruits that grew spontaneously in that climate. These served us for food on the way. At night we all lay down together in the most secure place we could find and reposed ourselves until morning. Though there were many noxious animals there, yet so kind was our Almighty protector that none of them were ever permitted to hurt or molest us.

Thus we went on our journey until the second day after our departure from Dukandarra, when we came to the entrance of a great desert. During our travel in that, we were often affrighted with the doleful howlings and yellings of wolves, lions and other animals. After five days' travel we came to the end of this desert, and immediately entered into a beautiful and extensive interval country. Here my mother was pleased to stop and seek a refuge for me. She left me at the house of a very rich farmer. I was then, as I should judge, not less than one hundred and forty miles from my native place, separated from all my relatives and acquaintances. At this place, my mother took her farewell of me and set out for her own country. My new guardian, as I shall call the man with whom I was left, put me into the business of tending sheep immediately after I was left with him. The flock, which I kept with the assistance of a boy, consisted of about forty. We drove them every morning between two and three miles to pasture, into the wide and delightful plains. When night drew on, we drove them home and secured them in the cote. In this round I continued during my stay here. One incident which befel me when I was driving my flock from pasture, was so dreadful to me at that age, and is to this time so fresh in my memory, that I cannot help noticing it in this place. Two large dogs sallied out of a certain house and set upon me. One of them took me by the arm and the other by the thigh, and before their master could come and relieve me, they lacerated my flesh to such a degree that the scars are very visible to the present day. My master was immediately sent for. He came and carried me home, as I was unable to go myself on account of my wounds. Nothing remarkable happened afterwards until my father sent for me to return home.

Before I dismiss this country, I must first inform my reader what I remember concerning this place. A large river runs through this country in a westerly course. The land for a great way on each side is flat and level, hedged in by a considerable rise in the country at a great distance from it. It scarce ever rains there, yet the land is fertile; great dews fall in the night which refresh the soil. About the latter end of June or first of July, the river begins to rise, and gradually increases until it has inundated the country for a great distance, to the height of seven or eight feet. This brings on a slime which enriches the land surprisingly. When the river has subsided, the natives begin to sow and plant, and the vegetation is exceeding rapid. Near this rich river my guardian's land lay. He possessed, I cannot exactly tell how much, yet this I am certain of respecting it, that he owned an immense tract. He possessed likewise a great many cattle and goats. During my stay with him I was kindly used, and with as much tenderness, for what I saw, as his only son, although I was an entire stranger to him, remote from friends and relatives. The principal occupations of the inhabitants there were the cultivation of the soil and the care of their flocks. They were a people pretty similar in every respect to that of mine, except in their persons, which were not so tall and stout. They appeared to be very kind and friendly. I will now return to my departure from that place.

My father sent a man and horse after me. After settling with my guardian for keeping me, he took me away and went for home. It was then about one year since my mother brought me here. Nothing remarkable occurred to us on our journey until we arrived safe home. I found then that the difference between my parents had been made up previous to their sending for me. On my return, I was received both by my father and mother with great joy and affection, and was once more restored to my paternal dwelling in peace and happiness. I was then about six years old.

Not more than six weeks had passed after my return, before a message was brought by an inhabitant of the place where I lived the preceding year to my father, that that place had been invaded by a numerous army, from a nation not far distant, furnished with musical instruments, and all kinds of arms then in use; that they were instigated by some white nation who equipped and sent them to subdue and possess the country; that his nation had made no preparation for war, having been for a long time in profound peace; that they could not defend themselves against such a formidable train of invaders, and must, therefore, necessarily evacuate their lands to the fierce enemy, and fly to the protection of some chief; and that if he would permit them they would come under his rule and protection when they had to retreat from their own possessions. He was a kind and merciful prince, and therefore consented to these proposals.

He had scarcely returned to his nation with the message before the whole of his people were obligated to retreat from their country and come to my father's dominions. He gave them every privilege and all the protection his government could afford. But they had not been there longer than four days before news came to them that the invaders had laid waste their country, and were coming speedily to destroy them in my father's territories. This affrighted them, and therefore they immediately pushed off to the southward, into the unknown countries there, and were never more heard of.

Two days after their retreat, the report turned out to be but too true. A detachment from the enemy came to my father and informed him that the whole army was encamped not far from his dominions, and would invade the territory and deprive his people of their liberties and rights, if he did not comply with the following terms. These were, to pay them a large sum of money, three hundred fat cattle, and a great number of goats, sheep, asses, etc.

My father told the messenger he would comply rather than that his subjects should be deprived of their rights and privileges, which he was not then in circumstances to defend from so sudden an invasion. Upon turning out those articles, the enemy pledged their faith and honor that they would not attack him. On these he relied, and therefore thought it unnecessary to be on his guard against the enemy. But their pledges of faith and honor proved no better than those of other unprincipled hostile nations, for a few days after, a certain relation of the king came and informed him that the enemy who sent terms of accommodation to him, and received tribute to their satisfaction, yet meditated an attack upon his subjects by surprise, and that probably they would commence their attack in less than one day, and concluded with advising him, as he was not prepared for war, to order a speedy retreat of his family and subjects. He complied with this advice.

The same night which was fixed upon to retreat, my father and his family set off about the break of day. The king and his two younger wives went in one company, and my mother and her children in another. We left our dwellings in succession, and my father's company went on first. We directed our course for a large shrub plain, some distance off, where we intended to conceal ourselves from the approaching enemy, until we could refresh ourselves a little. But we presently found that our retreat was not secure. For having struck up a little fire for the purpose of cooking victuals, the enemy, who happened to be encamped a little distance off, had sent out a scouting party who discovered us by the smoke of the fire, just as we were extinguishing it and about to eat. As soon as we had finished eating, my father discovered the party and immediately began to discharge arrows at them. This was what I first saw, and it alarmed both me and the women, who, being unable to make any resistance immediately betook ourselves to the tall, thick reeds not far off, and left the old king to fight alone. For some time I beheld him from the reeds defending himself with great courage and firmness, till at last he was obliged to surrender himself into their hands.

They then came to us in the reeds, and the very first salute I had from them was a violent blow on the head with the fore part of a gun, and at the same time a grasp around the neck. I then had a rope put about my neck, as all the women in the thicket with me, and were immediately led to my father, who was likewise pinioned and haltered for leading. In this condition we were all led to the camp. The women and myself, being submissive, had tolerable treatment from the enemy, while my father was closely interrogated respecting his money, which they knew he must have. But as he gave them no account of it, he was instantly cut and pounded on his body with great inhumanity, that he might be induced by the torture he suffered to make the discovery. All this availed not in the least to make him give up his money, but he despised all the tortures which they inflicted, until the continued exercise and increase of torment obliged him to sink and expire. He thus died without informing his enemies where his money lay. I saw him while he was thus tortured to death. The shocking scene is to this day fresh in my memory, and I have often been overcome while thinking on it. He was a man of remarkable stature. I should judge as much as six feet and six or seven inches high, two feet across the shoulders, and every way well proportioned. He was a man of remarkable strength and resolution, affable, kind and gentle, ruling with equity and moderation.

The army of the enemy was large, I should suppose consisting of about six thousand men. Their leader was called Baukurre. After destroying the old prince, they decamped and immediately marched towards the sea, lying to the west, taking with them myself and the women prisoners. In the march, a scouting party was detached from the main army. To the leader of this party I was made waiter, having to carry his gun, etc. As we were a-scouting, we came across a herd of fat cattle consisting of about thirty in number. These we set upon and immediately wrested from their keepers, and afterwards converted them into food for the army. The enemy had remarkable success in destroying the country wherever they went. For as far as they had penetrated they laid the habitations waste and captured the people. The distance they had now brought me was about four hundred miles. All the march I had very hard tasks imposed on me, which I must perform on pain of punishment. I was obliged to carry on my head a large flat stone used for grinding our corn, weighing, as I should suppose, as much as twenty-five pounds; besides victuals, mat and cooking utensils. Though I was pretty large and stout of my age, yet these burdens were very grievous to me, being only six years and a half old.

We were then come to a place called Malagasco. When we entered the place, we could not see the least appearance of either house or inhabitants, but on stricter search found that instead of houses above ground they had dens in the sides of hillocks, contiguous to ponds and streams of water. In these we perceived they had all hid themselves, as I suppose they usually did on such occasions. In order to compel them to surrender, the enemy contrived to smoke them out with faggots. These they put to the entrance of the caves and set them on fire. While they were engaged in this business, to their great surprise some of them were desperately wounded with arrows which fell from above on them. This mystery they soon found out. They perceived that the enemy discharged these arrows through holes on the top of the dens directly into the air. Their weight brought them back, point downwards, on their enemies heads, whilst they were smoking the inhabitants out. The points of their arrows were poisoned, but their enemy had an antidote for it which they instantly applied to the wounded part. The smoke at last obliged the people to give themselves up. They came out of their caves, first spatting the palms of their hands together, and immediately after extended their arms, crossed at their wrists, ready to be bound and pinioned. I should judge that the dens above mentioned were extended about eight feet horizontally into the earth, six feet in height, and as many wide. They were arched overhead and lined with earth, which was of the clay kind and made the surface of their walls firm and smooth.

The invaders then pinioned the prisoners of all ages and sexes indiscriminately, took their flocks and all their effects, and moved on their way towards the sea. On the march, the prisoners were treated with clemency, on account of their being submissive and humble. Having come to the next tribe, the enemy laid siege and immediately took men, women, children, flocks, and all their valuable effects. They then went on to the next district, which was contiguous to the sea, called in Africa, Anamaboo. The enemies' provisions were then almost spent, as well as their strength. The inhabitants, knowing what conduct they had pursued, and what were their present intentions, improved the favorable opportunity, attacked them, and took enemy, prisoners, flocks and all their effects. I was then taken a second time. All of us were then put into the castle and kept for market. On a certain time, I and other prisoners were put on board a canoe, under our master, and rowed away to a vessel belonging to Rhode Island, commanded by Captain Collingwood, and the mate, Thomas Mumford. While we were going to the vessel, our master told us to appear to the best possible advantage for sale. I was bought on board by one Robertson Mumford, a steward of said vessel, for four gallons of rum and a piece of calico, and called VENTURE on account of his having purchased me with his own private venture. Thus I came by my name. All the slaves that were bought for that vessel's cargo were two hundred and sixty.

CHAPTER II.

CONTAINING AN ACCOUNT OF HIS LIFE FROM THE TIME OF HIS LEAVING AFRICA TO THAT OF HIS BECOMING FREE.

AFTER all the business was ended on the coast of Africa, the ship sailed from thence to Barbadoes. After an ordinary passage, except great mortality by the small pox, which broke out on board, we arrived at the island of Barbadoes; but when we reached it, there were found, out of the two hundred and sixty that sailed from Africa, not more than two hundred alive. These were all sold, except myself and three more, to the planters there.

The vessel then sailed for Rhose Island, and arrived there after a comfortable passage. Here my master sent me to live with one of his sisters until he could carry me to Fisher's Island, the place of his residence. I had then completed my eighth year. After staying with his sister some time, I was taken to my master's place to live.

When we arrived at Narraganset, my master went ashore in order to return a part of the way by land, and gave me the charge of the keys of his trunks on board of the vessel, and charged me not to deliver them up to anybody, not even to his father, without his orders. To his directions I promised faithfully to conform. When I arrived with my master's articles at his house, my master's father asked me for his son's keys, as he wanted to see what his trunks contained. I told him that my master intrusted me with the care of them until he should return, and that I had given him my word to be faithful to the trust, and could not, therefore, give him, or any other man, the keys without my master's directions. He insisted that I should deliver to him the keys on pain of punishment. But I let him know that he should not have them, let him say what he would. He then laid aside trying to get them. But notwithstanding he appeared to give up trying to obtain them from me, yet I mistrusted that he would take some time when I was off my guard, either in the daytime or at night, to get them, therefore, I slung them round my neck, and in the daytime concealed them in my bosom, and at night I always slept with them under

me, that no person might take them from me without my being apprized
of it. Thus I kept the keys from everybody until my master came home.
When he returned he asked where VENTURE was. As I was within
hearing, I came and said, "Here, sir, at your service." He asked for his
keys, and I immediately took them off my neck and reached them out to
him. He took them, stroked my hair, and commended me, saying in
presence of his father that his young VENTURE was so faithful that he
never would have been able to have taken the keys from him but by
violence; that he should not fear to trust him with his whole fortune, for
that he had been in his native place so habituated to keeping his word, that
he would sacrifice even his life to maintain it.

The first of the time of living at my master's own place, I was pretty
much employed in the house, carding wool and other household business.
In this situation I continued for some years, after which my master put me
to work out of doors. After many proofs of my faithfulness and honesty,
my master began to put great confidence in me. My behavior had as yet
been submissive and obedient. I then began to have hard tasks imposed on
me. Some of these were to pound four bushels of ears of corn every night
in a barrel for the poultry, or be rigorously punished. At other seasons of
the year, I had to card wool until a very late hour. These tasks I had to
perform when only about nine years old. Some time after, I had another
difficulty and oppression which was greater than any I had ever
experienced since I came into this country. This was to serve two masters.
James Mumford, my master's son, when his father had gone from home in
the morning and given me a stint to perform that day, would order me to
do *this* and *that* business different from what my master had directed me.
One day in particular, the authority which my master's son had set up had
like to have produced melancholy effects. For my master having set me off
my business to perform that day and then left me to perform it, his son
came up to me in the course of the day, big with authority, and
commanded me very arrogantly to quit my present business and go
directly about what he should order me. I replied to him that my master
had given me so much to perform that day, and that I must faithfully
complete it in that time. He then broke out into a great rage, snatched a
pitchfork and went to lay me over the head therewith, but I as soon got
another and defended myself with it, or otherwise he might have murdered
me in his outrage. He immediately called some people who were within
hearing at work for him, and ordered them to take his hair rope and come
and bind me with it. They all tried to bind me, but in vain, though there

were three assistants in number. My upstart master then desisted, put his pocket handkerchief before his eyes and went home with a design to tell his mother of the struggle with young VENTURE. He told that their young VENTURE had become so stubborn that he could not control him, and asked her what he should do with him. In the meantime I recovered my temper, voluntarily caused myself to be bound by the same men who tried in vain before, and carried before my young master, that he might do what he pleased with me. He took me to a gallows made for the purpose of hanging cattle on, and suspended me on it. Afterwards he ordered one of his hands to go to the peach orchard and cut him three dozen of whips to punish me with. These were brought to him, and that was all that was done with them, as I was released and went to work after hanging on the gallows about an hour.

After I had lived with my master thirteen years, being then about twenty-two years old, I married Meg, a slave of his who was about my own age. My master owned a certain Irishman, named Heddy, who about that time formed a plan of secretly leaving his master. After he had long had this plan in meditation, he suggested it to me. At first I cast a deaf ear to it, and rebuked Heddy for harboring in his mind such a rash undertaking. But after he had persuaded and much enchanted me with the prospect of gaining my freedom by such a method, I at length agreed to accompany him. Heddy next inveigled two of his fellow-servants to accompany us. The place to which we designed to go was the Mississippi. Our next business was to lay in a sufficient store of provisions for our voyage. We privately collected out of our master's store, six great old cheeses, two firkins of butter, and one batch of new bread. When we had gathered all our own clothes and some more, we took them all about midnight and went to the water side. We stole our master's boat, embarked, and then directed our course for the Mississippi River.

We mutually confederated not to betray or desert one another on pain of death. We first steered our course for Montauk Point, the east end of Long Island. After our arrival there, we landed, and Heddy and I made an incursion into the island after fresh water, while our two comrades were left a little distance from the boat, employed in cooking. When Heddy and I had sought some time for water, he returned to our companions and I continued on looking for my object. When Heddy had performed his business with our companions who were engaged in cooking, he went directly to the boat, stole all the clothes in it, and then travelled away for East Hampton, as I was informed. I returned to my fellows not long after.

They informed me that our clothes were stolen, but could not determine who was the thief, yet they suspected Heddy, as he was missing. After reproving my comrades for not taking care of our things which were in the boat, I advertised Heddy and sent two men in search of him. They pursued and overtook him at Southampton and returned him to the boat. I then thought it might afford some chance for my freedom, or at least be a palliation for my running away, to return Heddy immediately to his master, and inform him that I was induced to go away by Heddy's address. Accordingly, I set off with him and the rest of my companions for my master's, and arrived there without any difficulty. I informed my master that Heddy was the ringleader of our revolt, and that he had used us ill. He immediately put Heddy into custody, and myself and companions were well received and went to work as usual.

Not a long time passed after that before Heddy was sent by my master to New London gaol. At the close of that year I was sold to a Thomas Stanton, and had to be separated from my wife and one daughter, who was about one month old. He resided at Stonington Point. To this place I brought with me from my late master's, two johannes, three old Spanish dollars, and two thousand of coppers, besides five pounds of my wife's money. This money I got by cleaning gentlemen's shoes and drawing-boots, by catching muskrats and minks, raising potatoes and carrots, etc., and by fishing in the night, and at odd spells.

All this money, amounting to near twenty-one pounds York currency, my master's brother, Robert Stanton, hired of me, for which he gave me his note. About a year and a half after that time, my master purchased my wife and her child for seven hundred pounds old tenor. One time my master sent me two miles after a barrel of molasses, and ordered me to carry it on my shoulders. I made out to carry it all the way to my master's house. When I lived with Capt. George Mumford, only to try my strength I took upon my knees a tierce of salt containing seven bushels, and carried it two or three rods. Of this fact there are several eye witnesses now living.

Towards the close of the time I resided with this master, I had a falling out with my mistress. This happened one time when my master was gone to Long Island a-gunning. At first the quarrel began between my wife and her mistress. I was then at work in the barn, and hearing a racket in the house, induced me to run there and see what had broken out. When I entered the house, I found my mistress in a violent passion with my wife, for what she informed me was a mere trifle—such a small affair that I forbear to put my mistress to the shame of having it known. I earnestly requested my wife to beg pardon of her mistress for the sake of peace, even if she had given no just occasion for offence. But whilst I was thus saying, my mistress turned the blows which she was repeating on my wife to me. She took down her horse whip, and while she was glutting her fury with it, I reached out my great black hand, raised it up and received the blows of the whip on it which were designed for my head. Then I immediately committed the whip to the devouring fire.

When my master returned from the island, his wife told him of the affair, but for the present he seemed to take no notice of it, and mentioned not a word of it to me. Some days after his return, in the morning as I was putting on a log in the fireplace, not suspecting harm from any one, I received a most violent stroke on the crown of my head with a club two feet long and as large around as a chair post. This blow very badly wounded my head, and the scar of it remains to this day. The first blow made me have my wits about me as you may suppose, for as soon as he went to renew it I snatched the club out of his hands and dragged him out of the door. He then sent for his brother to come and assist him, but I presently left my master, took the club he wounded me with, carried it to a neighboring justice of the peace, and complained of my master. He finally advised me to return to my master and live contented with him till he abused me again, and then complain. I consented to do accordingly. But before I set out for my master's, up he came and his brother Robert after me. The Justice improved this convenient opportunity to caution my master. He asked him for what he treated his slave thus hastily and unjustly, and told him what would be the consequence if he continued the same treatment towards me. After the justice had ended his discourse with my master, he and his brother set out with me for home, one before and the other behind me. When they had come to a by-place, they both dismounted their respective horses and fell to beating me with great violence. I became enraged at this and immediately turned them both under me, laid one of them across the other, and stamped them both with my feet what I would.

This occasioned my master's brother to advise him to put me off. A short time after this, I was taken by a constable and two men. They carried me to a blacksmith's shop and had me handcuffed. When I returned home my mistress enquired much of her waiters whether VENTURE was handcuffed. When she was informed that I was, she appeared to be very contented and was much transported with the news. In the midst of this content and joy, I presented myself before my mistress, showed her my handcuffs, and gave her thanks for my gold rings. For this my master commanded a negro of his to fetch him a large ox chain. This my master locked on my legs with two padlocks. I continued to wear the chain peaceably for two or three days, when my master asked me with contempuous hard names whether I had not better be freed from my chains and go to work. I answered him, "No." "Well, then," said he, "I will send you to the West Indies, or banish you, for I am resolved not to keep you." I answered him, "I crossed the waters to come here and I am willing to cross them to return."

For a day or two after this not anyone said much to me, until one Hempstead Miner of Stonington asked me if I would live with him. I answered that I would. He then requested me to make myself discontented and to appear as unreconciled to my master as I could before that he bargained with him for me, and that in return he would give me a good chance to gain my freedom when I came to live with him. I did as he requested me. Not long after, Hempstead Miner purchased me of my master for fifty-six pounds lawful. He took the chain and padlocks from off me immediately after.

It may here be remembered that I related a few pages back that I hired out a sum of money to Mr. Robert Stanton, and took his note for it. In the fray between my master Stanton and myself, he broke open my chest containing his brother's note to me and destroyed it. Immediately after my present master bought me, he determined to sell me at Hartford. As soon as I became apprized of it, I bethought myself that I would secure a certain sum of money which lay by me safer than to hire it out to Stanton. Accordingly I buried it in the earth, a little distance from Thomas Stanton's, in the road over which he passed daily. A short time after, my master carried me to Hartford, and first proposed to sell me to one William Hooker of that place. Hooker asked whether I would go to the German Flats with him. I answered, "No." He said I should; if not by fair means, I should by foul. "If you will go by no other measures, I will tie you down in my sleigh." I replied to him, that if he carried me in that manner no person would purchase me, for it would be thought he had a murderer for sale. After this he tried no more, and said he would not have me as a gift.

My master next offered me to Daniel Edwards, Esq., of Hartford, for sale. But he not purchasing me, my master pawned me to him for ten pounds, and returned to Stonington. After some trial of my honesty, Mr. Edwards placed considerable trust and confidence in me. He put me to serve as his cup-bearer and waiter. When there was company at his house, he would send me into his cellar and other parts of his house to fetch wine and other articles occasionally for them. When I had been with him some time, he asked me why my master wished to part with such an honest negro, and why he did not keep me himself. I replied that I could not give him the reason, unless it was to convert me into cash and speculate with me as with other commodities. I hope that he can never justly say it was on account of my ill conduct that he did not keep me himself. Mr. Edwards told me that he should be very willing to keep me himself, and that he would never let me go from him to live, if it was not unreasonable and inconvenient for me to be parted from my wife and children; therefore, he would furnish me with a horse to return to Stonington, if I had a mind for it. As Miner did not appear to redeem me, I went, and called at my old master Stanton's first to see my wife, who was then owned by him. As my old master appeared much ruffled at my being there, I left my wife before I had spent any considerable time with her, and went to Col. O. Smith's. Miner had not as yet wholly settled with Stanton for me, and had before my return from Hartford given Colonel Smith a bill of sale of me. These men once met to determine which of them should hold me, and upon my expressing a desire to be owned by Colonel Smith, and upon my master's settling the remainder of the money which was due to Stanton for me, it was agreed that I should live with Colonel Smith. This was the third time of my being sold, and I was then thirty-one years old.

As I never had an opportunity of redeeming myself whilst I was owned by Miner, though he promised to give me a chance, I was then very ambitious of obtaining it. I asked my master one time if he would consent to have me purchase my freedom. He replied that he would. I was then very happy, knowing that I was at that time able to pay part of the purchase money by means of the money which I some time buried. This I took out of the earth and tendered to my master, having previously engaged a free negro man to take his security for it, as I was the property of my master, and therefore could not safely take his obligation myself. What was wanting in redeeming myself, my master agreed to wait on me for, until I could procure it for him. I still continued to work for Colonel Smith. There was continually some interest accruing on my master's note to my friend, the free negro man above named, which I received, and with some besides, which I got by fishing, I laid out in land adjoining my old master Stanton's. By cultivating this land with the greatest diligence and economy, at times when my master did not require my labor, in two years

I laid up ten pounds. This my friend tendered my master for myself, and received his note for it.

Being encouraged by the success which I had met in redeeming myself, I again solicited my master for a further chance of completing it. The chance for which I solicited him was that of going out to work the ensuing winter. He agreed to this on condition that I would give him one-quarter of my earnings. On these terms I worked the following winter, and earned four pounds and sixteen shillings, one quarter of which went to my master for the privilege, and the rest was paid him on my account. I was then about thirty-five years old.

The next summer I again desired he would give me a chance of going to work. But he refused and answered that he must have my labor this summer, as he did not have it the past winter. I replied that I considered it as hard that I could not have a chance to work out when the season became advantageous, and that I must only be permitted to hire myself out in the poorest season of the year. He asked me after this what I would give him for the privilege per month. I replied that I would leave it wholly to his own generosity to determine what I should return him a month. Well then, said he, if so, two pounds a month. I answered him that if that was the least he would take I would be contented.

Accordingly I hired myself out at Fisher's Island, earning twenty pounds; thirteen pounds six shillings of which my master drew for the privilege and the remainder I paid for my freedom. This made fifty-one pounds two shillings which I paid him. In October following I went and wrought six months at Long Island. In that six month's time I cut and corded four hundred cords of wood, besides threshing out seventy-five bushels of grain, and received of my wages down only twenty pounds, which left remaining a larger sum. Whilst I was out that time, I took up on my wages only one pair of shoes. At night I lay on the hearth, with one coverlet over and another under me. I returned to my master and gave him what I received of my six months' labor. This left only thirteen pounds eighteen shillings to make up the full sum of my redemption. My master liberated me, saying that I might pay what was behind if I could ever make it convenient, otherwise it would be well. The amount of the money which I had paid my master towards redeeming my time, was seventy-one pounds two shillings. The reason of my master for asking such an unreasonable price, was, he said, to secure himself in case I should ever come to want. Being thirty-six years old, I left Colonel Smith once more for all. I had already been sold three different times, made considerable money with seemingly nothing to derive it from, had been cheated out of a large sum of money, lost much by misfortunes, and paid an enormous sum for my freedom.

CHAPTER III.

CONTAINING AN ACCOUNT OF HIS LIFE FROM THE TIME OF PURCHASING HIS FREEDOM TO THE PRESENT DAY.

MY wife and children were yet in bondage to Mr. Thomas Stanton. About this time I lost a chest, containing, besides clothing, about thirty-eight pounds in paper money. It was burnt by accident. A short time after I sold all my possessions at Stonington, consisting of a pretty piece of land and one dwelling house thereon, and went to reside at Long Island. For the first four years of my residence there, I spent my time in working for various people on that and at the neighboring islands. In the space of six months I cut and corded upwards of four hundred cords of wood. Many other singular and wonderful labors I performed in cutting wood there, which would not be inferior to the one just recited, but for brevity's sake I must omit them. In the aforementioned four years, what wood I cut at Long Island amounted to several thousand cords, and the money which I earned thereby amounted to two hundred and seven pounds ten shillings. This money I laid up carefully by me. Perhaps some may inquire what maintained me all the time I was laying up my money. I would inform them that I bought nothing which I did not absolutely want. All fine clothes I despised in comparison with my interest, and never kept but just what clothes were comfortable for common days, and perhaps I would have a garment or two which I did not have on at all times, but as for superfluous finery, I never thought it to be compared with a decent homespun dress, a good supply of money and prudence. Expensive gatherings of my mates I commonly shunned, and all kinds of luxuries I was perfectly a stranger to; and during the time I was employed in cutting the aforementioned quantity of wood, I never was at the expense of six pence worth of spirits. Being after this labor forty years of age, I worked at various places, and in particular on Ram Island, where I purchased Solomon and Cuff, two sons of mine, for two hundred dollars each.

It will here be remembered how much money I earned by cutting wood in four years. Besides this, I had considerable money, amounting to all to near three hundred pounds. After this I purchased a negro man, for no other reason than to oblige him, and gave for him sixty pounds. But in a short time after he ran away from me, and I thereby lost all that I gave for him, except twenty pounds which he paid me previous to his absconding. The rest of my money I laid out in land, in addition to a farm which I owned before, and a dwelling house thereon. Forty-four years had then completed their revolution since my entrance into this existence of servitude and misfortune.

Solomon, my eldest son, being then in his seventeenth year, and all my hope and dependence for help, I hired him out to one Charles Church, of Rhode Island, for one year, on consideration of his giving him twelve pounds and an opportunity of acquiring some learning. In the course of the year, Church fitted out a vessel for a whaling voyage, and being in want of hands to man her, he induced my son to go, with the promise of giving him on his return, a pair of silver buckles, besides his wages. As soon as I heard of his going to sea, I immediately set out to go and prevent it if possible. But on my arrival at Church's, to my great grief, I could only see the vessel my son was in, almost out of sight, going to sea. My son died of the scurvy in this voyage, and Church has never yet paid me the least of his wages. In my son, besides the loss of his life, I lost equal to seventy-five pounds.

My other son being but a youth, still lived with me. About this time I chartered a sloop of about thirty tons burthen, and hired men to assist me in navigating her. I employed her mostly in the wood trade to Rhode Island, and made clear of all expenses above one hundred dollars with her in better than one year. I had then become something forehanded, and being in my forty-fourth year, I purchased my wife Meg, and thereby prevented having another child to buy, as she was then pregnant. I gave forty pounds for her.

During my residence at Long Island, I raised one year with another, ten cart loads of watermelons, and lost a great many besides by the thievishness of the sailors. What I made by the watermelons I sold there, amounted to nearly five hundred dollars. Various other methods I pursued in order to enable me to redeem my family. In the night time I fished with setnets and pots for eels and lobsters, and shortly after went a whaling voyage in the service of Col. Smith. After being out seven months, the vessel returned laden with four hundred barrels of oil. About this time I became possessed of another dwelling house, and my temporal affairs were in a pretty prosperous condition. This and my industry was what alone saved me from being expelled that part of the island in which I resided, as an act was passed by the selectmen of the place, that all negroes residing there should be expelled.

Next after my wife, I purchased a negro man for four hundred dollars. But he having an inclination to return to his old master, I therefore let him go. Shortly after, I purchased another negro man for twenty-five pounds, whom I parted with shorty after.

Being about forty-six years old, I bought my oldest child, Hannah, of Ray Mumford, for forty-four pounds, and she still resided with him. I had already redeemed from slavery, myself, my wife and three children, besides three negro men.

About the forty-seventh year of my life I disposed of all my property at Long Island, and came from thence into East Haddam, Conn. I hired myself out first to Timothy Chapman for five weeks, the earnings of which time I put up carefully by me. After this I wrought for Abel Bingham for about six weeks. I then put my money together and purchased of said Bingham ten acres of land lying at Haddam Neck, where I now reside. On this land I labored with great diligence two years, and shortly after purchased six acres more of land contiguous to my other. One year from that time I purchased seventy acres more of the same man, and paid for it mostly with the produce of my other land. Soon after I bought this last lot of land, I set up a comfortable dwelling house on my farm, and built it from the produce thereof. Shortly after I had much trouble and expense with my daughter Hannah, whose name has been before mentioned to this account. She was soon married after I redeemed her, to one Isaac, and shortly after her marriage fell sick of a mortal disease. Her husband, a dissolute and abandoned wretch, paid but little attention to her illness. I therefore thought it best to bring her to my house and nurse her there. I procured her all the aid mortals could afford, but notwithstanding this she fell a prey to her disease, after a lingering and painful endurance of it. The physician's bill for attending her illness amounted to forty pounds.

Having reached my fifty-fourth year, I hired two negro men, one named William Jacklin, and the other, Mingo. Mingo lived with me one year, and having received his wages, run in debt to me eight dollars, for which he gave me his note. Presently after he tried to run away from me without troubling himself to pay up his note. I procured a warrant, took him, and requested him to go to Justice Throop's of his own accord but he refusing, I took him on my shoulders and carried him there, distant about two miles. The justice asking me if I had my prisoner's note with me, and replying that I had not, he told me that I must return with him and get it. Accordingly, I carried Mingo back on my shoulders, but before we arrived at my dwelling, he complained of being hurt, and asked me if this was not a hard way of treating our fellow-creatures. I answered him that it would be hard thus to treat our honest fellow-creatures. He then told me that if I would let him off my shoulders, he had a pair of silver shoe-buckles, one shirt and a pocket handkerchief, which he would turn out to me. I agreed, and let him return home with me on foot; but the very following night he slipped from me, stole my horse and has never paid me even his note. The other negro man, Jacklin, being a comb-maker by trade, he requested me to set him up, and promised to reward me well with his labor. Accordingly I bought him a set of tools for making combs, and procured him stock. He worked at my house about one year, and then ran away from me with all his combs, and owed me for all his board.

Since my residence at Haddam Neck, I have owned of boats, canoes and sail vessels, not less than twenty. These I mostly employed in the fishing and trafficking business, and in these occupations I have been cheated out of considerable money by people whom I traded with taking advantage of my ignorance of numbers.

About twelve years ago, I hired a whale boat and four black men, and proceeded to Long Island after a load of round clams. Having arrived there, I first purchased of James Webb, son of Orange Webb, six hundred and sixty clams, and afterwards with the help of my men, finished loading my boat. The same evening, however, this Webb stole my boat and went in her to Connecticut river and sold her cargo for his own benefit. I thereupon pursued him, and at length recovered the boat, but for the proceed of her cargo I never could obtain any compensation.

Four years after I met with another loss, far superior to this in value, and I think by no less wicked means. Being going to New London with a grandchild, I took passage in an Indian's boat and went there with him. On our return, the Indian took on board two hogsheads of molasses, one of which belonged to Captain Elisha Hart, of Saybrook, to be delivered on his wharf. When we arrived there, and while I was gone, at the request of the Indian, to inform Captain Hart of his arrival and receive the freight for him, one hogshead of the molasses had been lost overboard by the people in attempting to land it on the wharf. Although I was absent at the time and had no concern whatever in the business, as was known to a number of respectable witnesses, I was nevertheless prosecuted by this con-scientious gentleman (the Indian not being able to pay for it) and obliged to pay upwards of ten pounds lawful money, with all the costs of court. I applied to several gentlemen for counsel in this affair, and they advised me, as my adversary was rich, and threatened to carry the matter from court to court till it would cost me more than the first damages would be,—to pay the sum and submit to the injury, which I accordingly did, and he has often since insultingly taunted me with my unmerited misfortune. Such a proceeding as this committed on a defenceless stranger, almost worn out in the hard service of the world, without any foundation in reason or justice, whatever it may be called in a Christian land, would in my native country have been branded as a crime equal to highway robbery. But Captain Hart was a *white gentleman*, and I a *poor African*, therefore it was *all right, and good enough for the black dog.*

I am now sixty-nine years old. Though once straight and tall, measuring without shoes six feet, one inch and an half, and every way well proportioned, I am now bowed down with age and hardship. My strength, which was once equal if not superior to any man whom I have ever seen, is now enfeebled so that life is a burden, and it is with fatigue that I can walk a couple of miles, stooping over my staff. Other griefs are still behind, on account of which some aged people, at least, will pity me. My eye-sight has gradually failed, till I am almost blind, and whenever I go abroad one of my grandchildren must direct my way; besides for many years I have been much pained and troubled with an ulcer on one of my legs. But amidst all my griefs and pains, I have many consolations; Meg, the wife of my youth, whom I married for love and bought with my money, is still alive. My freedom is a privilege which nothing else can equal. Notwithstanding all the losses I have suffered by fire, by the injustice of knaves, by the cruelty and oppression of false-hearted friends, and the perfidy of my own countrymen whom I have assisted and redeemed from bondage, I am now possessed of more than one hundred acres of land, and three habitable dwelling houses. It gives me joy to think that I *have* and that I *deserve* so good a character, especially for *truth* and *integrity*. *(While I am now looking to the grave as my home, my joy for this world would be full—IF my children, Cuff for whom I paid two hundred dollars when a boy, and Solomon who was born soon after I purchased his mother—If Cuff and Solomon—Oh! that they had walked in the way of their father. But a father's lips are closed in silence and in grief!—Vanity of vanities, all is vanity.)

* Note, the closing words in parentheses were omitted in the later editions. It is probable that both improved later, especially so in the case of Solomon, who is well spoken of by elderly men now living, as having maintained a good character.

CERTIFICATE.

STONINGTON, CONN., November 3, 1798.
THESE may certify, that VENTURE is a free negro man, aged about 69 years, and was, as we have ever understood, a native of Africa, and formerly a slave to Mr. James Mumford, of Fisher's Island, in the State of New York, who sold him to Mr. Thomas Stanton, 2d, of Stonington, in the State of Connecticut, and said Stanton sold said VENTURE to Col. Oliver Smith, of the aforesaid place. That said VENTURE hath sustained the character of a faithful servant, and that of a temperate, honest and industrious man, and being ever intent of obtaining his freedom, he was indulged by his master after the ordinary labor on the days of his servitude, to improve the nights in fishing and other employments to his own emolument, in which time he procured so much money as to purchase his freedom from his late master, Colonel Smith; after which he took upon himself the name of VENTURE SMITH, and has since his freedom purchased a negro woman, called Meg, to whom he was previously married, and also his children who were slaves, and said VENTURE has since removed himself and family to the town of East Haddam, in this State, where he hath purchased lands on which he hath built a house, and there taken up his abode.

NATHANIEL MINOR, ESQ.
ELIJAH PALMER, ESQ.
CAPT. AMOS PALMER.
ACORS SHEFFIELD.
EDWARD SMITH.

TRADITIONS

–OF–

VENTURE!

–KNOWN AS–

VENTURE SMITH.*

–COMPILED BY–

H.M. SELDEN.

SEVERAL editions of the Life of Venture have been published succes-
sively by his family, and by them circulated throughout the county, but
more in the towns contiguous to his home, where the subject was well
known for his abnormal strength, industry and goodly character, con-
firmatory of the personal narrative. Copies of the remarkable autobiography were also sent by purchasers to friends abroad. It has long been out
of print. To meet the demand for a new edition and to include traditions
gathered by correspondence, personal intercourse with the aged and
supplemented by some account of his family, is the object of the compiler.
Tradition says Venture's amanuensis was Elisha Niles, of Chatham, who
had been a school-teacher, and also a Revolutionary soldier, like one of the
sons of Venture.

The reader of this new edition will find much in confirmation of the
truthfulness of Venture's statements.

Among the different homes of Venture, the later and favorite one was in
Haddam Neck, near the western shore of Salmon River, on higher ground
and overlooking the cove. His farm was excellent land, fine mellow soil
and very easy to till. In illustration of its fertility an old and current
tradition says: "A black snake was once seen moving on and over the
heads of the standing rye on one of the fields." His house was a one-story
unpainted building, in the upper portion of which he had a room that he
called his office. Here, after his decease, his younger son, Solomon,

---

*Venture assumed the name of Smith in compliment to his latest master, Col.
Oliver Smith, who generously permitted him to secure his freedom by his own
earnings.

continued to live many years. A few rods from where it stood Wells C. Andrews built a large two-story house now owned by John H. Cone.

Venture presented a noble appearance. In mention of himself he says, "Though once straight and tall, measuring, without shoes, six feet one inch and a half, and every way well proportioned," etc. Tradition says he weighed over three hundred pounds and measured six feet around his waist. The tradition of the waist measure was received by the compiler from two sources. The first, from Mr. Orville Percival of Moodus, in 1894, then over 80 years of age, who said Venture measured six feet around his waist, that his feet were very large and twice the width of his (Mr. Percival's) father's feet.

The incident Venture relates of taking upon his knees a tierce of salt has with variation passed into tradition, or the act has been repeated. Mr. Percival gave it as occurring in a store at East Haddam, when Venture burst both of his brogan shoes in carrying the salt across the floor. Mr. Percival added: "A noted wrestler tried his skill in wrestling with Venture, but found he might as well try to remove a tree."

Mr. Alex. M. Clark of Haddam Neck, over 82 years of age, says that Venture worked occasionally for his grandfather, Robert Clark, and with his father, Benajah Clark, at the same time, and that he had often heard them say that Venture measured six feet around his waist, and one or both saw him measured; that Gersham Rowley, a brother of the late Eleazar Dunham Rowley of Young Street, Chatham, was present and assisted in the measurement. Mr. G. Rowley afterward moved to Farmersville, N. Y., where Mr. A. M. Clark visited and heard him relate the occurrence. Mr. A. M. Clark says he heard his father say that Venture weighed over 300 pounds; that his axe weighed nine pounds; that his usual day's work was seven cords of wood, but had cut nine cords in a day; that with his canoe he went often to Long Island, a distance of forty-five miles, to chop, and bring back clams on his return; that by his great strength he made the canoe go very straight and fast. Mr. Clark says that Venture called one day on his grandfather, Robert Clark, for him to stack some wheat, saying in disparagement of himself, "Nigger never know nothing!" Mr. Clark also related the tradition of the salt lifting and mentioned it as occurring in a store in East Haddam. Traditions vary sometimes.

Daniel Cone of Moodus gives the tradition of Venture's axe as weighing six pounds, and that he cut six cords of wood a day. He also repeated the salt-lifting tradition. Another tradition current over forty years ago was that Venture while chopping never raised his axe higher than his head, but forced it into the wood up to the eye at every blow, and further that he said he did not believe in chopping air. This appears to confirm the greater weight of his axe.

Mr. Robert S. Cone of Moodus writes: "About the weight of Venture's axe have no knowledge, but should think six pounds a light weight, for my father used a five and one-half pound weight." Mr. Cone adds: "I have heard father say that he and his brother Horatio cut wood for Venture at thirty-four cents per cord to pay for the use of his scow. When they went to get the scow she was well up on the beach. They thought it impossible to get her off. Venture said, 'Lead me down. True, I am blind, but I can give you a lift.' They led him to the water's edge. Father said the timbers fairly cracked as his great hands touched the scow. She swept into the water like a bird on the wing."

Another tradition, received from various sources, says that when Venture purchased oxen after his sight failed, his method of examining them, besides feeling, was to seize each ox by its hind legs and raise it up to estimate the weight. Again, that Venture while in the house of Ansel Brainerd, Sr., in Haddam Neck—who weighed two hundred or more—stooped down and, placing his hands palm upward on the floor, said to Mr. Brainerd, "You put your feet into my black paws and clasp your hands in my wool and I will raise you up!" This was done and Venture raised him up.

Among the early recollections of the compiler is his visiting an old, unoccupied gambrel-roofed house—the early home of his great-grandfather, Robert Chapman—having narrow outside doors. Tradition said that whenever Venture called, which he often did, he invariably turned sidewise to pass through.

Dea. E. C. Hungerford of Chester, in a letter of April 22, 1895, wrote: "The history of Venture will be interesting, I believe, to a great many. I shall want a copy, perhaps more than one.

"You ask me to rewrite my father's recollections of him. My father (born in 1777) told me that, when he was young, Venture often came to his father's house, and, as he was too heavy a burden to ride on a horse's back, he rode in a sort of two-wheeled cart. Sometimes his horse did not behave well, and then, Venture would put one hand in front of his horse's fore legs and one behind them and jounce the fore parts of the horse up and down a few times and remark, 'There!' The horse would usually behave well after such a jouncing. Father said he used to go behind Venture when he sat in an ordinary chair to look at his broad back and hips, which projected beyond the chair on each side, showing what a large man he must have been."

There is a tradition that the owner of a valuable wood or timber lot, wishing to have some of it cut, had engaged Venture to do it. He arrived later than expected, for which the owner reproved him. Venture, displeased, replied, "You will have cut all you want." At noon the owner came, and to his great surprise and disgust found nearly the whole of his beautiful grove laid low. Robert S. Cone thinks the party whose wood Venture nearly demolished was Capt. Elisha Cone of East Haddam, as his home was Venture's headquarters when he was on that side of the river, but he must have been aware of Venture's peculiarities. It is easy to suppose similar instances and in a different location.

Dr. A. B. Worthington of Middle Haddam, born in 1819, relates that tradition says Venture had engaged to cradle a field of grain. At noon he returned bearing the cradle, having finished the field, to the great surprise of the owner, who expected it would require more than a day to complete it.

Mrs. Philo Bevin of East Hampton, in her letter of March 12, 1895, which we copy in full, gives a similar occurrence which, perhaps, may have originated the former:

East Hampton, Conn., March 12, 1895.

Mr. H. M. Selden:

Dear Sir—I have been quite interested in the history of Venture, and my mother, who is living with me, at the age of 96 years and 9 months, is possibly the only living person in this vicinity who has personal recollections of him. Mother is the widow of Alfred I. Loomis of Westchester. Her maiden name was Abigail Foote, born in June, 1798, and in her childhood lived in S. W. district, known as Waterhole. Venture used to visit at a neighbor's, Mr. Bigelow, grandfather of D. S. Bigelow, who lives where his grandfather did when she was young. She says Venture froze his feet, and she remembers well that he walked on his knees and could travel quite fast, and for sport used to chase the children. She was afraid of him, and would never allow him to catch her, but Polly Bigelow would let him catch her. She says he was a very powerful man, and Mr. Bigelow one morning set him to cut down trees before breakfast and he hurried to call him away, fearing he would cut down the whole grove of timber. Perhaps you have heard all this, but I don't remember to have seen anything about his going on his knees, and possibly it may have been for only a little while. Mother is very bright and clear in her mind and her memory is better than the average of young folks, so I am sure she cannot be mistaken about this. I have promise of the loan of "Life of Venture" from a lady who lives here.

I don't suppose I have given you any points of interest, except to tell you there is one person living who remembers Venture, and I thought I would venture to write, peradventure it might add to your history.

Very respectfully yours,
MRS. PHILO BEVIN.

It is natural to suppose that the grove cutting on the Bigelow place was later than the one previously mentioned (thought to have been on the Capt. Elisha Cone farm), from the solicitude of the owner. The incident of the salt lifting related of Venture may have been reënacted by him (as mentioned in the tradition) on being appealed to by curious doubters. It is related of Venture that on the occasion of his marriage he threw a rope over the house of his master, where they were living, and had his wife go to the opposite side of the house and pull on the rope hanging there while he remained and pulled on his end of it. After both had tugged at it awhile in vain, he called her to his side of the house and by their united effort the rope was drawn over to themselves with ease. He then explained the object lesson: "If we pull in life against each other we shall fail, but if we pull together we shall succeed." The success of his later life implies that the lesson was not forgotten by his true and loving wife.

At length, borne down with the weight of years and increasing infirmities, he sickened and died September 19, 1805, in his seventy-seventh year. His heavy body was conveyed in a boat across the Cove and carried thence on a bier, a distance of some three miles, to the cemetery adjoining the First Congregational Church in East Haddam, for burial, by four strong men fittingly chosen. The two in front were white, proving the respect he had won, while two of his own race assisted in the rear. Robert S. Cone writes of the pallbearers: "When Venture was buried, my father was one of the pall-bearers. He was six feet three inches high. Uri Gates was six feet two inches high. Hannawell, a slave of Doctor Moseley, was five feet six inches high, and a slave of Gen. Epaphroditus Champion, about the same height, was his helper. The negroes being behind threw the weight upon themselves, and as they were mounting the long Olmsted hill the darkies complained bitterly. Hannawell exclaimed, 'Durned great nigger! Ought to have quartered him and gone four times. It makes the gravel stones crack under my feet.' "

His grave is marked by a brown-stone slab inscribed:

SACRED TO THE MEMORY OF
VENTURE SMITH,
AFRICAN.
Though the son of a King, he was kidnapped
and sold as a slave, but by his industry
he acquired money to purchase
his freedom.
WHO DIED SEPT. 19, 1805,
IN YE 77TH YEAR OF HIS AGE.

A similar slab at the adjoining grave is inscribed:
SACRED TO THE MEMORY OF
MARGET SMITH,
RELICT OF VENTURE SMITH,
WHO DIED
DEC. THE 17TH, A. D. 1809,
IN THE 79TH YEAR OF HER AGE.

CHILDREN OF VENTURE AND MARGET SMITH.

* Their names with supposed approximate dates of birth are gathered from the autobiography of their father.

1. HANNAH, born about 1752. Her freedom was purchased for £44. She married a free negro named Isaac, and died——. No mention of children.

2. SOLOMON, born about 1756; died about 1773, in his 17th year. His freedom was purchased for $200.

3. CUFF, born about 1758. His freedom was purchased for $200. Was a soldier in the Revolutionary War, credited to town of East Haddam, enlisted January 29, 1781, as a private for three years in Col. Heman Swift's Battalion. He married, but to whom is to the compiler unknown. Had seven children: 1st–Cuff; 2d–George; 3d–Daniel; 4th–Cynthia; 5th and 6th–twins, Jack and Alice; 7th–Venture, Jr., called Young Venture. Most of these were born in East Haddam. R. S. Cone thinks Cuff died in East Haddam. He was a very strong man, over six feet high. While he lived in Haddam Neck he worked some in the

---

* Venture in the closing words of his autobiography disparages his sons Cuff and Solomon. The compiler, on inquiry among the elderly people who remembered them well, fails to find sufficient warrant for the language of criticism. Evidently, if any youthful foibles early appeared, they were soon overcome.

quarries and assisted in loading vessels from the quarries with his brother Solomon. While so engaged, they together alone carried aboard some very heavy stone, which on being unloaded in New York those assisting could not believe were carried aboard by two men alone. George, the second son of Cuff Smith, married and had several children, one of whom was Nelson of Haddam, the father of Charles, who was born in Haddam in 1847, and married Ascenath Hurd of East Haddam. They have eight children and reside in Cobalt, worthy decendants of Venture.

4. SOLOMON, 2d, born 1773 or 1774, was a very strong man and over six feet high.

Mr. Robert S. Cone of Moodus, says: "Solomon had seven children. He was married twice. First, to Tamar, a worthy, useful woman. A friend to everybody, every one her friend. Think she had two children. One, William, lived to grow to manhood, a straight, handsome fellow, well formed and well spoken. Died in Hartford, unmarried.

"I recollect a short episode which occurred in my boyhood days in connection with the above William. We, that is, Tom Summers with others and myself when a lad, were sailing up the Cove in a scow. Summers was tall and very conceited of his strength, thinking himself more than a match for the strong. Solomon's place was noted at that time for its early peaches, delicious apples and fine vegtables, far ahead of his neighbors. As we moved along, when the scow stood opposite Solomon's place, Summers remarked, 'Now for a bag of Sol's apples!" He jumped ashore, sprang up the hill into the orchard and began to gather. William soon appeared, tall, well dressed and very comely. He very politely asked Mr. Summers to go away. Instead, Mr. Summers showed his two fists in fighting array. William again said, 'Will you go? Will you go?' Summers still showed fight. William, with a cat-like movement, seized him by the nape of the neck and seat of his pants and tossed him down the bank to the Cove with as little effort as we would manage a little child.

"Solomon's second wife was as unlike Tamar as possible. Her name was Peggy. She had six children. Hannah first; then two daughters. Don't recollect their names.* 4th—Henry; 5th—Oliver; then Eliza, for many years head chambermaid on the Hartford and New York line of boats, later on the largest of the Fall River line, the 'Puritan.' Solomon, the father, died

* Mary and Harriet.

in East Haddam at the home of George Palmer, where his daughter Eliza was brought up."

Mrs. L. E. Sexton of Turnerville writes: "I well remember Solomon and his wife Peggy. They came often to the store at Rock Landing kept by John L'Homedieu. One day she came alone and Mr. L'Homedieu kindly inquired after her husband, calling him Sol. (He was often called Sol Venture.) She repeated the name after him in anything but a pleased manner, saying, 'Why, Sol and Solomon are no more alike than Hagar and Phyllis," giving him a lecture for speaking of her husband in such a disrespectful manner.

"I remember Solomon as tall, straight and broad-shouldered, but I think she carried her head quite as high as he did. I think only two of their children attended school on Haddam Neck—two boys, one named George Oliver Washington Smith. The other one had a name equally as long, but I only remember one of them, Henry. The winter that Azariah Wheeler taught the school they attended and were his pet class. He had them come and stand by the table. First, he would drill them to get the right kind of bow, then each one had to give his name in full. By that time the whole school was interested, but if any smiled too broadly he would try to look severe and rap on the table with his ruler to call the house to order, but I think he enjoyed the fun with them and was quite willing the school should, too. He was a good teacher, and helped to make all the children happy, and that is half the battle whether at school or at home."

The compiler remembers both Solomon and George Oliver W. Smith. The former as being tall and straight, the latter a very bright young man, who married, lived in Middletown and died there several years since, leaving children.

It is related of Solomon that, calling at Capt. Justin Sexton's while he and his boys were engaged in butchering, he quoted the words, "Where the carcass is, there the eagles will be gathered together," and added, "among them comes a black crow and begs a piece of liver." He received some liver. There is a tradition that a large colored family called at Solomon's home early one morning, to remain through the day. They were unwelcomed by Mrs. Peggy, who did not wish a visitation. She placed a small pot inside a larger one and both over the fire. Noon came, long passed, and night succeeded in turn; the pot boiled without ceasing and the hungry visitors at length withdrew. The father remarked later, that for all he knew the "pawt" was still boiling.

Several have claimed, or been claimed by others, as decendants of

Venture. Yet the omission of their names from his autobiography casts doubt upon their claims. Among these was Diana, or Dinah Caples, more generally called Dian, and remembered by the elderly people. She often boasted of being a grand-daughter to the king. She made and sold baskets and artificial birds. Of the latter she feared some might learn the manufacture. In person she was of unusual proportions, about five feet in height and nearly as broad.

Robert S. Cone writes: "Tradition says Gideon Quash was Venture's son. He was near the age of Cuff. Both were Revolutionary soldiers. Gid, so said, resembled Venture in form, speech and feature. He was by far the most intelligent negro for miles; accumulated thousands of dollars; married a white wife, whom he told me he obtained her consent to become his, by himself showering into her lap a bag containing ninety-six hard dollars, one year's pay from government. His decendants still live in Colchester, owners of property and respected."

Dr. A. B. Worthington says that Quash called at Isham's store in Colchester and wanted to purchase a "book-tionary and a diction," for his son Jim to learn the meaning of words. Jim later showed his ability by teaching in Colchester.

Alex. M. Clark says, "Sanford, who lived with Solomon, was a son of Solomon's first wife previous to her marriage with Solomon, and that he attended school in Haddam Neck and lived with the family."

LIFE

OF

JAMES MARS,

A SLAVE

BORN AND SOLD IN

CONNECTICUT.

WRITTEN BY HIMSELF.

HARTFORD:

PRESS OF CASE, LOCKWOOD & COMPANY.

1864.

TO WHOM IT MAY CONCERN:

These will certify that the bearer, DEA. JAMES MARS, has been known to me and to the citizens of this town for a long period of years, as an honest, upright, truthful man,—a good citizen, an officer in his church, and a man whose life and character have gained the approbation, the esteem, and the good wishes of all who know him. Born a slave, the good providence of God has long since made him free, and, I trust, also taught him that "where the Spirit of the Lord is, there is liberty."

JNO. TODD.

PITTSFIELD, Mass., June 23, 1868.

INTRODUCTION

WHEN I made up my mind to write this story, it was not to publish it, but it was at the request of my sister that lived in Africa, and has lived there more than thirty years. She had heard our parents tell about our being slaves, but she was not born until a number of years after they were free. When the war in which we have been engaged began, the thought came to her mind that her parents and brothers and sisters were once slaves, and she wrote to me from Africa for the story. I came to Norfolk on a visit at the time the war broke out, and some in Norfolk remember that I was once a slave. They asked me about it; I told them something about it; they seemed to take an interest in it, and as I was in Norfolk now, and having an opportunity to write it, I thought I would write it all through. In telling it to those, there were a great many things that I did not mention that I have written. After I had written it out, I saw that my brother and my other sister would think that I might give them the same; and my children had often asked me to write it. When I had got it written, as it made more writing than I was willing to undertake to give each of them one, I thought I would have it printed, and perhaps I might sell enough to pay the expenses, as many of the people now on the stage of life do not know that slavery ever lived in Connecticut.

A SLAVE BORN AND SOLD IN CONNECTICUT

THE treatment of slaves was different at the North from the South; at the North they were admitted to be a species of the human family. I was told when a slave boy, that some of the people said that slaves had no souls, and that they would never go to heaven, let them do ever so well.

My father was born in the State of New York, I think in Columbia county. He had, I think, three different masters in that State, one by the name of Vanepps, and he was Gen. Van Rensaeller's slave in the time of the Revolution, and was a soldier in that war; he was then owned by a man whose name was Rutser, and then was owned in Connecticut, in Salisbury, and then by the minister in North Canaan.

My mother was born in old Virginia, in Loudin county; I do not remember the name of the town. The minister of North Canaan, whose name was Thompson, went to Virginia for a wife, or she came to him; in some way they got together, so that they became man and wife. He removed her to Canaan, and she brought her slaves with her, and my mother was one of them. I think there were two of my mother's brothers also. The Rev. Mr. Thompson, as he was then called, bought my father, and he was married to my mother by him. Mr. Thompson ministered to the people of Canaan in holy things; his slaves worked his farm. For a short time things went on very well; but soon the North and the South, as now, fell out; the South must rule, and after a time the North would not be ruled. The minister's wife told my father if she only had him South, where she could have at her call a half dozen men, she would have him stripped and flogged until he was cut in strings, and see if he would do as she bid him. She told him, You mind, boy, I will have you there yet, and you will get your pay for all that you have done. My father was a man of considerable muscular strength, and was not easily frightened into obedience. I have heard my mother say she has often seen her mother tied up and whipped until the blood ran across the floor in the room where she was tied and whipped.

Well, as I said, the South and the North could not agree; the South seceded and left the North; the minister's wife would not live North, and she and her husband picked up and went South, and left my father and mother in Canaan to work the farm, and they lived on the farm until I was eight years old. My mother had one child when she came from the South; I was the first she had after she was married. They had five children born in Canaan,—three died in infancy. I was born March 3d, 1790.

Mr. Thompson used to come up from Virginia and talk about our going South. He would pat me on the head and tell me what a fine boy I was. Once when he was in Canaan, he asked me if I would not like to go with him and drive the carriage for my mistress. He said if I would go he would give me twenty-five cents, or as it was then called, twenty-five coppers. I told him I wanted the money first. He gave me a quarter, and then I would not agree to go, and he put me in the oven; that I did not like, and when I got out I would not give him the money, but his business I did not yet know. He had come to sell his farm and to take us all South. My father said he would not go alive; the minister told him he must go; my father said he never would. Well, the man that had formerly ministered to the people in holy things, sold the farm, and stock, and tools, and effects, with a few exceptions. He kept a pair of horses and harness, a wagon, a bed, and a few such articles. The harness and wagon he kept to take us to the South with. After he sold his place, he took us all to a wealthy friend of his, until he had settled up all his affairs, so as to show to the world that he was an honest and upright man. He would have them think that he feared God and let alone evil; for he was born or raised in the State of New York, and had taught the people of North Canaan they way to do, as you will see, for in former days he spoke to the people from the pulpit morally, and they thought much of the man. He had taught them slavery was right, and that the Great Almighty God had sanctioned the institution, and he would practice it. He now made his arrangements to set out on his journey; the day was fixed to leave his much-loved people and home for his southern home, where he had obtained a new home and friends and acquaintances.

My father, although a slave without education, was intensely watching the movements of the teacher of the people, but kept all that he saw to himself, yet he was steadily planning his escape. The set day had now within about thirty-six hours come; all went on well with the man from the South. He had had no thought but all was well; those fine chattels were his, and would fetch him in a southern market, at a moderate estimate, two thousand dollars; they would furnish him pocket change for some time, and also his loving wife could have a chance to wreak her vengeance on my father for what she called disobedience.

It was a matter of doubt with my father what course to take,—how he could get away with his family the best and safest; whether to go to Massachusetts, which joined Canaan on the north, or to Norfolk, which joined Canaan on the east. Very fortunately for us, there was at that time an unpleasant feeling existing between the two towns or the inhabitants of Canaan and Norfolk. He said that the people of Canaan would side with their former pastor, and he found that the people of Norfolk would take sides against Canaan and their pastor; then he thought the best that he could do would be to take his family to Norfolk, where they would be the safest. He concluded to take them to Norfolk, but how was he to get them there with what he wanted to take with them? He came to the conclusion that the horses he had for a long time driven might as well help him now in this hour of distress as not. He got a colored man to help him that was stout and healthy. They hitched up the parson's team, put on board what few things he had and his family, in the still of a dark night, for it was very dark, and started for Norfolk, and on the way we run afoul of a man's wood-pile, for it was so dark he could not see the road; but we got off from the wood-pile without harm, and arrived in Norfolk about one o'clock. I think we stopped at a tavern kept by Mr. G. Pettibone, and in him we found a friend. We unloaded what we had, and father and the man that was with him took the team back to Canaan, so that the parson might set out on his journey and not have to wait for his team, and father returned to where he had left his family. He felt that he had done all for the parson that he well could, for he had taken away his family off from his hands, so that the parson would be relieved from the care that must necessarily occur in such a long journey with a family on his hands to see to, and my father thought that the parson's old Jewel would be relieved from some of her pardoned habits and from a promise she had so often made to him when she got him South. Well, how the parson felt when he had got himself out of bed, and found that he was left to pursue his journey alone, the reader can tell as well as I, for he was a big and bristle man; but I will leave him for a while, and see what is to be done with us.

It was soon known in the morning that we were in Norfolk; the first inquiry was, where will they be safe. The place was soon found. There was a man by the name of Phelps that had a house that was not occupied; it was out of the way and out of sight. After breakfast, we went to the house; it was well located; it needed some cleaning, and that my mother could do as well as the next woman. We all went to work and got it cleaned, and the next day went into it and stopped some time. Father did

what work he could get out of the way, where he would not be seen, and
it was necessary for him to keep out of sight, for Norfolk was the
thoroughfare to Hartford. Days and weeks passed on, and we began to feel
quite happy, hoping that the parson had gone South, as we heard nothing
from him. At length we heard that he said he would have the two boys at
all hazards. It was thought best that the boys should be away. So one dark
night we heard that the parson was coming out with his men to find the
boys, for have them he would. A man that lived near to us said he would
take the boys where they would be safe. His name was Cady. It was agreed
on, and he went with us over a mountain, over rocks and logs. It was very
rough and steep, and the night was so dark that we could only see when it
lightened. At last we got through the woods on the top of what is called
Burr Mountain. We could look down in low grounds and see logs that were
laid for the road across the meadow; at every flash they could be seen, but
when it did not lighten we could not see anything; we kept on,—our pilot
knew the way. At last we arrived at the place. The name of the family was
Tibbals. The family consisted of an old man, a middle-aged man and his
wife and four children, and a very pleasant family it was. We had not been
there long before it was thought best that my brother should be still more
out of the way, as he was about six years older than I, which made him an
object of greater search, and they were at a loss where to send him as he
was then about fourteen years of age. There was a young man by the name
of Butler, from Massachusetts; he was in Norfolk at the time, studying law;
he said he would take him home with him, and he did so, as I supposed,
and I saw him no more for more than two years.

I stopped with the family a few days, and then went home, or what I
called home. It was where my parents and sister were. I found them very
lonely. I had not been home many days before our quiet was disturbed,
for the parson had his hunters out to find our whereabouts. He somehow
found where we were. My sister and myself were at play out at the door;
we saw two men in the woods, a little from the house, coming very fast,
and they came into the house. My father was not far from the house;
mother was in the house. The men were Captain Phelps, the man who
owned the house, and Mr. Butler, the law-student. They told us that we
must now say whether we would go with the parson or not, and we must
decide quick, for the parson was coming, and he would soon be on the
spot, and there was no time to lose. Mother had said she was not unwilling
to go herself, if it was not for father and the children, and the parson had
made her such promises that she was somewhat inclined to go. The parson

talked so fair to her, he beguiled her, I suppose, somewhat as our first mother was beguiled in the garden. The beguilers were both, I do not say preachers, but they were both deceivers, and he talked so smooth to mother that he beguiled her. He told her if she would go to Canaan and see to his things and pack them up for him, then if she did not want to go, she need not. Mother talked with father; he did not incline to go, but finally he consented. The parson ordered a wagon, and it was soon on the spot; but where was Joseph?—he is not here. "I want him to go with us, that we may be all together," said the parson. Father saw what the parson's plan was: he told him the boy was on the way,—he could get him when we got to Canaan. I should have said that those two men that came to tell us that the parson was coming, hid in the barn before the parson arrived, and were not seen by him. They had a few words with my father while the parson went for his team. We set off for Canaan, and in the land of Canaan we arrived that day. Where is Joseph? Father said he would go for him the next day in the morning, or in the day. Father went, as the parson supposed, for Joseph. The parson was loading; mother was packing; all was now going on well. Night came, and when all was still, for father had told some one it would be late before he got back, he came and took the parson's horses, and took mother and the two children on horseback, and instead of going South, went to Norfolk, and got there about two o'clock in the morning. We stopped at a tavern kept by Captain Lawrence. The horses were sent back for the parson, for he said he should start the next day; but it seemed that he did not start for old Virginia, for we often heard of him after that day.

We stopped with Capt. Lawrence a few days. It was thought best by our friends that we should not all be together, for it was found that the parson was still in the land, and on the lookout for us. I was sent to a woman in the neighborhood, by the name of Darby—a poor woman. I stopped with her a few days, with instructions to keep still. The old lady had but one room in her house. You may wonder why I was sent to such a place; most likely it was thought she had so little room that she would not be suspected of harboring a fugitive.

A man by the name of Walter lived near by; he was in the habit of coming in to see how his boy did, as he called me. He told me when any one came there I must get under the bed. I used to sit in the corner of the room, so that I should not be seen from the window. I stayed there a number of days,—I do not now remember how many. One day I ventured to take a peep through the key-hole; the door was locked. Some one came to the door; I made a bound, and then a roll, and I was out of sight. The door was opened, and it was my friend Mr. Walter. He was quite amused to hear the performance; he said he would take me with him the next day, he was going to work in a back lot where it would be out of sight. So the next day I went with him; it was quite a treat. At noon we ate our dinner in the field; that was new to me. After dinner Mr. Walter lay down on the ground; he told me he should go to sleep, and I must keep a look-out to see if any one came in sight. If I saw any one, I must wake him. I kept watch, but there was none came to disturb him in his repose. The day passed away, and we returned home at night—all well, as I supposed; but it seemed that the parson had his pickets out, and had got an idea that I was somewhere in the street. That night I had to leave my place at Mrs. Darby's, and went about a mile to a man's house by the name of Upson; he lived on a back street. I thought him to be a friend; I do not know but he was,—but as I find that men now act in relation to slavery, I am inclined to think otherwise. The next morning the man went to his work; he was painting for the minister in Norfolk. Mrs. Upson sent me to the brook, a little way from the house, to fetch a pail of water. I did not like going into the street very much, but being taught by my parents to obey, I went without any words. As I got to the brook, a man rode into the brook with a cocked hat on. I did not much like his looks. I did not know who he was. Said he,—"My boy, where is your father and mother?" I said, "I don't know, sir." "Where is your brother?" "I don't know, sir." "Where do you live?" "I don't know, sir." "Whom do you stay with?" "I don't know, sir." I did not then know the name of the man. He rode off, or rather I left him asking questions. He looked after me till I got to the house, and rode up. I asked Mrs. Upson who it was that came to the brook when I was there. She said it was Mr. Robbins, the minister. I thought nothing of it, for I thought all the people in Norfolk were our friends. In a few hours, the woman sent me to the neighbor's to get some water from the well. It was a widow woman where I went to get the water, and there I found my father. He said that Capt. Lawrence had been there and told him that Mr. Robbins had sent his son to Canaan to tell parson Thompson that he had seen one of his boys, and we must go in the woods, for he thought the parson would come out to look for me. Father took the water and went with it to the house that I brought the pail from. The family where I went for the water, I shall always remember with the kindest feelings. We have ever, from that day to the present, been on the best terms, and I believe three of them are living now. Two of them live in that same house that they then lived in, and the transactions of this narrative took place sixty five years ago. Their name is Curtiss.

When father came back, we set off for the woods pointed out by our friends; we went across the lots and came to a road, and crossed that into another open field. The woods were in the backside of the field. As we went on, we ascended a ridge of land, and we could see the road that led from Canaan to Norfolk. The road then went past the burying-ground, and we could see it from where we were. We saw fourteen men on horseback; they were men we knew; the parson was one of them. We hid behind a log that was near us until they got out of sight; we then went into the woods, and there we found my mother and sister; they had been sent there by the man that had told us of the parson's information of where I was. We all remained there. This I should think was about two or three o'clock in the afternoon. Very soon the thought of night came to mind; how we were to spend the night, and what we should do for something to eat; but between sundown and dark a man passed along by the edge of the woods, whistling as he went. After he had passed on, father went up where the man went along, and came back with a pail or basket, and in it was our supper. We sat down and ate. The man we saw no more that night, but how were we to spend the night I could not tell; it was starlight, yet it was out in the woods, but father and mother were there, and that was a comfort to us children, but we soon fell asleep and forgot all our troubles, and in the morning we awoke and were still in the woods. In due time the man that passed along the night before, came again with more food for us, and then went his way; his name was Walter. We spent several days in the woods,—how many I do not remember. I think it was the fore part of the week when we went into the woods; we were there over the Sabbath, for I well remember a man by the name of Bishop had a shop where he fulled and dressed cloth not very far from where we were, and he came to the back door of his shop and stood and looked out a while, and went in and shut the door. I felt afraid he would see us. We kept very still, but I think he did not know that we were there; if he did, it did us no hurt. We were fed by kind friends all the time we were in the woods.

One afternoon, or towards night, it was thought it would be safe to go to a barn and sleep. After it was dark we went to a barn belonging to a Mr. Munger and slept, but left it while the stars were shining, and so for a few nights, and then it was thought we might sleep in the house. The next night after dark, we went in the house of Mr. Munger for the night. My sister and myself were put up in a back chamber, behind barrels and boxes, closely put together, out of sight for safe-keeping. We had not been there long before mother came and told us we must get up, for Captain Lawrence, our friend, had sent word that the parson said he would have the boys at any rate, whether he got the parents or not. His pickets were going to search every house within a mile of the meeting-house that night, or search until he found them. But we went into the woods again; we were there awhile again; when it rained, we went sometimes into a barn when we dared. After a time it was rather still, and we were at one house and sometimes at another. We had pickets out as well as the parson. It was thought best that I should not be with the rest of the family, for the hunt seemed to be for the boys. My brother, I have said, was out of the State. I was sent to one family, and then to another, not in one place long at a time. The parson began to think the task harder than he had an idea; it rather grew worse and more perplexing; he did not know what to do. He was outwitted in all his attempts; every effort or trial he had made, had failed. He now thought of giving my father and mother and sister their freedom if they would let him have the boys to take with him; this they would not do.

After some time was spent, the parson or his pickets had an idea that we were all at Capt. Lawrence's house, shut up there; how to find out if we were there or not, was the puzzle. They contrived various plans, but did not succeed. Finally there was one thing yet. They knew that Mr. Lawrence loved money; they thought they would tempt him with that; so they came to his house and made trial. They met together one day and wanted to search his house; he would not consent for a time; they urged and he refused. He finally told them on certain conditions they might go into every room but one. They went into all the rooms but one. They then wanted to go into the room that they had not been into; they offered him money to let them go into the room,—how much he did not tell, as I know of. He finally consented. The much-desired room was a chamber over the kitchen. Mr. Lawrence opened the door at the foot of the stairs, and called and said, "Jupiter! (for that was my father's first name,) you must look out for yourself now, for I can not hide you any longer." He then told the parson's pickets they must take care, for Jupiter says he will kill the first man that lays hands on him. They hesitated some; they then went up stairs still, and stopped a short time, and then with a rush against the door, it gave way, and they all went in. They found the landlady sitting there as composed as summer, with her knittingwork, unconscious of an arrest to go south as a slave! but they found us not, although the room they last went into was the one we had occupied all the time we were in that house, sometimes one night, sometimes a week, and then in the woods or elsewhere, as was thought best to keep out of the way.

The pickets returned to the land of Canaan to see what was to be the next move. The parson then proposed to give my father and mother and sister their freedom, if they would let him have the boys. That they would not do; but the boys he said he must have. As my brother was away, it was thought best that I should be away. I was sent to Mr. Pease, well-nigh Canaan, and kept rather dark. I was there for a time, and I went to stay with a man by the name of Camp, and was with him a time, and then I went to stay with a man by the name of Akins, and stayed with him a few days, and went to a man by the name of Foot, and was with him a few days. I went to another man by the name of Akins, and was there some time. The parson was not gone south yet, for he could not well give up his prey. He then proposed to sell the boys until they were twenty-five, to somebody here that my parents would select, for that was as long as the law of Connecticut could hold slaves, and he would give the other members of the family their freedom. It was finally thought best to do that if the purchasers that were acceptable could be found. Some friends were on the lookout. Finally a man by the name of Bingham was found; it was a man that my father was once a slave to; he would take my brother,—then a man by the name of Munger would buy me if they could agree. Mr. Bingham lived in Salisbury, Mr. Munger lived in Norfolk; the two men lived about fifteen miles apart, both in Connecticut.

The trade was made, and we two boys were sold for one hundred pounds a head, lawful money,—yes, sold by a man, a minister of the gospel in Connecticut, the land of steady habits. It would seem that the parson was a worshiper with the Athenians, as Paul said unto them when he stood on Mars Hill, he saw an inscription on one of their altars; and it would seem that the parson forgot or passed over the instruction of the apostle that God made of one blood all nations of men for to dwell on all the face of the earth.

The parson was a tall man, standing six feet in his boots, and had no legitimate children to be heirs to his ill-gotten gains. The bargain was made on the 12th of September, 1798. Then I was informed that I was sold to Mr. Munger, and must go and live with him. The man I did not know, but the thought of being sold, not knowing whether I was ever to see my parents, or brother, or sister again, was more than I could endure; the thought that I was sold, as I did not then know for how long, it was hard to think of; and where were my parents I knew not: It was a sad thought, but go I must. The next morning (I was to go the morning of the 13th) was a sad morning to me. The morning was clear, without a cloud. I was told where the man lived, and I must go, for he had bought me. I thought of my parents; should I, oh! should I never see them again? As I was taught to obey my superiors, I set out; it was a little over a mile. The way was long. I was alone. Tears ran down my cheeks. I then felt for the first time that I was alone in the world, no home, no friends, and none to care for me. Tears ran, but it did no good; I must go, and on I went. And now sixty-five years have passed away since that time; those feelings are fresh in my memory. But on my way to my new home I saw my father; I will not attempt to describe my feelings when he told me he had taken rooms in the same neighborhood, and should be near me. That made the rough way smooth. I went on then cheerful and happy. I arrived at the place. I found a man with a small family; it consisted of himself and wife and three daughters. The oldest was near my age. The family appeared pleasant. I ate a bowl of bread and milk, and was told to mount a horse that was at the door with a bag of rye on his back, and ride to the field; that was about a mile off. The man went with me, and on the way we passed the house of Mrs. Curtiss, where I mentioned in the former part of this narrative of going for well-water for Mrs. Upson. We went to the field and worked that day; went home at night. The family appeared very pleasant, and I felt pleased to think that the parson had gone, for I was told that he went the same day that I went to my new home. In a short time my father and mother and sister came into the neighborhood to live. I was allowed to go and see them one evening in two weeks. They lived about sixty rods from where I lived. Things went on well. I was very contented, and felt glad that the fear of being carried south was at an end. The parson was out of town and out of mind. I soon became acquainted with Mrs. Curtiss' boys, for I passed the house where they lived every day, as Mr. Munger's farm was beyond where they lived. I soon was feeling contented and happy. There was one thing that was unfortunate for me; Mr. Munger was not a stout, strong man, and not very healthy, and had no other help but me, and of course I had many things to do beyond my strength. I do not complain of many things, yet there are two things more I will mention. One of them I feel to this day, and that I feel the most is that I did not have an opportunity to go to school as much as I should, for all the books I ever had in school were a spelling-book, a primer, a Testament, a reading-book called Third Part, and after that a Columbian Orator. My schooling was broken and unsteady after the first and second winters, as Mr. Munger had no help, and had to go something like two miles for his wood. He would take me with him to the woods, and he would take a load and go home, and leave me to chop while he was gone. The wood was taken off from a fallow where he had sowed rye. It was in piles. Some had to be cut once, and some twice, and some three times. I went to school the most of the first winter; after that my schooling was slim. The other thing was, he was fond of using the lash. I thought so then, and made up my mind if I ever was the strongest I would pay back some of it. However, things went on, and I thought a good deal of Mr. Munger; yet I wonder sometimes why I was not more contented than I was, and then I wonder why I was as contented as I was. The summers that I was thirteen and fourteen, I was sick; they began to think I had the consumption. They sometimes would say to me, "If you should die we should lose a hundred pounds." I do not know as Mr. Munger ever said that, but it was said to me. But I will pass on with my story.

I soon found out that I was to live or stay with the man until I was twenty-five. I found that white boys who were bound out, were bound until they were twenty-one. I thought that rather strange, for those boys told me they were to have one hundred dollars when their time was out. They would say to me sometimes, "You have to work four years longer than we do, and get nothing when you have done, and we get one hundred dollars, a Bible, and two suits of clothes." This I thought of.

Some of the family or friends of the family would tell me what a good boy I should be, because Mr. Munger saved me from slavery. They said I must call him Master; but Mr. Munger never told me to, so I never did. If he had told me to, I should have done so, for I stood greatly in fear of him, and dreaded his displeasure, for I did not like the lash. I had made up my mind that I would not stay with him after I was twenty-one, unless my brother did with the man he lived with. My brother had been home to see. us, and we went once to see him. I asked my brother how long he was going to stay with Mr. Bingham. He said Mr. Bingham said he should have his time when he was twenty-one. Well then, I would have my time, I said to myself. Things went on, and I found Mr. Munger to be a very good sort of a man. I had now got to be fifteen years of age. I had got my health, and had grown to be a big boy, and was called pretty stout, as the word is, yet I was afraid of Mr. Munger. I actually stood in fear of him.

I had now got to be in my sixteenth year, when a little affair happened, which, though trivial in itself, yet was of consequence to me. It was in the season of haying, and we were going to the hayfield after a load of hay. Mr. Munger and I were in the cart, he sitting on one side and I on the other. He took the fork in both of his hands, and said to me very pleasantly, "Don't you wish you were stout enough to pull this away from me?" I looked at him, and said, "I guess I can;" but I did not think so. He held it toward me with both his hands hold of the stale. I looked at him and then at the fork, hardly daring to take hold of it, and wondering what he meant, for this was altogether new. He said, "Just now see if you can do it." I took hold of it rather reluctantly, but I shut my hand tight. I did as Samson did in the temple; I bowed with all my might, and he came to me very suddenly. The first thought that was in my mind was, my back is safe now. All went on well for two months or more; all was pleasant, when one day he—or Mr. Munger, I should have said—was going from home, and he told me, as was usual, what to do. I went to my work, and did it just as he told me. At night, when he came home, he asked me what I had been doing. I told him, but he did not seem satisfied. I told him I had done just what he told me. He said I had not done what I ought to have done. I told him I had done what he told me. That was more than I had ever said before. He was angry and got his horsewhip, and said he would learn me. He raised his hand and stood ready to strike. I said, "You had better not!" I then went out at the door. I felt grieved to see him in such a rage when I had done just as he told me, and I could not account for it. If he had been a drinking man, I should not have wondered; but he was not, he was a sober man. I could not get over my feeling for some time, but all was pleasant the next day. I said to his daughters that I would not stay there a day after I was twenty-one, for I did not know what their father meant. I did just as he told me, and thought I was doing what he would be satisfied with. They told me not to mind it. Things went on from that time as well as I could wish. From that time until I was twenty-one, I do not remember that he ever gave me an unpleasant word or look. While I lived with him, after that time, I felt that I had now got as good a place as any of the boys that were living out. I often went with his team to Hartford and to Hudson, which the other boys did not that lived in the neighborhood. I now felt that I could do anything for the family; I was contented and happy.

The year that I was eighteen, Mr. Munger was concerned in an iron establishment, manufacturing iron. He had a sister living in Oneida county, and he learned that iron was high or brought a good price there. He told me he thought he would send a load out there and get a load of wheat, and asked me if I would go out with a load. I told him I would if he wished me to; he said he did. He got every thing ready, and I set out the 17th day of October, and thought it would take me about two weeks or thereabouts. On I went, and when I got there I could exchange my iron for wheat readily, but none had their wheat out, and their barn-floors were so full that they could not thrash. I had to wait a week. As soon as I got my load, I set out for home. I was gone a day or two over three weeks. After I got to Norfolk, I passed the house where my parents lived. They told me that it was very current with the people that I had sold the horses and wagon, and was seen by some one that knew me, and was on my way to Canada. They said that Mr. Munger said he did not believe it,—he said he should not trouble himself. Yet I went on home. He was glad to see me; asked if I had any bad luck. I told how it was, and he was satisfied, and said when he saw the team that they were in better condition than they were when I left home. "Now they may talk as much as they please; you and the team, wagon and load are here." And when I told him what I had done, he said he was perfectly satisfied, I had done well; he had no fault to find. Every thing went on first-rate. I did my best to please him, and it seemed to me that the family did the same. I now took the hardest end of the work. I was willing to do what I could. I was willing to work, and thought much of the family, and they thought something of me. Mr. Munger was receiving his share of offices of the town, and was from home a portion of his time. I felt ambitious to have our work even with others. He said his work went on as well as if he was there.

When I was in my twentieth year, a nephew of Mr. Munger came to board with him; he was studying law. Mr. Munger and I were accustomed to talk about my term of service with him. I told him I did not mean to stay with him until I was twenty-five. He said he thought I would if I meant to do what was fair and just. I told him that my brother had his time when he was twenty-one, and I wanted my time. He finally had some talk with his nephew, who said that he could hold me. But finally Mr. Munger made me an offer of what he would give me if I would stay. I thought the offer was tolerably fair. I had now become attached to the family. I told him that I would stay, as he had often said he thought I ought to stay after I was twenty-one. I thought I would divide the time with him in part, as the offer he made would not cover the whole time. All was fixed, and I worked on. Nothing more was said for a long time about it; then the thing was spoken about, and the same mind was in us both, and I felt satisfied. The fall previous to my being twenty-one came; all was right, as I thought. The winter came and nothing was said. The last of February came. I heard it hinted that Mr. Munger had said that he should not make any bargain with me, but if I left him he would follow me. The thing was understood by us, and I paid no attention to it. March came, and nothing was said. The third of March was my birthday. All was quiet, and I kept on as before until the first of April. It was told me that Mr. Munger said that his nephew had examined the law and found that he could hold me, and what he gave me would be his unless he was bound by a written agreement. As there were no writings given, I began to think it was time to know how it was. There was another thing now came to mind.

When I was thirteen years old, Mr. Munger bought a calf of my father, and gave it to me, and said he would keep it until it was two years old, and then I might sell it and have what it brought. He kept it. He had a mate for it, and when the steers were two years old he sold them for twenty-four dollars. He then told me that he would give me a heifer of the age the steer was, and when she had a calf he would take her to double in four years. When I was seventeen he gave me a heifer, and she had a calf that spring, and the first of April he said he would take her, and at the end of four years from that time he would give me two cows and two calves. That was agreed on. The next year, in March or April, one of his oxen hooked my cow; it hurt her so that the cow died. Well, now, what was to be done? He said at the time agreed on I should have my cows. I was content with that and worked on, feeling that all would be made right. I thought I should have two cows with those calves when I was twenty-one, and that would be a beginning. Afterward I agreed to stay with him until I was twenty-five; I could let them until that time. I will now go on with my story. I asked him for my cows and calves. He said he should not let me have any. He said if I stayed and did well perhaps he would give me a cow. I asked him if that was all that I was to have if I stayed until I was twenty-five. He said he would see. I asked when he would see. He said when the time came. I then told him I had been told that Warren (that was the name of his nephew) had told him not to give me what he had agreed to, and I wanted to know if he would do as he had agreed to or not. He said I belonged to him, and I could not help myself. I told him I would stay with him as I had said if he would give me a writing obligating himself to give me the sum we had agreed upon. After hesitating a short time, he said he would not give a writing; he would not be bound. I told him I had got that impression, "and if you say you will not give me what you said you would, I will not work another day." He then said if I left him he would put me in jail and keep me there a year at any rate. This was on Saturday. The next day I picked up what few duds I had, and at evening, as it was the Sabbath, I told him I had done all the work for him that I should do. I then bade him good night and left his house, and went to my father's. The next day in the afternoon, Mr. Munger and nephew came to my father's with a sheriff. I was not in the house. He told my father that he would pay my board in jail for one year, and I could not help myself. They took what few clothes I had, and went away before I got home. It was well it was so. I told my father that I would stay in jail as long as Mr. Munger would find money. I sent the word to Mr. Munger. He sent me word that I should have an opportunity to. My people wanted to have me go away for a time. I thought at first I would. Then I saw that I had nothing to go with, and had no clothes for a change. I would not leave. I told them I would go to jail. I thought perhaps I could get the liberty of the yard, and then I could earn something to get some clothes, and then I would leave for Canada or some other parts.

A few days after, I heard that Mr. Munger said he would leave it to men how it should be settled, and he sent me such word. I sent word to him, no, I was going to jail, if he would keep his word. He finally said as I had always been faithful, he would not or had rather not put me in jail. My parents said so much, they did not want to have me go to jail, that I finally said I would leave it to three men if they were men that I liked: if they were not, I would not. He said I might name the men; their judgment was to be final. The men were selected, the time and place specified. The day came, the parties met, and the men were on hand. Mr. Munger had his nephew for counsel; I plead my case myself. A number of the neighbors were present. Mr. Munger's counsel began by saying that his uncle had bought me, and had paid for me until I was twenty-five, and that he had a right to me. I then told his nephew that I would have a right to him some day, for he was the cause of all the difficulty. He said no more. The arbitrators asked Mr. Munger if he had anything against me. He said he had not. They asked him, in case they gave him anything, if he wished me to work it out with him; he said he did. They went out a few moments, and returned and said that I must pay Mr. Munger $90. He then asked me to go home with him, and he would hire me. I told him I would go and get my clothes, for that was in the decision. He said I could have them. His nephew did not want me to live with his uncle, if he boarded with him. I told Mr. Munger that I would not work for him. I hired to another man, and went to work in the same neighborhood. This nephew kept an eye on me for a long time, and always gave me the road whenever he saw me coming. Mr. Munger and family always treated me with attention whenever I met them; they made me welcome to their house and to their table. If that nephew had not interfered, there would have been no trouble.

Things all went on pleasantly. In about four years I went there again to work, and in a short time Mr. Munger and his two daughters joined the church of which his wife was a member. I joined the same church, and was often at his house. Mr. Munger was unfortunate and lost his property, not as people lose their property now. He was poor and not very healthy, and his wife and the daughter that was not married, not being healthy, and he being a man advanced in life, it wore upon him and his family, and his daughter went into a decline. I went west, and was gone about three months, and on my return went to see the family, and found the daughter very much out of health and wasting away. I called again the next day but one. As I had been accustomed to take care of the sick, she asked me to stop with her that night. I did so, and went to my work in the morning. The second day after, I called again to see her, and she made the same request. I staid and watched with her that night. She asked what I thought of her; I told her I feared she would never be any better. She then asked me to stay with her if she did not get any better, while she lived. I told her I would. A cousin of hers, a young lady, was there, and we took the care of her for four weeks. I mention this because it was a time to be remembered and cherished by me while I live. We were in the daily habit of speaking of her prospects and how she felt. She would speak of death with as much apparent composure as of any other subject. She said very little to her friends about her feelings. The day that she died was the evening of the Sabbath. About six o'clock in the afternoon, or rather all that day, she did not appear to be as well; but at the time just mentioned she sunk away and seemed to be gone for a short time, when she revived as one out of sleep, suddenly, and seemed surprised, and said, "There is nothing that I want to stay here for; let me go." She then bade her friends farewell, and told them not to weep for her, for she was going. Her countenance seemed as if lit up with heavenly love, and for a short time she seemed to be away from the world, and then was still and said but little. About eleven o'clock she wanted to be moved. She was moved. She then wanted to drink. I gave her, or put the glass to her lips. She did not swallow any. I saw there was a change, and before her friends could get into the room her spirit had fled.

That was a scene that I love to think of. It makes me almost forget that I ever was a slave to her father; but so it was. I staid until she was buried, and then I went West again. Her parents were broken-hearted indeed. I returned from the West, and spent a part of the summer with Mr. Munger.

I afterwards worked where I chose for a few years. I was frequently at Mr. Munger's house. He seemed depressed, his health rather declined, and he finally sank down and was sick. He sent for me; I went to him, and he said he wished to have me stay with him. I told him I would, and I staid with him until he died, and closed the eyes of his daughter when she died, and his also. And now to look back on the whole transaction, it all seems like a dream. It is all past, never to be re-acted. That family have all gone, with one exception.

APPENDIX.

This Appendix is by request of those that have read what is before it:—

After the death of Mr. Munger, I married a wife and lived in Norfolk a few years; we had two children. We went to Hartford after a while; I worked for the then known firm of E. & R. Terry. There was a man came to Hartford from Savannah, with his family; he came to school his daughter. He brought a slave girl with him to care for the smaller children. My wife washed for the family. All went on well for about two years. The Southern man's name was Bullock, and the slave's name was Nancy. One day when I was at work in the store, a gentleman came where I was; he asked if this was deacon Mars. I said "Yes, sir." He said Mr. Bullock was about to send Nancy to Savannah, "and we want to make a strike for her liberty, and we want some man to sign a petition for a writ of habeas corpus to bring Mr. Bullock before Judge Williams; they tell me that you are the man to sign the petition." I asked him who was to draw the writ; he said Mr. Wm. W. Ellsworth. I went to Mr. Ellsworth's office with the man. I signed the petition. I then went to my work. I told Mr. Ellsworth that it would cause an excitement; if he wanted me at any time, I would be on hand. The writ was served on Mr. Bullock, and he was brought before Judge Williams, but Nancy could not be found. The court adjourned till eight o'clock the next morning. At night Nancy came to the house where they were boarding; she had been out as she was accustomed to go with the children. Mrs. Bullock told Nancy to go to bed. She somehow had an idea that all was not right; she opened the door, and gave it a swing to shut, but it did not shut, as she said afterwards. She thought she would see what they were talking about. She said Mrs. B. told Mr. Bullock to start in the morning at 4 o'clock with Nancy for New York; "never mind the bond, and send Nancy South." I omitted to mention that the court put Mr. Bullock under a bond of $400 to appear the next morning at 8 o'clock. The plan to send Nancy South was fixed on. Nancy said to herself, "When you come where I be, I wont be there." She went out of the house, and went to the house of a colored man and stopped for the night. The next morning the court sat; master and slave were both there. The court said it was the first case of the kind ever tried in the State of Connecticut, and the Supreme Court of Errors was to meet in ten days, and was composed of five judges; he would adjourn the trial until the session of that court.

During those ten days I had a fair opportunity to see how strong a hold slavery had on the feelings of the people in Hartford. I was frowned upon; I was blamed; I was told that I had done wrong; the house where I lived would be pulled down; I should be mobbed; and all kinds of scarecrows were talked about, and this by men of wealth and standing. I kept on about my work, not much alarmed. The ten days passed away; the Supreme Court of Errors sat; Judge Williams was chief judge. The case was argued on both sides. When the plea was ended, then came the decision:—two of the court would send Nancy back to slavery; two were for her release; we shall hear from Williams to-morrow at eight o'clock.

At the time appointed all were in attendance to hear from Judge Williams. The Judge said that slavery was tolerated in some of the States, but it was not now in this State; we all liked to be free. This girl would like to be free; he said she should be free,—the law of the State made her free, when brought here by her master. This made a change in the feelings of the people. I could pass along the streets in quiet. Nancy said when she went into the court-house on the last day she had two large pills of opium; had she been sentenced to go back, she should have swallowed both of them before she left the court-house.

Now to my family. I have said I had two children born in Norfolk, and six in Hartford. One died in infancy. I lived in Hartford about sixteen years. I took a very prominent part in the organization of the Talcott Street Church. I moved from Hartford to Pittsfield, Mass. When I had been there three years and a half, my wife died in November; the May following I lost a son sixteen years of age. My oldest son enlisted in the U.S. Navy when he was eighteen, and has followed the sea ever since. I had another that went to sea, that I have not heard from for eight years. My oldest daughter went to Africa, to Cape Palmas; she went out a teacher, and has been there five years. I have one son who, when the war broke out, when the first gun was fired on Sumter, wanted to enlist, and did enlist in the navy, and went out on the brig Bainbridge, and served until she was stopped for repairs. He then went on the Newbern and served his time, and has an honorable discharge. Another, and the last one, enlisted in the artillery and went to New Orleans, but never, no, never came back, nor will he ever come again. I have a daughter in Massachusetts, of a frail constitution. She has a family to care for. I have none to care for me that has anything to spare, yet my children are willing to help as far as they are able. As they are not able I feel willing to do all that I can to help to get my living. The question is sometimes asked me if I have not any means of support. The fact is, I have nothing but what I have saved within the last three years. I have spent a portion of that time with my book about the country. I am now in my eightieth year of age, I cannot labor but little, and finding the public have a desire to know something of what slavery was in the State of Connecticut, in its time, and how long since it was at an end, in what year it was done away, and believing that I have stated the facts, many are willing to purchase the book to satisfy themselves as to slavery in Connecticut. Some told me that they did not know that slavery was ever allowed in Connecticut, and some affirm that it never did exist in the State. What I have written of my own history, seems to satisfy the minds of those that read it, that the so called, favored state, the land of good morals and steady habits, was ever a slave state, and that slaves were driven through the streets tied or fastened together for market. This seems to surprise some that I meet, but it was true. I have it from reliable authority. Yes, this was done in Connecticut.

August 22d, 1866, I had a fall and uncapped my knee, that laid me by ten months, so that I was unable to travel or do anything to help myself, but by the help of Him that does all things well, I have got so as to be able to walk with a staff. During the time that I was confined with my knee, I met with kind treatment, although I was away from home. I was in the state of New York at the time of my misfortune, away from any of my relations, still I was under the watchful care of a Friend that sticketh closer than a brother. He has thus far provided for me, and I feel assured that He will if I trust Him, with all my heart and soul and strength, and serve Him faithfully, which is my duty, the few years or days that are allotted to me, and it is my prayer that I may have grace to keep me, that I may not dishonor the cause of Christ, but that I may do that which will be acceptable in the sight of my Heavenly Father, so that I may do good to my fellow-men.

One thing in my history I have not mentioned, which I think of importance. Although born and raised in Connecticut, yes, and lived in Connecticut more than three-fourths of my life, it has been my privilege to vote at five Presidential elections. Twice it was my privilege and pleasure to help elect the lamented and murdered Lincoln. I am often asked when slavery was abolished in Connecticut; my answer is, the Legislature in

1788, passed an act that freed all that were born after 1792, those born before that time that were able to take care of themselves, must serve until they were twenty-five; my time of slavery expired in 1815. Connecticut I love thy name, but not thy restrictions. I think the time is not far distant when the colored man will have his rights in Connecticut.

LIFE

OF

WILLIAM GRIMES,

THE

RUNAWAY SLAVE,

BROUGHT DOWN

TO THE PRESENT TIME.

WRITTEN BY HIMSELF.

NEW HAVEN:

PUBLISHED BY THE AUTHOR.

1855.

TO THE PUBLIC.

THOSE who are acquainted with the subscriber, he presumes will readily purchase his history. Those who are not, but wish to know who Grimes is, and what is his history, he would inform them, generally, that he is now living in Litchfield, Connecticut, that he is about forty years of age, that he is married to a black woman, and passes for a negro, though three parts white; that he was born in a place in Virginia, has lived in several different States, and been owned by ten different masters; that about ten years since, he ran away, and came to Connecticut, where, after six years, he was recognized by some of his former master's friends, taken up, and compelled to purchase his freedom with the sacrifice of all he had earned. That his history is an account of his fortune, or rather of his suffering, in all these various situations, in which he has seen, heard, and felt, not a little.

To those who still think the book promises no entertainment, he begs leave to suggest another motive why they should purchase it. To him who has feeling, the condition of a slave, under any possible circumstances, is painful and unfortunate, and will excite the sympathy of all who have any. Such was my condition for more than thirty years, and in circumstances not only painful, but often intolerable. But after having tasted the sweets of liberty, (embittered, indeed, with constant apprehension,) and after having, by eight years labor and exertion, accumulated about a thousand dollars, then to be stripped of all these hard earnings and turned pennyless upon the world with a family, and to purchase freedom, this gives me a claim upon charity, which, I presume, few possess, and I think, none will deny. Let any one suppose himself a husband and father, possessed of a house, home, and livelihood: a stranger enters that house; before his children, and in fair daylight, puts the chain on his leg, where it remains till the last cent of his property buys from avarice and cruelty, the remnant of a life, whose best years had been spent in misery! Let any one imagine this, and think what I have felt.

WILLIAM GRIMES.

Litchfield, October 1st, 1824.

LIFE
OF
WILLIAM GRIMES.

I WAS born in the year 1784, in J——, County of King George, Virginia, in a land boasting its freedom, and under a government whose motto is Liberty and Equality. I was yet born a slave. My father, ——, was one of the most wealthy planters in Virginia. He had four sons; two by his wife, one, myself, by a slave of Doct. Steward, and another by his own servant maid. In all the Slave States the children follow the condition of their mother; so that, although in fact, the son of ——, I was in law, a bastard and slave, and owed by Doct. Steward. My father was a wild sort of man, and very much feared by all his neighbors. I recollect he shot a man by the name of Billy Hough, through the arm, who came to my master's and staid. He was, however, finally taken up and committed to Fredricksburg jail, for shooting Mr. Gallava, a gentleman of that county. He refused, however, to be taken, until a military force was called out. Then he gave up, went to jail, was tried and acquitted on ground of insanity. Doct. Steward's house was about a mile from my father's, where I went frequently, to carry newspapers, &c. He always used to laugh and talk with me, and send me to the kitchen to get something to eat. I also at those times saw and played with his other children. My brother, the mulatto, was sent to school, and I believe had his freedom when he grew up. My father, I have no doubt, would have bought and freed me, if I had not been sold and taken off while he was in jail. I supposed my father would have been hung; and whether wealth and powerful friends procured his escape, I know not. It is, however, a sufficient commentary upon that event, and upon my fortune, that I then thought and now speak on the subject with indifference. He died at his own house in J——, about the year 1804. That he suffered his blood to run in the veins of a slave, is the only reflection I would cast upon his memory, which is just none at all in the Slave States. He was a very brave man, I reckon; and when it was attempted to take him, armed his slaves, and would never have been taken alive, if some of his friends had not persuaded him to yield quietly. Mr.

Gallava was passing my father's when my father met him, and asked him to stop; he said, no, he could not. My father then drew his pistol and shot him dead. Mr. Gallava's servant came directly to Doctor Steward and gave the alarm. My father inherited the house and plantation where he lived from his father, who was a man of considerable notoriety, and I believe, both respected and beloved. His character I cannot give. His name, however, has been embalmed by the Muses, and lives in song; he being the very person on whom that famous song called, "Old Grimes," was written. The lines are as follows:

TUNE—"John Gilpin was a citizen."

Old Grimes is dead.—That good old man
    We ne'er shall see him more;
He used to wear a long black coat,
    All button'd down before.

His heart was open as the day;
    His feelings all were true;
His hair was some inclin'd to gray—
    He wore it in a queue.

Whene'er was heard the voice of pain
    His breast with pity burn'd—
The large, round head upon his cane,
    From ivory was turn'd.

Thus, ever prompt at pity's call,
    He knew no base design—
His eyes were dark, and rather small;
    His nose was aquiline.

He liv'd at peace with all mankind,
    In friendship he was true;
His coat had pocket holes behind—
    His pantaloons were blue.

Unharm'd—the sin which earth pollutes,
    He pass'd securely o'er:
And never wore a pair of boots,
    For thirty years or more.

But poor *Old Grimes* is now at rest,
    Nor fears misfortune's frown;

He had a double-breasted vest—
    The stripes ran up and down.

He modest merit sought to find,
    And pay it its desert:
He had no malice in his mind—
    No ruffles on his shirt.

His neighbors he did not abuse,
    Was sociable and gay;
He wore large bukcles in his shoes,
    And chang'd them every day.

His knowledge hid from public gaze,
    He did not bring to view—
Nor make a noise town-meeting days,
    As many people do.

His worldly goods he never threw
    In trust to fortune's chances;
But liv'd (as all his brothers do)
    In easy circumstances.

Thus, undisturb'd by anxious care,
    His peaceful moments ran;
And ev'ry body said he was
    A fine old gentleman.

Good people all, give cheerful thought
    To Grimes' memory:
As doth his cousin, ESEK SHORT,
    Who made this poetry.

Such, according to Esek Short, was the character of my grandfather; and, if it is impartially given, I think the family has degenerated. One would think, though, Mr. Short admired old Grimes' virtues more than he lamented his death.

Doct. Steward kept me until I was ten years old. I used to ride behind the carriage to open gates, and hold his horse. He was very fond of me, and always treated me kindly. This made my old mistress, his wife, hate me; and when she caught me in the house, she would beat me until I could hardly stand. Young as I was then, I can yet remember her cruelty with emotions of indignation that almost drove me to curses. She is dead, thank God, and if I ever meet her again, I hope I shall know her.

When I was ten years of age, Col. William Thornton came down from the mountains, in Culpepper County, to buy negroes, and he came to my master's house, who was his brother-in-law, and seeing me, thought me a smart boy. He asked my master what he would take for me; he replied, he thought I was worth £60. Col. Thornton immediately offered £65, and the bargain was made. The next morning I started with him for Culpepper. It grieved me to see my mother's tears at our separation. I was a heart-broken child, although too young to realize the afflictions of a tender mother, who was also a slave, the hopes of freedom for her already lost; but I was compelled to go and leave her. After two days travel on horseback, we arrived at my new master's plantation, which was called Montpelier. After residing there a few weeks, my mistress, finding me an honest servant boy, I was then intrusted with all the keys, which made some of the other servants jealous, who had, when in the situation which I held, pilfered from the stores entrusted to their care, for the purpose of giving to their acquaintances and relations; one in particular, my mistress's head servant and seamstress, who had as many children as my mistress, and who were then working on the plantation. They fared much harder there than they would in my situation. She tried every art she could invent to set my master and mistress against me. As I had to make the coffee every morning in the nursery, where this servant, whose name was Patty, sat sewing, she would, when I was out, often take medicine from the cupboard, and put it in the coffee; and her object in doing this, was to compel me to go on the plantation, and have one of her children in my place. But as I was a poor friendless boy, without any connexions or inducements to that, if I had been disposed, my mistress was determined to keep me in my present situation. But the favorable opinion my mistress had of my integrity (which was correct) has cost me many a severe flagellation, in the manner which I will now relate. I had always made the coffee to the satisfaction of my mistress, until one morning my young master, George Thornton, after taking two or three sips at it, observed, this coffee has a particular taste; and Doct. Hawes, whom I shall hereafter mention, being then at the table, observed the same, adding that it tasted as if some medicine has been put in it. Upon this remark of the Doctor, my mistress rose up from the table and went to the cupboard where the medicine was kept; and after examining said, "Here is where he has just taken it from this morning." My master then rose up in anger, and took me behind the ice-house, and whipped me severely in the following manner: First, he caused me to be what they call horsed up, by being raised upon the shoulders of another slave, and the slave to confine my hands around his breast; in this situation they gave me about forty or fifty lashes; they whipped me until I had hardly any feeling in me. The crime was sufficiently deserving the punishment, but for a young boy who had tried and exerted himself to the utmost to give good satisfaction to his master, mistress, and all the family, never intending to injure any other servant, but rather participate in their wrongs, and render assistance if it could lawfully be done; and all for the malicious temper and disposition of this same Patty, it was too much for me to bear. It indeed sometimes happened, that every morning I was taken and whipped severely, for this very act of that malicious (I must call her brute,) when I was entirely innocent. There, without friends, torn from the arms of my mother, who has since died in slavery, not being allowed to see me, her only son, during her last illness: (I knew of course she would suffer while confined and unable to help herself, and no one willing to help her that could be allowed to see her,) this, together with my sufferings, is sufficient to convince my readers, that any boy of my age would endeavor to find, and also improve an opportunity to clear themselves from the house of bondage.

Doct. Hawes, aforementioned, was present at the time I was whipped on account of the coffee, and advised my master not to whip me any more, as he thought I could not bear it much longer. He was my master's son-in-law, and a member of Congress, and married my master's eldest daughter. He did not whip me any more at that time, after the advice of the Doctor. Oftentimes, my mistress would have me make the coffee in the dining room, before her. At such times Patty had no opportunity for putting in the drugs, and the coffee was then good. I was satisfied in my own mind, that as she was the overseer of the house, and her husband of the plantation, there being about ten or fifteen servants about the house, and no one of them allowed to interfere with this business in which I was employed, that it must be through her machinations which she employed to injure me and get me severely flogged. One time they had what they call a spell, on the plantation, at which all the servants were compelled to turn out and assist in hoing corn. I then requested my master to let me go and assist them. He finally consented, and I went. After working there two days, they requested me to come back in the house again, but I refused; and in order that I should be punished for refusing to return, my master and mistress consented to my staying, thinking that my labor and fare would be so much harder that I would willingly return; but the fear of making the coffee and of the whipping I should receive, induced me still to refuse to return; although at the same time I longed to return on account of my food, (as did the children of Israel to the flesh pots of Egypt.) Patty and her husband were then better satisfied, for they had me just where they wanted me; that is, out of the house into the field, where I suffered everything but death itself. When I was in waiting at the house, Maj. Jones, brother-in-law to my master, saw me waiting about the house, and thinking me a smart active boy to wait about the house, asked my master if he would sell me. He refused, saying he wanted me to wait on his son, William Thornton, jr., who was studying with Lawyer Thompson, near Culpepper Court House, as soon as he should go into business for himself. So I was not sold this time.

I remained on the plantation about two years, under a black overseer by the name of Voluntine, who punished me repeatedly, to make me perform more labor than the rest of the boys. My master then procured another overseer, a white man, by the name of Coleman Thead; he treated us somewhat better than old Voluntine, but he was very severe, and flogged me severely several times, for almost nothing. The overseers have an unlimited control over the slaves on the plantation, and exercise their authority in the most tyranical manner. I was one day at work on the plantation, with nothing on but my shirt, when the overseer (Thead) came to me, threatening to whip me, and caught hold of me for that purpose. I clinched him and told him that if he struck me, I would inform my master about his riding a favorite horse without my master's consent; that my master had already enquired of me why the horse grew so poor, but I would not tell him; the fear of detection induced him to let me go, telling me to be a good boy, and he would not flog me. I worked under this overseer about nine months, when he left us and went to Georgia. I then worked under old Voluntine again for about six months, when my master engaged a new overseer by the name of *Burrows*: he was more severe than either of the former. After working with him some time, he set us to making fence, and would compel us to run with the rails on our backs, whipping us all the time most unmercifully. This hard treatment continuing for some time, I at length resolved to run away. I accordingly repaired to the cabin of a slave called *Planter George*, and informed him that I intended to run away the next morning. I asked him for an old jacket and some meal, both of which he promised to give me. I then baked what meal I had for my supper, and went to sleep. Old George immediately repaired to the house of the overseer and informed him of my intention to run away in the morning. The overseer came directly to the cabin and sent in George to question me, while he should listen without. George asked me if I intended to run away provided he would give me the jacket and some meal; being partly asleep I answered that I did not know. He repeated the question several times and still received the same answer. The overseer then hallooed out, "Hey, you son of a bitch, you are going to run away, are you? I'll give it to you; bring him out here." So they brought me out and horsed me upon the back of Planter George, and whipped me until I could hardly stand, and then told me if I did not run away he would whip me three times a day, and make me carry three rails to one all day.

In this manner do the overseers impose on their planters, and compel their slaves to run away, by cruel treatment. The next morning came, and I knew not what to do. If I went to the field, I was sure to be whipped, and to run away I did not like to. However, like most, I presume in my situation, I chose the latter alternative, so away I ran for the mountain. I passed close by the field where my young master, Philip Thornton, was shooting. His gun burst and blew off part of his thumb. I crept along under the fence, and got to the mountains, where I staid until night: then I began to be hungry, and thought I would go to some of the neighbors to get something to eat. I went to Mr. Pallam's and asked for some tobacco seed for my master for an excuse, and staid there all night. I got some corn bread for my supper, and picked up a little about the kitchen for the next day. The next morning I went to the mountains and staid till night again, when I went down to Mr. Pallam's to get something to eat, pretending that I had come on an errand from my master. Mr. Pallam immediately seized me and called to Daniel to bring the hame strings. He had been down to my master's that day and they told him I had gone off, and if I came there again, to take me, which he did, and would have carried me home that night, but his wife persuaded him to wait till morning. I was then put under the care of old Daniel. Mr. Pallam told me if I ran away from him he would catch me with his dogs, for they would track me any where. Daniel took me to his hovel, and for greater security took away my shoes. I lay peaceable till near morning. When the fear of my master came over me again, and I wished to get away. I begged old Daniel to let me go out, under pretence of necessity, but he refused. He finally gave me one of his shoes, and I went to the door to look out. It was just the dawn of day. I had been waiting the cock crowing all night, and it was now time to go if I went at all. The ground was covered with a light snow. I gave a jump and Daniel after me, but my step was as light as the snow flake, and the last glimpse I had of Daniel showed him prostrate over a log. I escaped to a corn field in sight of my master's house, and secreted myself in an old log which I had picked out before. While in the log I fell asleep, and dreamed they had caught and was tying me to be whipped; and such was my agony that I awoke, from a dream, indeed, but to reality not less painful. I staid in that place about three days, when I became so pinched with hunger, that I thought I might as well be whipped to death as to starve; so I concluded to give myself up, if I could get to my master before the overseer should get me. In that I succeeded. They gave me something to eat, and Doct. Hawes, my master's son-in-law, who was at the house, advised them not to whip me. My master asked me what made me go off: I told him the cruelty of the overseer. He then told the overseer not to whip me again without his knowledge. I was so hungry that they were afraid to give me as much as I wanted, lest I should kill myself. Not long after, however, the overseer came into the field where we were at work, and after trying to find some fault, whipped us all around. This was the first time he had done it since my master told him not; but I dare not tell my master, for if I did, the overseer would whip me for that. If it were not for our hopes, our hearts would break; we poor slaves always cherish hopes of better times. We are human beings, sensible of injuries, and capable of gratitude towards our masters. This overseer whipped me a great many times before I escaped from his hands. Shortly after this I recollect my master came home late at night, and getting off his horse, got entangled, and would have fallen if I had not been near, and caught him; and being a very large man, the fall might have injured him very much, nay, killed him. Afterwards, when he was angry with me, I could sometimes appease him somewhat by hinting this to him. There is a holiday which our master gave us, called Easter Sunday or Monday. On one of those days I asked my young master, Stuart Thornton, to let me go and see Miss Jourdine, a mulatto girl who was brought up with me and sold by Doct. Steward to Mr. Glassel. It was eight years before that when I saw her last. She was then a beautiful girl. I cannot describe the emotions of pleasure with which her presence filled my bosom, nor forget the hour when fate parted us forever. I presume the heart and the feelings of an illiterate peasant or an ignorant slave, are as susceptible and as ardent as those of men more enlightened, at least when warmed and excited by the influence of female attractions. The last look of a woman whom you know loves you, which is given through tears and with a consciousness that you are leaving her forever, troubles my heart beyond any thing I have since experienced. My young master did not like me to go, but I did. On the way my bosom burned and my heart almost leaped from me, as I thought on this girl. I felt as though I could, unarmed, have flogged half a dozen lions if they had crossed my path. I did not find her at Mr. Glassel's, she having been sold to Mr. Jourdine, who had bought her and kept her for his wife; but I did not return without seeing her. One of the Miss Glassels sent a book to my young mistress, to whom I presented it on my return. She asked me where I had been: I told her I had been to see Miss Jourdine. And because I called the girl Miss instead of Betty, my young mistress was extremely angry with me, and said she would have me whipped in the morning. In the morning Burrows, the overseer, came after me to Aaron's cabin, where I staid. As I came towards the house, my master came out, The little rascal, says he, had the impertinence to call that wench Miss Jourdine to his mistress; take him and give it to him. So they took me and tied me on a bench, and as soon as they began to whip, I would slip out from the rope, until my master told the overseer to horse me upon another's back, and after he had whipped me a while to stop and let me rest; for he said he wanted to whip me about a month. They began to whip again in a few minutes, though not so hard, and kept it up three or four hours; I begging all the while to be forgiven, and promising to offend no more. I was so weak after this, I could hardly stand, but they would not have got me to whip if it had not snowed, and prevented me from running away to the mountain. My master gave me many very severe floggings; but I had rather be whipped by him than the overseer, and especially the black overseers. Oh, how much have I suffered from these black drivers!

Sometime during this year, my master's son, George, wanted me to wait on him. He came to the field where I was at work, to see me. I had been fighting with Moses, and had cut off my hair as close as possible, for the purpose of having the advantage. Seeing this, he refused to take me, I looked so bad. So I was obliged to remain in the field and live on my peck of meal a week. Colonel Thornton was a severe master, and he made his' slaves work harder than any one about there, and kept them poorer. Sometimes we had a little meat, or fish, but not often anything more than our peck of meal. We used to steal meat whenever we could get a chance; and such was my craving for it, that if the punishment had been death, I could not have resisted the temptation. How much I suffered, I will not pretend to say; but I recollect one Saturday I had been to work hard all day: in the evening, I found, back of the garden, some hog's entrails which had been thrown out a few days before. I was so hungry for meat, that I took these guts, washed them, and put them into a skillet and boiled them. I then wet some corn meal in cold water, put it in the ashes, and made a fire over it. After it had baked, I mixed it with the guts and eat it; but before morning, I was so much swollen that I liked to have died. When any of the hogs died, we always eat them. But we did not wait for pigs and geese to die of old age, when we could get a chance to steal them. Steal? Yes, steal them. Why, I have been so hungry for meat that I could have eat my mother.

One instance of cruelty from my mistress I can never forget. It was my turn to beat homony that night. So I began at dark and beat most all night. Having been at work hard all day, before morning I was so hungry that I took and fanned the chaff and husks from the corn I was beating, wet it up with water, and baked it, and this without one grain of salt or fat. I had worked as hard as I could, and beat the homony as I thought sufficiently. About an hour before day, I lay down and went to sleep. In the morning, my mistress sent to the overseer to give me a severe whipping, for she said the homony was not beat quite enough, though very good. Notwithstanding I had worked all night as hard as I could spring, I was taken and flogged. (Homony is a kind of food used at breakfast and dinner. It is made of corn pounded till the skin is all off, then boiled, mashed and fried.) It seems as though I should not forget this flogging when I die; it grieved my soul beyond the power of time to cure. I should not have been alive now if I had remained a slave, for I would have resisted with my life, when I became older, treatment which I have witnessed towards others, from the overseers, and such as I should probably have met with, nay, such as I have received when a boy from overseers.

While I was with Col. William Thornton, a great many of his slaves were taken sick and died. Doct. Hawes married one of Col. Thornton's daughters, Fanny Thornton. My master gave him a tract of land in Culpepper, on which he built himself a house, about a mile from my master's, and came up there to live, from Caroline, Spotsylvania county. We always supposed that some of his slaves poisoned my master's; and I heard one of the servants say, that he saw an old woman of Doct. Hawes' put something like red earth into the bread. Several of the servants in the spinning room died, and after that there was a groaning heard in that room; and I have myself heard the spirits groan in that room. If ever there was a room haunted it was that. I will believe it as long as I have my breath to draw. I slept in the passage, close by the door of my master and mistress. Sometimes when I was as wide awake as I am now, the spirits would unlock the doors, and come up stairs, and trample on me, press me to the floor, and squeeze me almost to death; I should have screamed, but the fear of my master, who would not believe, but would have whipped me, prevented.

There was, not long after this, a great hurricane and earthquake; and I saw the sky part and it looked as red as crimson. The earth shook, and every thing that was on it; and I heard them talk of many thousands who were drowned.

There was, I recollect, at my master's, two gentlemen from Connecticut, Parson Beebe and Doct. Goodsell. They staid there sometime, and it was supposed Doct. Goodsell was courting my young mistress. One of my young masters came on to court with them. I heard them talk about New Haven, but I little thought I should ever see it.

While I was at work under Burrows, the overseer, my master's son, George, returned from Philadelphia, where he had been studying physic. He went to Northumberland County to practice, and took me from the plantation to wait on him.

In going to Northumberland, we passed through Leedstown, where I saw my mother and brothers. It was, I suppose, ten years since I had seen my mother. She was living with her old mistress, Doct. Steward's former wife, but now married to George Fitchue, Doct. Steward being dead. There is nothing in slavery, perhaps, more painful, then the unavoidable separation of parents and children. It is not uncommon to hear mothers say, that they have half a dozen children, but the Lord only knows where they are. Oh! my poor mother! but she is gone, and I presume her skin is now as white as that of her mistress.

Master George hired a house in Northumberland, and I took care of the house when he was gone. I always had been praying to God, ever since I knew what God was; and I thought, like Peter, I had faith. One day, when I was alone in the house, I shut all the doors in the house, and went up into the third story to pray; and just as I entered the room, I saw, to my astonishment, a number of skeletons hanging up about it. It was a terrible sight to me, and I was so frightened that I could not stop. The holes in the skull, where the eyes are, seemed to look right at me. I turned round as slowly and softly as possible, without taking my eyes from them until I shut the door. I have often thought it strange, that a skeleton or a corpse should terrify us, though they might shock our feelings. But my poor heart never walloped so before; and I had never thought our garret was a sepulchre.

My master sent me to Fredericksburg to get another doctor to come and help him cut off a woman's thigh. I had helped him once. but I almost fainted. When I had got in town and done my errand, I put out my horse at the tavern, and went into the kitchen, where, who should I find but my old master's cook, Philip. He told me that my brother Benjamin was in town. I went to see him, and told him who I was. He gave me seventy-five cents. With this I went and bought some cake and rum, and drank, not thinking, until I got drunk and fell down in the street. Some of my friends took me up and carried me in, and I slept till most night, when I started for home, and rode with all haste, lest my master should flog me for staying. I pretended to him that I rode slow. However, as I did not let him see the horse he never found out my scrape, and it is well he did not, for if he had, I might not have been here to record it. He was cross to me and I feared him like death. I recollect once his whipping me, after our return from Northumberland, so severely on the naked back, that I carry the stripes to this day, and all because his mother told him that I had been telling his younger brother something that was done when he lived at Northumberland. He gave me once a tumbler of spirits, and made me drink it, which almost killed me. This he did to conceal from my knowledge a scrape which he was going to have, as I supposed. If the cook had not blown tobacco smoke through me, I believe I should have been a corpse before morning.

After staying at Northumberland six or eight months, master George left there, and I went back to his father's plantation—I went sorrowing, too. Master George was going to Philadelphia again, so there was no other place for me but his father's plantation, where I must work all day, and sometimes most all night, with my peck of meal a week, and the hell-hound Burrows to flog me, for he gloried in doing it. One instance in which my master disappointed his savage heart, I remember. He told Burrows to take me down to the stable, tie my legs, put a rail between them, then stretch me up and whip me. While going down to the stable, which was about thirty or forty rods distant, I thought if the order was put in execution, I could not endure it, but must die in the operation. My master and Burrows went forward, and I followed behind. I looked up to heaven and prayed fervently to God to hear my prayer, and grant me relief in this hour of adversity; expecting every moment to be whipped until I could not stand; and *blessed be God* that he turned their hearts before they arrived at the place of destination: for, on arriving there, I was acquitted. God delivered me from the power of the adversary. Blessed be his name, he heard my prayer in the hour of adversity, and delivered me from the enemy. I will here inform my readers, that in the time of going down to the stable, I did not make a feeble attempt to induce my master not to flog me; but put my trust, and offered my prayers to my heavenly Father, who heard and answered them.

On my arriving at the stable, I was surprised to hear my master express himself in terms that I could not reasonably from former treatment expect. He said to me, "go, behave yourself well and you shall not be whipped." In the meantime, Burrows, the overseer, who had stood by wanting and waiting for the privilege of whipping me, stood in suspense and astonishment at the lenity of my master in not having me flogged after he, Burrows, had everything prepared for the purpose; such as a bundle of hickories, ropes to bind me, and a good stout hand to lay it on; ah! and a good resolution.

At one time my master having caused on oven to be built in the yard, for the purpose of baking bread for the negroes, I went there and finding it not quite dry, made impressions with my fingers, such as letters, &c., on it, while the mortar was green on the outside. Gabriel, one of the servants, a son of old Voluntine, was ordered to strip my shirt up and whip me; (the word severely has been so many times used it needs no repetition;) my master stood by to see the thing well executed: and as he thought he did not be severe enough, he ordered me to strip him and perform the same ceremony, which I did. He then ordered Gabriel to try to whip me harder than he did before. Then Gabriel knew what the old man meant, to wit, to whip me as severely as lay in his power, which he effected on the second trial, exerting all his strength and agility to the utmost to make me suffer, only to please his master. This being so often the case, the negro drivers and indeed the slaves, show much less humanity in punishment, than the masters themselves.

Again, while living with my present, or old master, Col. William Thornton, I had the care of some cows, two of which had calves; and I tried to invent some method to get some milk from these cows, to eat my corn bread; but dared not let any person know that I did it, fearing that if I did I should receive a severe whipping. But a stratagem occurred to me. We had gourds growing on the side of the fence. I had often used and seen used, the shell of the gourd for a ladle, or scoup dish, and I took a gourd that was green, and excoriated a part, took out the seeds, &c., and without any further cleansing, I filled it with milk from the cow, and then hid it in the chaff pen. I then went home and baked some bread, and got another gourd and carried there the milk. Being in an open place and it requiring straining, I had nothing at all to strain it through; but being under necessity, I took a part of my shirt tail, which being made of coarse tow cloth, and not having been washed for five or six weeks, I being a poor motherless boy, and no one to wash it but myself, and I all the time kept busy in the field, under the overseer; my shirt was what would be generally termed, full of lice at the time; but as I had no other cloth for straining I made use of that. But when I went to get the milk, the gourd being green, the milk had contracted a bitterness of which no one can judge, unless they have had a trial. I was however driven to the necessity of eating it, or eating my bread dry. I was quite fearful of being taken by old James, a black servant, who was very much respected by master and mistress, although very deceitful, but escaped his vigilance. He died before I began to wait on any of my young masters; and peace be to his soul.

Master George returned from Philadelphia in about a year. He courted his cousin, who lived about six miles from his father's, and married her. His father gave him a plantation, a mile from his own, where I was now placed. My master lived at my wife's father's, intending to move in the spring; this being the fall season. The name of his overseer was Bennet. This Bennet and his mother, had lived on land rented to them by my former master, Col. Thornton. They were then very poor, and secretly bought things from the negroes which they had stolen from my master. This Bennet, having now become overseer, was severe. My master had a servant by his wife's estate called James. I saw Bennet strip off James' shirt, and whip his naked back as if he had been cutting down a tree. I thought what was to be my fate.

One day I was sick and did not go to ploughing. Bennet came after me, and told me he would whip me if I did not. I took up a stick, and told him if he put his hand upon me I would strike him; and marched towards him as bold as a lion. But he knew that I had lived so poor that I had not much strength; and seeing that he did not fear but was in a great rage, I took to my heels. But he caught me and dragged me up to the negro houses, and called two of them to come and assist him. While they were tying me, I made one pitch at Bennet with my head. I missed him, but he hit me with a club, and knocked me speechless. The blood ran from my mouth and nose very fast. I was then so weak that I could hardly stand; so I gave up, and told the overseer to whip me as much as he pleased, but if he did not whip me to death he should drink sorrow for it. When I was tied, James brought the sticks. I spoke out brave, and said to the overseer, why don't you get some better ones; whip me till your soul is satisfied, but I'll remember every stick. He began to whip, and I counted out loud every stroke. After he had struck me eleven times, he said, if you will say that you are drunk, and hold your peace, I will stop. I said, you might as well whip me to death; for if you don't master will, when he hears of this. But he promised me that if I would hold my tongue, and say nothing about this, he would see that I should not be whipped. He knew that it was for his interest to keep me from exposing their buying things which they knew the slaves had stolen. My master, however, heard something about this scrape, and was going to whip me, but Mr. Bennet interfered, and told him that I was drunk, as I said, and that he had whipped me enough.

I ought, perhaps, to blame slavery more than my master's. The disposition to tyrannize over those under us, is universal; and there is no one who will not occasionally do it. I had too much sense and feeling to be a slave; too much of the blood of my father, whose spirit feared nothing. I was therefore, perhaps, difficult to *govern in the way in which it was attempted*. I was at this time the property of George Thornton, to whom I was given by his father. Doct. P. T., an older brother, at this time came up from his father's plantation to buy me, which he did.

I was then in the ice-house; he called me up, and the moment I saw him my heart leaped for joy. He asked me if I was willing to go and wait on him, as it would be much easier for me than it would to work on the plantation? I answered, yes sir, if you please. He then said he had bought me, and was going to Port Royal, to practice physic, and wanted me to go with him on another horse, carry his portmanteau and wait on him. He then sent me to the tailor's to get some clothes, and fitted me out very handsomely. We traveled on to Port Royal, where he went into practice. I had two horses to take care of. After remaining there a couple of months, he formed an acquaintance with a young lady, who he afterwards married. After he had been married one month and four days, his wife died. Soon after that we returned to his father's plantation in Montpelier. After remaining there a few days we went on to Frederickstown in Maryland, where we staid a short time, and returned again to his father's. After a short stay there, we went to Monticello, and resided at the house of Thomas Jefferson, formerly President of the United States, for a few weeks. While we were there he met with his brother-in-law, from Port Royal, and we returned to that place, when he stayed long enough to settle up his business, and then went to Richmond, Virginia, to practice physic, where he had a very good run of business. After some time, having an opportunity to earn something, I had laid up a few dollars, and being very fond of having my fortune told, I was anxious to know whether I should be a free man or not. I went to an old woman who told fortunes, in order to have her tell mine, a number of times. She told me that I should be sold to a gentleman, and be taken to the south. I asked her what kind of a man he was: she told me his head was white, which I afterwards found to be true, for he used powder. What she told me proved to be true: she told me he was a crabbed sort of a man and that I should be severely dealt with. She said to me, don't you go, your master will not compel you to go, but you will finally consent to it, and will go. I told her I would not go. She again told me that I would. I have since thought it strange how this old creature could tell me exactly as it was; but it was so. The man who bought me was at this time in New York, some hundreds of miles off.

Some months after this, one morning as I was busily engaged about the yard, cleaning my master's boots, and doing other work as usual, a gentleman came into the yard at the bell tavern, where my master boarded, and enquired of one of the servants for Doct. Thornton. He told him he did not know where he was, but pointing to me said, there is his servant, sir. He then said to me, are you his servant boy? I answered him that I was. He then told me to go up and tell my master (who was then in bed) that he wanted to see him. I went and told my master there was a gentleman below who wished to see him. He told me to invite him up into his room. I did so and showed him the way up, where I left them together. A short time after this he came down and asked me if I should be willing to go to Savannah with him, provided he should buy me. I told him I did not know where it was. He then told me to go up and see my master. I did so, and he asked me if I wanted to go with that gentleman. I told him I was very well contented to live with him. (He had always treated me perfectly well, we never had any difficulty.) I found that this gentleman had enquired on the road for a good servant, and being informed that my master had one that he would sell, he came to buy me. My master told me that this gentleman was rich and would be likely to give me my time after a few years, but I did not agree to go still. The gentleman again returned from the eagle tavern to our boarding house, the bell tavern. He then slipped two dollars into my hand and said, here, boy, take this and say you will go; and after a great deal of coaxing and flattering, I finally consented to go, for which I have many a time and often heartily repented. He then went to my master and I followed him. He told him that I had consented to go. My master said he would not force me to go, but if I was willing he would consent to it. Mr. A——, (for that was my new master's name, who was a Jew,) then paid him five hundred dollars. Doct. Thornton then ordered his horse up: he would not stay to see me start, but bade me good bye, and rode off with tears in his eyes. I then started with my new master for Savannah, with a carriage and four horses; we traveled about twelve miles the first day. I was dissatisfied with him before I had got two miles. We traveled the next day twenty-five miles, as far as Petersburgh. I was so much dissatisfied with him, that I offered a black man at that place, two silver dollars to take an axe and break my leg, in order that I could not go on to Savannah; but he refused, saying he could tell me a better way. I asked him how? He said run away. I told him I would not run away unless I was sure of gaining my freedom by it. We then traveled on the next day about thirty miles, and put up for the night. I then attempted to break my leg myself. Accordingly I took up an axe, and laying my leg on a log, I struck at it several times with an axe endeavoring to break it, at the same time I put up my fervent prayers to God to be my guide, saying, "if it be thy will that I break my leg in order that I may not go on to Georgia, grant that my blows may take effect; but thy will not mine be done." Finding I could not hit my leg after a number of fruitless attempts, I was convinced by my feelings then, that God had not left me in my sixth trouble, and would be with me in the seventh. Accordingly I tried no more to destroy myself. I then prayed to God, that if it was his will that I should go, that I might willingly. My old master and mistress in Virginia had often threatened to sell me to the negro buyer from Georgia, for any trifling offence, and in order to make me dislike to go there, they would tell me I should have to eat cotton seed and make indigo, and not have corn bread to eat as I did in Virginia. The next day we went as far as Columbia, in South Carolina. This was Saturday evening.

I was quite fatigued, and after taking care of the horses, I laid myself down in the stable to rest. I soon fell asleep, and slept for an hour or two. My master missing me, and thinking I had run away, made a thorough search for me, but could not find me until I awoke and went into the house. He was very angry with me: he cursed me and asked me where I had been. I told him I had been asleep in the stable. He told me I lied, and that I had attempted to make my escape; threatening to whip me. I told him I had not attempted any thing of the kind; but he would not believe me. Here, again, I was in great trouble. I went to bed and slept as well as I could, which was but little.

The next day we pursued our journey, and nothing of any consequence occurred, different from what had before taken place, until we arrived at

Savannah, which was in about six weeks. As we entered the city, we were about to pass a man who had a gun on his shoulder, loaded with shot. It accidentally went off, the contents within a very few inches of me. Here, again, I escaped a wound, if not death. After residing in Savannah for a few months, and perceiving that he grew more severe and inhuman with me every day, I began to despair of ever living with him in peace. I however found some friends in Savannah, after a short time, and they advised me (after being made acquainted with the manner in which I was used) to get away from him as soon as possible. He would never allow me to leave the yard, unless it was for the purpose of taking out his horses to exercise them. At such times, I would often go to the fortune-teller, and by paying her twenty-five cents, she would tell me what she said my fortune would be. She told me I should eventually get away, but that it would be attended with a great deal of trouble; and truly, I experienced a vast deal of trouble before I could get away.

I will state to my readers some facts relative to the treatment I received from him, and others, during the time I lived there. He had an old black female slave whom he called Frankee. I always believed her to be a witch: circumstances to prove this, I shall hereafter state. He also had, at one time, a number of carpenters at work in his yard. One of them was a man about my size, and resembling me very much in dress, being dressed in a blue roundabout jacket. He came into the yard to his work one morning, with an umbrella in his hand. This old woman saw him come in, and thinking it was me, or pretending so to do, was the cause of my receiving a severe whipping, in the following manner. My master having mislaid his umbrella, had been looking for it for some time, and on inquiring of her about it, she told him that she saw me come into the yard with it in my hand. I was then in the yard; he called to me, and said, where have you been, sir? I replied, only to work about the yard, sir. He then asked me where I was all night with his umbrella? I told him I had not been out of the yard, nor had I seen his umbrella. He said I was a liar, and that I had taken his umbrella away, and was seen to return with it in my hand this morning when coming into the yard. I told him it was not so, and that I knew nothing about it. He immediately fell foul of me with a large stick, and beat me most unmercifully, until I really thought he would kill me. I begged of him to desist, as I was perfectly innocent. He not believing me, still continued to beat me, until his strength was entirely exhausted. Some time after this, my mistress found his umbrella where she had placed it herself, having removed it from the place where he had left it, and gave it to him, saying, you have beat him for nothing—he was innocent of it. I was afterwards informed by another servant of the circumstance. I then went to my master, and told him that he had beaten me most unmercifully for a crime I was not guilty of, all through the insinuation of that old woman. He replied, "No, by Gad, I never hit you a blow amiss: if you did not deserve it now, you did some other time." I told him she must have been drunk or she would not have told him such a story. He said that could not be, as she never was allowed to have any liquor by her. I told him to look in her chest, and convince himself. He then inquired of her if she had any rum. She said, no, sir, I have not a drop. I then told him that if he would look in her chest he would find it. He accordingly went, and found it. He then said to her, hey, you old bitch, I have caught you in a lie. On this same account she appeared to be determined to kill me, by some means or other. I slept in the same room with her, under the kitchen. My blankets were on the floor. She had a straw bed on a bedstead about four paces from mine. My master slept directly over my head. I have heretofore stated that I was convinced that this creature was a witch, and would turn herself into almost any different shape she chose. I have at different times of the night felt a singular sensation, such as people generally call the night-mare. I would feel her coming towards me, and endeavoring to make a noise, which I could do quite plainly at first; but the nearer she approached me the more faintly I would cry out. I called to her, aunt Frankee! aunt Frankee! as plain as I could, until she got upon me and began to exercise her enchantments on me. I was then entirely speechless; making a noise like one apparently choking or strangling. My master had often heard me make this noise in the night, and had called to me to know what was the matter; but as long as she remained there I could not answer. She would then leave me and go to her own bed. After my master had called to her a number of times, Frankee! Frankee! what ails Theo? (a name I went by there, cutting short the name Theodore,) she answered, hag ride him, sair. He then called to me, telling me to go and sleep with her. I could then, after she had left me, speak myself, and also have use of limbs. I got up and went to her bed, and tried to get under her coverlid; but could not find her. I found her bedclothes wet. I kept feeling for her, but could not find her. Her bed was tumbled from head to foot. I was then convinced she was a witch, and that she rode me. I then lay across the corner of her bed without any covering, because I thought she would not dare to ride me on her own bed, although she was a witch. I have often, at the time she started from her own bed, in some shape or other, felt a shock, and the nigher she advanced towards me, the more severe the shock would be. The next morning my master asked me what was the matter of me last night? I told him that some old witch rode me, and that old witch is no other than old Frankee. He cursed me, and called me a damned fool, and told me that if he heard any more of it, he would whip me. I then knew he did not believe in witchcraft. He said, why don't she ride me? I will give her a dollar, Ride me, you old hag, and I will give you a dollar. I told him she would not dare to ride him.

One morning after he had given me such a severe pounding concerning the umbrella, and I was determined not to stay with him long, but to get away from him as soon as possible, he ordered me to fetch up my horse and saddle him, and put the other horse to the chaise, in order to go out to Bonaventure. I did so, and whilst I was gone I tried to invent some project, to make him believe me unwell. The next morning I prentended to be sick. He asked me what was the matter with me? I told him I had a pain in my side. He then said to Miss A — , go and weigh out a pound of salts for him, She did so. He then came to me with the salts in a cup, and said, do you see this, sir–do you see this? By Gad, you shall take every bit of this. He then mixed up a slight dose and gave it to me, which I took. He then sent for a doctor, who came and felt my pulse, and then said it would be well enough to put a blister plaister on my side. He accordingly went home, spread a very large plaister, and sent it over, which my master caused to be put on my side, which drew a large blister there. All this I bore without being sick or unwell, in the least. There was a man who had been to him repeatedly to see if he would sell me. He always refused, saying, no, I did not buy him to sell; and I will be damned if I do sell him,–I bought him for my own use. I saw that he knew I was determined to get a new master, and he was the more determined to keep me. At length I refused to eat any thing, at all. He would often ask me why I would not eat. I answered him that I could not, I was very weak and unwell. Still he invented every method he could to induce me to eat, often setting victuals by my bedside, &c. At length, one day he wanted me to go and fetch a load of wood. He said, come, make haste and get your dinner ready, I want you to be a clever fellow, and eat your dinner, then to take the horse and cart, and go out and fetch in a load of wood. The dinner was soon ready: he cut off some meat and other victuals, and gave me before he eat himself, saying, here now, take this, be a clever fellow; eat it, and go and fetch a load of wood. I told him I did not want it. He says, take it, sir, and eat it. I replied, I thank you, sir, I don't want it. Got tam your soul, you don't want it; ha, you Got tam son of a bitch, you don't want it, do you? He then took up a chair and came towards me, threatening to kill me. His wife being afraid he would, called to him in order to prevent him, saying, do not kill him; do not strike him with that chair. He set it down and called to Frankee, fetch me a rope, Got dam you, fetch me a rope. I will bind him fast, send him to jail, and let him have Moses' law, (which is thirty-nine lashes on the naked back.) She fetched the rope, and he bound me, and was on the point of having me taken to jail when I, dreading the whipping I knew I should be obliged to take if I went there, finally consented to eat my victuals, which I relished exceedingly well. Then I went to the woods, and fetched home a load of wood. After that I again refused to eat anything, at all; but pretended to be sick all of the time. I also told Frankee to tell my master that I was subject to such turns every spring, and I should not live through this. She told him, which frightened him very much, thinking he should lose me, (which would grieve him as much as it would to lose a fine horse of the same value.) He then again tried to make me eat by the same means, often leaving victuals by my bedside at night, or order Frankee to do it. He would then inquire of her if I had eaten anything yet. She replied, no, sir, I have not seen him eat anything since last Friday noon. I had his horse to water every day; and as I went out of, or across the yard, where I knew he would see me, I would pretend to be so weak that I could scarcely go. I would stagger along, to make him think that I should fall every moment. He one time called his wife to the window, saying, Misses, Misses, by Gad, come here, do you see him? He is almost gone; by Gad, I shall lose him; see how he staggers. By Gad, he has not eat a mouthful now for these three weeks. I must lose him, by Gad; do you see that? I would, however, have it understood, that during all this time I did not go without victuals. I sometimes could steal a little provision; and after driving my master to his plantation, I could sometimes run into the potatoe house, where I could find a few of them, which I ate raw. At other times I could find a bone, not quite stripped clean, which, together with what I stole, made me a comfortable subsistence; or as much so as the slaves generally receive. I was determined not to eat anything in his sight, or to his knowledge, in order to make him think he must either sell me or lose me. One morning he sent me to eat my breakfast. I told him I did not want any. He said, go along and get your breakfast. I went, and returned. When I came back, he asked me if I had eaten my breakfast? I told him, no, sir, I thank you, I did not wish for any. You did not, did you? Gad dam you, you are sick are you? You may die and be damned, by Gad;—you may die and be damned;—your coffin shall not cost me a quarter of a dollar, by Gad;—you shall be buried on your face, by Gad;—you may die and be damned.

Which of us is most likely to receive that part of this blessing which is to take effect in the next life, I will not say. However, being determined to change my situation if possible, I went to one Major Lewis, a free black man, and very cunning. I gave him money to go to my master and run me down, and endeavor to convince him that I was really sick, and should never be good for anything. In a few days from this, my master came down in the kitchen and says, boy get up; there, boy, (holding it out in his hand,) there is the very money I gave for you: I have got my money again, and you may go and be damned; and don't you never step into my house again; if you do, I will split your damned brains out. I then went to my new master, Mr. Oliver Sturges, who came from Fairfield, Connecticut. He bought me to drive his carriage. A new coachman's dress, which he gave me, would have felt much better, if it had not been for the large blister that had been drawn upon my side. However, I rode down by my old master's, and cracked my whip with as much pride, spirit and activity, as one of Uncle Sam's mail carriers, who drives four horses, on a general post road, drunk or sober. My old master happening to see me pass in this manner, was very much chagrined to think he had sold me under the impression that I was just ready to die. He called his wife to the window and complained to her that she had urged him to sell me, and swore and cursed outrageously. I was now under my sixth master, Mr. Sturges, who bought me from the Jew. Mr. Sturges was a very kind master, but exceedingly severe when angry. He had a new negro, by the name of Cato, with whom I got a fighting, and bit off his nose, just as my master was going to sell him, which injured the sale of Cato very much. For this I had to beg very hard to escape being whipped. I went to the fortune tellers, who told me that my master said that if he should take me on with him to New York, I should be free; so I knew that I should not go with him. I had always been in the habit of praying, ever since I knew what it meant; and whenever I went to church, to drive the carriage, I used to stand upon the steps and listen to the preaching. About this time I began to realize that I was a sinner, and that hell would be my portion if I should die in my present situation; and afterwards while I was living with Dr. Collock, and under the advice of the Rev. Mr. Collock, whose voice and preaching harrowed up my soul with awful apprehensions, I sought and obtained the hope of salvation. Blessed be God, I know the path to heaven. I have had sweet communion with the Lord; but alas! I have erred, and gone astray from holiness.

My conscience used sometimes to upbraid me with having done wrong, after I had run away from my master and arrived in Connecticut; and while I was living in Southington, Conn. (where I spent some time, as will afterwards be told,) I went up on a high mountain and prayed to the Lord to teach me my duty, that I might know whether or not I ought to go back to my master. Before I came down I felt satisfied, and it did seem to me that the Lord heard my prayers, when I was a poor, wretched slave, and delivered me out of the land of Egypt, and out of the house of bondage; and that it was His hand, and not my own artfulness and cunning, which had enabled me to escape: therefore, if we trust in God, we need have no fear of the greatest trials; and though my heart has been pierced with sufferings keen as death, and drank from the cup of slavery the bitterest dregs ever mingled in it, yet, under the consolations of religion, my fortitude never left me.

As Mr. Sturges was intending to remove to New York, he sold out all his property, and every thing he could wish to part with. He talked very strong of taking me on with him to New York; but after consideration altered his mind, and hired me out to a Mr. Wolhopter, a printer, in Savannah. I lived with Mr. Wolhopter all that summer, and drove his horses and carriages all about there, and out to White Bluff, where he had hired a seat for the summer, supposing it to be a healthy situation, which indeed it was; but we were tormented with mosquitoes and such other insects as infest that country, (called by different names,) to a great degree, so that we could hardly sleep at nights. We were alternately at this place and at Savannah for the space of four or five months. At the expiration of that time, Mr. Wolhopter removed back to Savannah, with his family, and I accompanied them. I will here mention that during the time I resided at White Bluff, at the request of Mr. Wolhopter I often went a fishing, and the rays of the sun beating down more severe there than where I had formerly lived, it created an ague and fever, which reduced me so low that even my attending physician, Dr. Collock (who attended me strictly for about four months,) despaired of my life; and often since that time being borne down under the afflictions that a slave often experiences—and indeed too often—I have wished his predictions had proved true. But after Dr. Collock perceived I was convalescent, and gaining my health and strength rapidly, he inquired of me, that provided he should buy me, if I would be contented to live with him, drive his horses and carriage, occasionally wait in the house and at the table, and do such other business as is necessarily required in a family.

With but few remarks I endeavor to give my readers but a faint representation of the hard treatment, ill-usage and horrid abuse the poor slave experiences while groaning under the yoke of bondage:—that yoke which is not easy, nor the burden light; but being placed in that situation, to repine is useless; we must submit to our fate, and bear up, as well as we can, under the cruel treatment of our despotic tyrants. After Dr. Collock made this proposition to me, I replied that I had been sold from my parents in Virginia, and felt anxious to see them again once more; but if he would buy me, I would serve him faithfully and freely for the term of five years, provided that at the expiration of that time he would grant me my freedom, to be specified in writing; to which he consented, and promised to have it done, and give me the writing to keep; but he never fulfilled his promise. He, however, wrote to Mr. Sturges, in New York, and told me that he had received a letter from him, in which he consented I should go and live with him, and directed me to leave Mr. Wolhopter's house and come to his place of residence, which I accordingly did; being then very low in health, not having recovered from the ague and fever, but after living with him for some time I recovered my health, so far as to be able to perform my duty. When I first went there, on account of my being unwell my mistress did not like to have me sleep in the house, and so gave me a room up over the carriage house to sleep in. In this room there was a bedstead, or bunk, made of boards. I understood, by some of the servants, that a man lately died there in a fit. In the course of the day I laid myself down on the bedstead with a blanket to rest, not being able to be about, as a very little exercise overcame me. After lying there about an hour, I was looking very steady up towards the roof of the building, when to my great horror and surprise I could plainly perceive a large, bright, sparkling pair of eyes intently fixed on me, staring me full in the face. It instantly occurred to me that the bedstead I was then lying on belonged to the man who had died there, and that I (not having any liberty to use it) was doing wrong, and that this was a token for me to leave it. I accordingly took my blanket, spread it on the floor, and slept on that. Presently after the cook, Jane, came up to fetch me something to eat, she inquired of me why I left the bedstead and lay on the floor. I replied to her that I was afraid I had done wrong in lying on it as long as I already had done, for I had received no liberty from any person so to do, and I was convinced in my own mind that the bedstead placed there belonged to the man who had died there; and that I thought I had seen a token for me to leave it, which I accordingly had done. I then told her the circumstances of the eyes and of my conjectures at the time, that I had no business there. She replied to me, sleep on it if you please, you are perfectly welcome to the use of it. My mistress not knowing anything of what had happened, sent me word that I might have a lamp there to keep burning through the night. She then was very kind to me and used me well; but I could not endure the thoughts of sleeping there, and as soon as bed-time came, I took my blanket and went into the house, and slept in the parlor with the two boys who were then waiting in the house, named Sandy and Cyrus, (commonly called Cy.) This being all unknown to my mistress at that time, but she afterwards consented to have me sleep in the house, which I did during the time I lived there. My readers, or many of them who are not credulous, will very likely be apt to disbelieve the assertion already made, but I can assure them that the whole is true. Where is the person who would be made easily to believe a story of this kind, unless he positively did know it to be a fact, and the circumstances can be attested to even now. Although they did not see what I did, there were some of them acquainted with the circumstances. This cook, who brought me my victuals, told me the place was said to be haunted. She had her information from the other servants, who also told me the same; also, that strange noises were heard, which had been heard by other persons who were sick and put up there by my master's orders to be taken care of; many of them had been removed on the same account, as they told that they were positive of hearing strange noises, and also seeing frightful sights. These stories, combined with what I myself saw, warranted me in my opinion to make this assertion. I think the house, without any doubt, is what people in general would call haunted. My readers may put their own constructions and draw inferences, I can barely state that I tell the truth.

   This circumstance happened in the winter. The next summer my master, Dr. Collock, ordered me to get the horses and carriage ready, to take all the family off to Darien, which I accordingly did. They went from thence to Cumberland Island, and I returned to Savannah with the horses and carriage, alone. My master gave me a piece of bacon, or shoulder, smoked, which I suppose would weigh about six or eight pounds, which was the whole he left me to last all summer. He also left a tierce of rice to be divided among us about the house, in all eight or ten of us. After the rice was gone, we were allowed to each of us eight quarts of Indian corn per week; this was all we had to subsist on during his absence, which was about six or seven months. I also had a great deal to do about the house, and out on the plantation I had as much mowing as I could attend to. At another time, when I was at work out in the country, at my master's country seat, I had slipped the head stalls or bridles over the horses heads in order to let them eat while they were harnessed to a wagon, as I had been using them to draw hay. I left them to eat while I went to eat my dinner. In the meantime, two or three small negro children got into the wagon and frightened the horses, so that they ran round the house in the yard a number of times; and in so doing, they dragged the wagon over, or so nigh a young tree which my master set great store by, that it was torn up or broken down. When my master returned from Cumberland Island, he inquired of the driver (Old Ben) what had become of the tree. Old Ben replied, the torm broke him down, massa; and my master knew no more afterwards about it. The wagon that was also badly broken, we mended up as well as we could among ourselves: the harness, which being considerably injured, I carried to Mr. Kitchen, who being used to make and repair harnesses for my master, fixed it so that he (my master) never found that it had been broken or injured. All of this passed unnoticed by my master.

At the time Dr. Collock left Savannah, he left in his office an old man called Dr. Sherman to take charge of his office, and attend on such persons as should request his attendance, when he was gone. There were also, at the same time, two young gentlemen in the office, studying with my master; one of them named James M'Call, and the other, a young man I think they called Mr. Ginneylack. He at different times had insulted these young gentlemen to such a degree, that they left the office. A short time after this he found a large paper containing a number of images drawn out with a pencil; one representing himself, and others representing ducks, with their bills open, apparently in the attitude of squalling. On the paper was written something like this:—"How do you do, my good old friend?—how do you do?—how are your sore legs? We know that ducks quack, and Sherman is a quack," &c. It was supposed that he was a quack in the greatest degree. Dr. Collock was considered one of the best physicians in Savannah; but as he was obliged to go to Cumberland Island, and could get no other person of any repute to remain in his office and take charge of his business readily, and this old man (or doctor) being an indigent person, he, out of charity, let him remain in his office until his return, and transact such business in his line as the people should see fit to set him about. The old man, not knowing to whom to ascribe the (what he termed) libel, vented his malice on me, by asserting that I was the author of it, of which I was perfectly innocent; but he made my master believe it. He wrote to him while he was at Cumberland Island, and persuaded him that I was actually the author. At the time my master wished to return to Savannah, he wrote to his brother-in-law, Edward Campbell, Esq., attorney-at-law, requesting him to come with me, with the carriage and horses, to Darien, in order to take him and his family home. We accordingly went on one day, met them there, and returned the next. After our return, my master took me into his office, and inquired of me about these images. I told him I knew nothing about it. He was very inquisitive about it, but I still told him I knew nothing about it; but as Sherman made him believe that I had done all this mischief, of course my mistress also believed it; and after that I could never please them, let me try my best endeavors, they still appeared to be dissatisfied.

I was one evening ordered to take my mistress and her sisters to Mr. Andrews'. I accordingly harnessed the horses, put them to the carriage, and drove (with the ladies) to the house where I was directed. They went in the house and stayed, I do not know how long. I stayed with the horses and carriage at the door, in order to take care of them. I waited for them until I fell asleep and was dreaming. When they came out of the house, they awoke me by their talking and laughing at the door. I did not know where I was, where I had been, nor where I was a going. I knew no more where I was than if I had been blindfolded. But I was afraid to let them know that I had been asleep, so I drove on directly towards the market, looking on the right hand and on the left, to see if I could recognize some house that I had before been acquainted with; but finding none I drove on. I had passed a number of turns which would have taken us directly home. My mistress observing this, enquired of me why I did not take that route home, but I made her no reply, then turned towards the bay, thinking I was driving towards the commons. I then saw Mrs. Telfure's house, and then I knew where I was. I then drove down to Judge Jones', and left her sisters there, and continued on home with my mistress to Broad street. I do not think that my mistress, or either of the ladies ever suspected the reason why I took such a roundabout road to get home; but it was owing entirely to my falling asleep in the carriage while waiting at the door, and on awaking not knowing where I was.

At another time I was severly attacked with a toothache. My master drew one of my teeth, which fractured my jaw, and made it ache worse. He had often given me a great many bottles to clean and scour, and at this time gave me a great number. I went down under the bluff to get some sand for the purpose of cleaning them. While I was there I kept drinking spirits, (in order to ease my jaw where the tooth was drawn,) till I got completely intoxicated, and did not return until nearly evening. *I was then a praying soul.* As I was returning back to my master's house, I called in at the Rev. Henry Collock's study or office. He seeing my condition, or the condition I then was in, immediately offered to attend prayers with me, which he did; we prayed there nearly half an hour. I went into his office with tears rolling down my bosom, and the floor of his office will be a witness to my tears until the day of judgment. After our prayers were ended I came out, and the next time I saw him, was within the walls of a cold prison; he came to the diamond hole, and spoke to me, and asked me how I did, (I was at the time lying down on my blanket on the floor.) I answered him, I had a very bad jaw-ache. I then asked him to give me a book containing the Psalms of David, such an one as I was then reading. The next day he sent me a Bible. I, however, at the time I left this Parson Collock at his office went directly home to my master, who was his cousin. One was a worldly man, the other was a Christian. Immediately after I went into the yard, my master had information of it, and then took me in his office; he asked me where I had been? I told him I had been after gravel to clean his bottles, and on account of the pain in my jaw, I had drank spirits until I was so much intoxicated that I dare not come back until then. He then, after having a long conversation with me, ordered me to go up stairs and lie down. I did so, but after I had lain there a few minutes, he came up, took me by the collar and ordered me to go into a room where he wanted to lock me up. At this time I suspected his intention of wishing to lock me up, in order that as soon as night came, he could send me to jail. I then pretended to be much more intoxicated than I really was, in hopes by that means to induce him to let me remain where I then was until morning; but he would not, and after a severe struggle, he effected the purpose he intended, and I was locked up in a room in the third story, or in the garret. After sitting sometime I began to consider my situation. I observed a bedstead with a cord in it, which I concluded best for me to take out and let myself down from the window, and clear myself for the woods; but upon examination, I found the window so high from the ground, (after I had taken the cord from the bedstead,) that I feared to attempt the leap; I threw back the cord with despair, and then determined to force the door; it was in me a desperate undertaking, but I finally effected it. After coming down the stairs as still and shy as possible, that creature, Jane the cook, perceived me and gave the alarm. Immediately the cry of stop thief! stop thief! re-echoed from every quarter. I ran and they pursued, caught me, and brought me back. I was then bound and pinioned, my hands were closely tied behind, and I was conducted in this manner (in a more shameful manner than one half the prisoners, malefactors, or highway robbers, after having the sentence of death pronounced upon them, are taken to the place of execution) to jail. There I staid eight long weeks, and what do you think my diet was during that time? Why, I will tell you, my reader, our allowance was to each person one quart of corn, ground and the husks fanned out of it, and then boiled, which we sometimes are allowed salt for, and at other times we are not. Oftentimes we were obliged to eat it without even salt or any other seasoning. As for meat, we are entirely a stranger to it, we know nothing about it, as an allowance either from our masters or the jailor. Our jailor having considerable to be done in and about the house, and knowing me to be expert in what he wanted to have done, released me from solitary confinement, and let me work for him about the prison at his own discretion; but one day Dr. Collock saw me out of jail on my ordinary business, while he was passing by, and came in and told Captain M'Call the jailor, that I would run away if he gave me such liberties. Mr. Griffin, then clerk of the jail, came and called to me and said, Grimes, your master says you will run away, and that you must be shut up again, for he does not like to see you out here. I was then conducted back to the cell again, where I remained until he again returned to Savannah; then I was restored as it were to liberty again, that is, to do what was necessary in and about the house; but I being a barber, fared rather better than the other prisoners.

I will state that I have seen women brought there and tied hand and foot, and their clothes turned up and tied there, up to their shoulders, leaving their bodies perfectly naked, then whipped with a keen raw-hide (or cow-skin sometimes called) until the blood ran down to their heels. I was then in expectation that my turn would be next, every moment looking for it. While I was in confinement, I myself, as well as the other prisoners, were used to the sound of Oh pray! Oh pray! which came from those poor slaves, then in preparation for being whipped, or experiencing then at the same time, the smart of the lash which was so often used without mercy. As large, stout and athletic a negro as I was ever acquainted with, was selected for the purpose of whipping those who were doomed to receive the lash. He himself being there confined for some crime he had committed. In a case of whipping, he was compelled to put it on as severely as lay in his power, or take a severe flogging himself. One man who was confined in the same room with me, by the name of Reuben, belonged to John Bolton, (one of the richest men in Savannah.) This poor man's back was cut up with the lash, until I could compare it to nothing but a field lately ploughed. He was whipped three times in one week, forty stripes, save one, and well put on by this athletic fellow. You may well think this poor negro's back was not only well lacerated, but brutally and inhumanly bruised.

I at this time was in such dread of the whipping post, where I daily saw so many human beings sacrificed to the lash of the tyrant, that it struck me with horror. I prayed constantly to my God (who had relieved me before in the hour of danger,) to protect and defend me in this adversity, being now in a prison, from whence I knew no means of escape. And early one morning, while pondering on the miseries I was compelled to endure, I thought, and indeed was convinced, that I heard a voice from heaven, saying, Be of good cheer; and other words, which I do not conceive necessary to mention in this history. At the same time I heard this, I had a glimpse of something most glorious to behold. I immediately felt a comfort in my soul, which cheered me up, and made me feel joyful. I was then convinced that my prayers had ascended to the high throne of Grace, for which I returned my most fervent thanks to the Almighty Ruler of the Universe.

After remaining some time in jail, Dr. Collock came and took me out, and said his reason for keeping me there so long was, that he had expected a ship from New Orleans, and intended to send me there to work on the sugar plantation; but as the ship did not arrive, and he having considerable mowing to do on his plantation, he would take me out and set me at work to do his mowing, the other slaves not understanding it. So, after remaining in my solitary cell for eight long weeks, I was then permitted to breathe the fresh air again, and put to my task in the meadows, where I continued during that season, cutting and curing his grass. The winter following, I was employed in clearing and grubbing new ground. The next summer I was kept on the plantation as usual, under the negro driver. When the season came for cutting oats, I was one day sent to mow them. I mowed one forenoon, and having a severe boil under each arm, did not feel able, nor indeed was I able to rake them up. I went to the room where I slept, it being out of from Savannah about two or three miles, in a large house, where the driver and his family slept. I there laid down to rest myself. After about half an hour, the old negro driver came to me, and asked me why I did not rake up my oats, or those I had cut. I replied that I had a large boil under each arm, and was unable to do it. He swore I should do it, and went for a stick to beat me, in order to compel me to do it. I heard him coming back, and when he burst open the door, I let him have it in old Virginia style, (which generally consists in gouging, biting and butting.) I drove my head against him, (hardly knowing what I was about, being so much terrified,) until he could scarcely stand or go. I then compelled him to give up the stick to me, which I kept in my hand, walking to and fro, while he as soon as he recovered from the bruising I had given him, called aloud to the other slaves to come to his assistance. They immediately gathered together, to the number of about twenty. He ordered them to seize me, and was in hopes they would; but one of the stoutest of them, on whom he placed the greatest reliance, came up to me to enquire what was the matter, and why I had treated the driver so. I asked how I had treated him. He replied, how did you. I then seized him by the shoulders, and said to him, I will show you. So I served him in the same way I had the driver, and almost as severe. The other negroes seeing me use this stout fellow so harshly, were afraid to touch me. I kept walking with the stick I had taken from my enemy, to and fro as before. They did not attempt after that to touch me. The driver then called to one of the slaves, to get a horse, and go to town, to give my master information; saying Robert, Robert, gitta up a horse, and go uppa town tella massa Pero a whippa me. But they not attempting to meddle with me any more, I went myself to town, to see my master first. I arrived there after Robert had been there a short time. I went into my master's office and told him the whole affair. He enquired of me very particularly concerning it. I convinced him of my innocence, and he sent me back to the plantation again, to work as before. During the conversation I had with my master, he asked me how I dare strike the driver, I replied that I must defend myself. He said to me, would you dare to strike me if I was out there? I answered, yes sir, I know my arm would be cut off if I should attempt to strike you; but sir, if you had been there you would not have used me in the way the driver did; he is an ignorant old African, or Guinea negro, and has not judgment sufficient to superintend any one in my present situation. I then showed him my boils. He was satisfied I was not able to rake the oats, but said, when I leave my driver there, I put him in my shoes; go gack to the plantation, I shall be there soon myself. I told him I had no friend, except it was himself, and if he did not whip me when he came to the plantation, I should be convinced he was my friend; and furthermore I was convinced that not one negro on the plantation was friendly to me. He knew me to be a stranger, and a man of good sense. After this conversation, I went back to the plantation, and staid there until he came. When he arrived there, he called the old driver, and talked to him very severely, saying, you should have examined into his situation before you undertook to whip him; you would then have been satisfied he was not able to work. He said not three words to me in anger. I continued to work on the plantation until towards winter, when I was again sent to the woods, and employed in cutting and splitting rails. I should have mentioned, that while working on the plantation the summer past, I undertook to raise for myself a small crop of rice, of perhaps twenty rods of ground. It being the first I had ever undertook to raise, it cost me considerable trouble. All that I knew about it, was what little information I could get from seeing the negroes raise here and there a small piece for themselves; and I was obliged to do it in the same way; that is, to take an opportunity occasionally, when not being observed by the driver, to slip in and do a little at it. After it was in a situation to cut, I reaped it and carried it to town, where I sold it for $1.25 per hundred, amounting in the whole to about 5 or $6. I kept this money, that in case of emergency, I could occasionally purchase a small piece of meat, or other necessary articles, for my subsistence. I sometimes went to town in order to procure something to eat with our common allowance, (a peck of corn per week) and have often carried on my head a bundle of wood, perhaps three miles, weighing more than one hundred pounds, which I would sell for twelve cents, in order to get a supply of necessary food. I would then, it being late in the evening, go to my master's house unknown to him, and lodge there. It has frequently been the case, that I have been so much fatigued with my day's work, and then carrying my bundle of wood that distance, that I have overslept myself, or slept longer than I intended. In that case, I have been obliged to get out at the window, or in some other way avoid my master, who used to visit his plantation early each morning, so that I could get there first. I would then, after running three miles, start the negroes out to work, telling them my master was coming. They would all go out at once, and by the time he arrived, be steadily engaged at their work. Thus I gained for my master a great many hours work in the course of the season, which he knew nothing about, and all for the purpose of clearing myself from blame, and perhaps a severe flogging.

By this manner, I was enabled to acquire a very comfortable subsistence through the winter, or during the time I lived with Dr. Collock. He sold me some time in the winter. To do the Doctor justice, I must say that he was the best and most humane man I ever lived with, or worked under. Some time previous to my master's selling me, I had heard that A. S. Bullock, Esq. agent for the navy, (who had engaged a carriage and pair of horses, coming on from New York, which he expected very soon,) wanted to buy a servant, to drive and take care of them. I went to see him, and enquired if he would buy me. He replied yes, if your master will sell you. I then went to my master and told him Mr. Bullock wished to buy me, provided he would sell me. He then said to me, where did you see Mr. Bullock? have you been there to try to induce him to buy you? I replied, no sir, he saw me in the street and enquired of me whether my master wished to sell me. I told him you did. He then said go and tell your master I will buy you if he will sell you; he then asked me what price my master would require for me, I told him $500 was the price for which I was last sold; he replied I will give that sum for you if Dr. Collock will accept of it. He added tell your master if he wants to sell you, that I wish him to come and see me. My master replied, if Mr. Bullock wants to see me, let him come here, I shall not go to see him. I then went and told Mr. Bullock the answer my master gave me; he asked me if my master would give me a recommend. I answered him that he said he would give me none. He then observed to me, I perceive your master does not want to sell you. He then called his little son to him (aged about twelve years) and gave him between five and six hundred dollars, telling him to go to Dr. Collock, give him the money and tell him if he was willing to sell Grimes, to take that and send back as much change as he pleased. He took $500, and sent back the remainder. I was now sold to Mr. Bullock, where I stayed without returning to see my old master. I felt very uneasy whilst the boy was gone, fearing my master would not sell me, as I was satisfied his intention was not to sell me in Savannah, but to send me off to New Orleans, or some other place at a distance, being as I was convinced in my own mind, so much prejudiced against me by that old quack (so called) *Sherman*, that he was determined if he sold me at all, that it should not be in Savannah. It is generally known that when a man sells a servant, he intends by that means to punish him, and endeavors to sell him where he shall never see him again. For this same reason I was afraid Dr. Collock would not sell me, my mistress also being opposed to my being sold in Savannah.

I shall here mention a very narrow escape I had while I lived with Dr. Collock. As I was occasionally tending his horses and driving them, I was exposed very often to be hurt by them, to be killed, bit, thrown off them, &c. He had one very ill-natured cross horse, no one could approach him or pass behind him with any safety. I was one day compelled to go in great haste in the reach of him. As I got almost past him, he threw both his feet against me with such violence, that my breath was entirely beat out of my body, and I was completely stunned; he sent me at a distance where I lay completely senseless for some time; I barely escaped with my life. After some time I got up, went and informed my master and mistress of the circumstances, when the necessary remedy was administered, and I finally recovered. This I mention, merely to inform my readers of the dangers and narrow escapes I have experienced during my slavery.

The same parson Collock, whom I have heretofore mentioned, was a very fine candid and humane man; he was beloved by every one who was acquainted with him; a friend to the poor slave, as well as the richest planter, or gentleman, he was in a habit of holding meetings in the evening, as often as two or three times each week, which I always attended to strictly, and very often it was as late as 10 o'clock, or later, before I reached my master's house. He had a number of times on finding me not at home in the evening, enquired of the other servants where I was, and was generally by them told that they did not know unless I was at meeting; he one evening after my return, appeared to be very angry with me, and asked me where I had been so late for a number of evenings. I replied, I have been to meeting, sir. He then said by what means do you escape the vigilance of the guard? (or what they term in the northern states *watch*.) I replied the guard do not meddle with me in returning from meeting. He then said, why do they not? they ought to. I said nothing to this, but I knew very well what he wished, that was, he would be very well pleased to have the guard take me up, and take me to jail, in order to punish me for attending meeting; but the guard never attempted to meddle with me—they always took me to be a *white man*.

I have frequently walked the streets of Savannah in an evening, and being pretty well dressed, (generally having on a good decent suit of clothes,) and having a light complexion, (being at least three parts white,) on meeting the guard, I would walk as bold as I knew how, and as much like a gentleman; they would always give me the wall. One time in particular, while walking home late in the evening, I saw two or three of them together. I was afraid, but summoned all my resolution, and marched directly on towards them, not turning to the right hand nor to the left, until I came up to them. They at first did not notice me, being engaged in conversation. I continued on, head up, walked past them and happening to brush one of them a little in passing, they immediately turned off the walk; one of them spoke and said we ask your pardon sir. At another time I deceived them in the following manner: One evening a colored man from Richmond, Virginia, called on me while sitting in the kitchen, and told me he had lately been waiting on my old master, Doct. Philip Thornton, of Richmond, and had taken him from there to his father's country-seat, at Monpelier, in Culpepper County, in a carriage with four horses, but was at present waiting on a gentleman from Richmond, then in town, who lodged at Col. Shelman's tavern, some distance from my master's. He told me his name was William Patterson, he was a free man, and was hired by people occasionally to drive their horses. He had heard of me while at Doct. Thornton's, and by enquiring of Major Lewis, a black man, who was a great groom in Savannah, he found where I lived. He stayed with me, taking something to drink, and smoked a cigar (my master knowing nothing of it) until about eleven o'clock, when he wanted to return to his lodgings. I told him the guard were all out at their posts, and it would be dangerous for him to attempt it alone; but if he would consent to walk behind me in the capacity of a servant, (to all appearances,) I would accompany him home, and I had no doubt but I could deceive the watch as I had done before. He readily consented to this, and I put on my best suit, took a rattan in my hand, he walked behind me and continued on until we reached the tavern, where we found about fifteen or twenty of the guard seated on the steps of the door; he trembled, but I walked directly on, when they rose up to make room for me to enter and him to follow. I opened the door and went in, he closed it. After he had followed me as a servant through the streets, and made the watch believe it, when we were alone by ourselves, he flourished his hands, and snapped his fingers a great number of times, saying, well done, well done for you; I will tell this when I get home to Virginia; I should not dared to have undertaken so desperate a thing.

During the time I lived with A. S. Bullock, Esq., the navy agent, at first he treated me very well. After living with him about a fortnight, the horses and carriage he had expected arrived. The horses were very low in flesh. I took them into my care, attended them strictly, and they soon began to thrive: in about three or four weeks they were in good order. By this time my master knew, or at least thought, I understood the business of taking care of horses, and was very well pleased with my performance, as I kept the carriage, horses and harness very clean and nice. During the winter and summer after, I used to drive the horses and carriage, carrying some part or the whole of his family out for a ride every evening, about five o'clock. The distance was generally from three to five miles. The winter following I was employed generally as during the one past. The next spring he sold his horses and carriage to Doct. Jones, who was an enemy to me, and exerted all the arts he could invent, to influence my master against me; but all availed nothing, my master being well pleased with me and I with him, he could not effect his purpose. At this time my mistress, her sister, Mrs. Hunter, with her daughter, Miss Catherine, and a brother of my mistress, Mr. Glen, took passage in a packet, with a great number besides, for New York. My master concluded to go by land, and to buy a light carriage, with a pair of horses; one Mr. Lyon to join with him, and for me to go and drive the horses. After having everything almost completed for the journey, they altered their minds, and concluded to take passage in the stage. If I had gone on with Mr. Bullock to the northward, I should have returned, had it been for no other purpose than to make out my enemies to be liars, who had instilled into my master a belief that if he took me with him I would never return, but run away and leave him. I was then left, by my master's order, to work out and pay him three dollars per week, and find myself. I then went to work for Mr. Irving, on board the Epervier, who was manager on board. He gave me one dollar for each day I worked there. The Epervier was a vessel taken from the British in the last war. I saw seven truck loads of gold and silver, in boxes, taken from her and carried to the bank in Savannah. I worked for Mr. Irving about a month, he paid me off, and I worked about town for a few days after. I then went out on a plantation and worked for a Mr. Houston. He also gave a dollar a day. I worked for him about a week at mowing. After that I came back and went to work on board the James Monroe, a national vessel, for Capt. Skinner, of New London, Connecticut. He gave me seventy-five cents a day. I acted as cook and steward on board of her. After this I went to work about town, and Mr. Burrows, a brother-in-law of my master, hired me to drive his horses and carriage. He gave me twenty dollars a month. I carried him and his family to Augusta. I resided with him all that summer, and drove his horses and carriage from there, up the same hills, back and forth, each day, when the weather was good, for about six months, which was as long as my master would spare me. Mr. Stephen Bullock, a relative of my master, (as he was left superintendent of his affairs during the time he was absent,) wrote to Mr. Burrows that he must send me home. Accordingly I went back on horseback. A few weeks after my return, my master and family arrived from New York, with a carriage and four elegant horses. I now had six horses to take care of, and the carriage to keep clean and in order. I took such good care of the horses, and kept the carriage so nice, that Mr. Bullock was well pleased with me. After I had got the four new horses in good order, and fat, he sold one pair of them, which relieved me from some trouble and labor. We have never had any disagreement, yet he had been on to the northward, and but just returned. Some time after this my master bottled up a few dozen of wine, counted them and delivered them into my care for keeping. At his time he had a number of workmen, joiners and carpenters at work about the house. When I took the wine into my care. I took it out of the cellar, and as I was gone after a basket, one of the workmen took a bottle and secreted it. My object in going after a basket was to carry it up into the garret, and this man passing that way, took that opportunity to steal a bottle of it, perhaps not considering at the same time that I was responsible for it, and should be liable to receive a severe punishment if the bottles were not all found: but he did not even return the bottle after drinking the contents. After I carried them up stairs, my master went and counted them, and finding one missing, called to me to know where it was. I told him I had set them all out of the cellar, and then went for a basket to carry them up; and I had carried the whole that I found up garret. He said there was one missing, and ordered me to fetch it immediately. I told him I thought I had carried up the whole of them. We then went together and counted them a number of times, but found one missing. He was very angry with me. I asserted my innocence repeatedly, but all to no purpose. I could not make him believe me not guilty. I was suspicious that some one of the mechanics had taken it. I went to them and enquired about it. One of them acknowledged that he had taken it, and was willing to pay my master for it. I then immediately went and informed my master, but he would not believe me. I returned to the man who took it, and requested him to go with me to my master, in order to convince him of my innocence. He consented, and we went together. He made a statement to him of the whole affair, and also told him he was willing to pay him to his full satisfaction. But whether my master had an idea that there was a connivance between us to clear myself, or what his motive was I cannot tell, but he did not appear to be any more satisfied than before; still telling me I took it. It grieved me very much to be blamed when I was innocent. I knew I had been faithful to him; perfectly so. At this time I was quite serious, and used constantly to pray to my God. I would not lie nor steal. My master knew nothing of that. I kept it a profound secret from him. When I considered him accusing me of stealing, when I was so innocent, and had endeavored to make him satisfied by every means in my power, that I was so, but he still persisted in disbelieving me, I then said to myself, if this thing is done in a green tree what must be done in a dry? I forgave my master in my own heart for all this, and prayed to God to forgive him and turn his heart. I was dissatisfied to think that my master had so bad an opinion of me at the time I was so honest; and tried by best endeavors to please him.

I then wanted some person to buy me, and let me work until I had paid $800. I accordingly applied to a man who promised me he would try to buy me. I must here state the circumstance that prevented him from doing so. Sometime previous to this, I had told the other servants that something would happen to me, that my master would be very angry with me for something, that he would beat me unmercifully and send me to prison. They were very much surprised to hear me talk in this manner as they well knew that we were on very good terms at that time. So after this happened concerning the wine, I having a number of articles in and about the yard, such as boxes, clothes, trunks, &c.; and as I have before mentioned, being determined to get some person to buy me, I used occasionally to carry some of them off and hide them in the woods, well knowing that if my master should sell me, he would never allow me to enter his yard again; and the things being my own, would be of service to me in another place, should I be so fortunate as to have a new master. After obtaining the promise of this man to buy me, he being unwilling to speak to him on the subject, fearing my master might think he was endeavoring to entice me away, he told me to ask my master if he wanted to sell me. I shall not mention the name of this man, for as it so happened he did not buy me, it might make some difficulty. Ever since the circumstance of the wine, my master not appearing to be satisfied with me about it, had treated me very severely. I determined one day when my master was in the parlor to ask him the question. So I went into the kitchen which was in the lower room where the other servants were, (having been myself in the stable attending to the horses,) and told them that what I had prophesied would soon take place, saying, my hour is come, I am now going up to see my master, and he will beat me and put me in prison. They then enquired of me what was the matter. I answered them that I was going to ask my master a question, for which I shall receive this. They endeavored to persuade me not to go, saying, you will only bring trouble on yourself by going. But being determined on doing it, I went, not heeding what they said, begging of me not to go. I went up. He was walking backwards and forwards (with his hands thrust in his pockets) across the room, waiting for his dinner. I stood for a few moments behind a chair, with my hand on the back of it, fearing to speak. At length he stepped up toward me, saying, well what's wanting, Grimes? I being so fearful to irritate him, dared not speak immediately. He repeated, well Grimes, what's wanting? I then with a great deal of diffidence (after many fruitless attempts to speak) said, master, are you willing to sell me? It was exactly as I had anticipated; he flew into a violent passion, caught hold of a chair and came towards me in the attitude of attempting to strike me; he made one or two passes at me with it, but dropping it, seized me by the collar and beat me with his fist most unmercifully; at the same time exclaiming, sell you? yes, you damned son of a bitch. God damn you, I'll sell you; I'll sell you by God; who wants to buy you? God damn you. who wants to buy you? I made no reply, but cleared myself from him and his house as soon as possible for the stable. While going towards the stable, not daring to turn my head, and expecting him every moment at my heels, I pretended to stop to pick up something, at the same time casting my eyes behind me, I saw him coming very rapidly towards me. I had hoped as his dinner was nigh ready, he would not undertake to come after me until after dinner, and had determined on quitting him immediately, thinking it best to go then, as I was convinced he would when he next saw me finish what he had begun, that is a severe beating; but seeing him so near, and pretending not to have seen him, I went into the stable, took my fork, and went to work stirring up the straw, not noticing him at all, or at least not letting him know that I did. He came into the stable and seized me by the collar with his left hand, while with his right fist clenched, he beat me with that in my breast and face, until all in a gore of blood. I dared not say a word, but pretended to be very much hurt; he all the time exclaiming, who wants to buy you? God damn you, I say, who wants to buy you, you rascal? He then dragged me to the platform under the Piazza, continuing all the time to beat me in the same manner, but calling frequently to Jack to bring a rope and bind me. He said, bring me a rope, Jack, bring a rope, God damn you, and bind this rascal? Jack went for a rope, but not being able to find one as soon as he wanted, my master was quite enraged at him, and fell to beating him severely. After some time Jack found a rope and fetched it to my master, but he was so much enraged at me, that he kept beating him, saying, tie him, you rascal, tie him sir. All that poor Jack could do was to smart under his chastisement, and keep saying, yes sir, yes sir, I will. I was then placed in such a situation that my arms were pinioned, and my hands tied behind.

He then sent Jack for a constable, saying, go, you rascal, and find a constable; have this damned rascal taken to jail. Jack went, but soon came back, saying, I could not find Master Nobie. He then told him to go and get any constable he could find. He soon came with another. My master told this constable to take me to jail, and give me a flogging, and lock me up. This man seeing my situation—my face all blood, my hands bound behind me, and I standing there trembling with the bruises I had received, together with the fear of another more barbarous flogging, appeared to take pity on me. He whispered to my master and said, I think, by his looks, you have given him a severe whipping; I would put him in jail without any more chastisement. My master replied, by God, I have not hurt him; all I have done was with my knuckles. I had repeatedly told my master before that my hands were so closely bound the blood was almost ready to start through my fingers. He replied, I don't care if it should. He then directed the constable (as he had persuaded him not to flog me any more) to take me to jail. We started and got as far as the gate, when he called him back, saying, let Jack wash the blood off his face; it has not been washed for six months, people will think I have been murdering him. He then told Jack to go and get my hat and put it on me, and also my coat, and spread it over my shoulders, which he did. I then went with the constable to jail, and was locked in. I knew my master's disposition so well, that I was convinced he did not wish to have me imprisoned; but only for me to make an acknowledgment and asked his pardon, for merely my asking him the question I did. I had before anticipated this, for I knew he could not do without me: all he wanted of me, to set me at liberty, was for me to ask his pardon, and promise never to ask him to sell me again. Had he (at the time the constable advised him not to have me whipped again) persisted in having his orders executed, which I knew to be Moses' law, that is, 40 stripes, save one, which I must receive before I entered the jail, I should have begged his pardon, and made almost any acknowledgment he should require, knowing my constitution could not bear it. But I pretended to be ignorant of the whole, and acted stupid and dull, not regarding what I knew to be his wish; and when I heard him order the constable to commit me without whipping, my heart leapt for joy, for I knew what I had to endure before I should be sold. After lying in jail some time, I sent word to this same man who had promised to buy me, to come and buy me out of jail; but he refused, thinking my master would conjecture he had enticed me to leave him, notwithstanding I had assured him that my master wished to sell me.

After that I was compelled to lie there in my solitary cell for the space of three weeks, before any person appeared to buy me. The room in which I was placed was so foul and full of vermin, it was almost insupportable. The lice were so thick and large that I was obliged to spread a blanket (which I had procured myself) on the floor, and as they crawled upon it, take a junk or porter bottle, which I found in the jail, and roll it over the blanket repeatedly, and in the same way that I have seen people grind or powder mustard seed on a board. I could always hear the death of some announced by their cracking. This I had to observe daily and indeed often two or three, and perhaps more times each day. Besides all this, I had often to take off my shirt, pick them out of my collar, pile them up as fast as I could, and take the bottle to crush them. My readers will here understand that this room had constantly, previous to my imprisonment therein, been occupied as a prison for negroes. They, no more than myself having a privilege of a change of linen, or water wherewith to cleanse it. Any person would naturally suppose the place to be (vulgarly speaking) filled with lice; and it was, when I went there, as nigh filled as any building I ever entered. I will here mention that a few days previous to the time that I told the servants something would take place between my master and myself dissatisfactory to us both, that for some trivial fault, which I cannot now recollect, he came to the stable, took the reins of the harness, bound my hands and led me along the stables (the doors being open,) backwards and forwards, for some time, threatening to whip me. The windows in the house being open, my mistress saw him. She then went to the back door and called Ben (a servant) from the kitchen. He came to her. She immediately seized him by his ear, and shaking him severely, pointing at the same time to me, (having a fair view and grinning horridly a ghastly smile,) said, you see there! you see there! Do you see how your master does with Grimes? he will do so with you, too. She then called Jack, a poor, honest Guinea negro, and a faithful servant, to her, and used him in the same way, saying, if you do not behave yourself well, you shall be served in the same manner. They replied, yes, mistress, I will! I will! It was a practice of my master to have a soup almost every day. My master Stephen usually went to market each day to procure meat for dinner for the family, and always purchased a shin of beef. Jack accompanied him with the market basket to fetch home what he bought. The richest part of the soup was consumed by the family, and the remainder, consisting of the lean meat, and the shin, and coarse pieces remaining on the bones, were then left for us in the kitchen. Gulla Jack, who was a servant about the house, to scour, &c., the same that fetched the meat home, after noticing this for a number of months, began to be dissatisfied with it. One day in particular we were standing together under the platform, back of the house, my master being in the necessary, but a few yards from us, heard his conversation, which amounted to nearly what I now am about to state. Jack said to me, (not knowing our master was so near,) be Gad, I don't want to stay here for my master to licka me, an licka me, an all he give me a sin of beef; he eata all de meat, and den he licka me wid de bone. Be Gad, me do not lika stay here to be usa so. Using such kind of broken language as he had often before used to me, when I would laugh and join with him, merely for sport, and to hear him talk; at this time I joined with him and laughed heartily. After this I went to the stable to work, and Jack went to his work. My master went into the house and went up stairs, when he told my mistress what he had heard. Whilst he was telling her, one of the servant girls happened to overhear him. She came directly and informed Jack and myself of it, saying our master was quite angry with us for it. We were both very much frightened at this information, and knew not what to do. I had cleaned his shoes for him, and sent them up by the girl; he sent them back again, saying, they were not half cleaned. I did it again, and made them very nice, and sent them up again. He sent them back a second time, with orders for me to fetch them up myself. I was now more afraid than before, but I took them up to him in the parlor. When I went in he was very angry: he snatched up the poker and thrust it hastily into the fire with the greatest fury, exclaiming, what! you are above cleaning my shoes, are you? By God, you are above cleaning my shoes; you can carry on with Jack about a shin of beef, but you are above cleaning my shoes. I replied that I did not mean any harm by that, but only laughed to hear Jack use his broken language. He then said Jack was not to blame, but it was me altogether, for I knew better; but he was a poor, ignorant Guinea negro, and therefore not so much to blame.

My master would always, when the weather was bad, order me to drive the horse and chaise to his office, and carry him home to dinner, precisely at two o'clock. One time I being detained longer than usual, did not arrive there until after the clock had struck. I met him about fifty yards from his office on his way home; I drove up to him in order to have him get in; but he took no notice of me at all, and continued on towards home; I drove a little forwards and turned about, overtook him, and asked him if he would ride. He looked at me very sternly and replied, no, I'll walk, as I began it. I then drove home and told Ben about it. He said to me, ah! you look out for that. I might mention a great many similar circumstances, but it would be too tedious a task, and I will leave it here.

After I had got through with all my troubles with Mr. Bullock, a Mr. White came and bought me out of jail for five hundred dollars. He came to the jail and spoke to me, saying he would buy me if I would consent to drive his horses. I told him I would. I was accordingly let out of jail soon after, and went to his house. I found him to be a cross, crabbed man. I did not stay with him long. I lived with him perhaps two or three months, when a certain Mr. Welman came to my master's and bought me. This was the eighth time that I had been sold for five hundred dollars each time. My master did not buy me for his present use. He hired me out to Mr. Oliver Sturges, the man who had owned me before. I worked for Mr. Sturges about four or five months. He had a man from New York, whom he hired for thirty dollars per month; he wanting to go home, Mr. Sturges offered Mr. Welman the same wages for me. Whilst I was there I drove his horses, took care of his carriage, and occasionally attended the people in the house.

I have experienced the sufferings of a slave in the Southern States. I have travelled from Frederickstown in Maryland, to Darien in Georgia, and from there to Savannah, from whence I made my escape in the following manner. While I belonged to Mr. Welman he went with his family to Bermuda, and left me to work for what I could get, by paying him three dollars per week. During this time the brig Casket, from Boston, arrived. I went with a number more to assist in loading her. I soon got acquainted with some of these Yankee sailors, and they appeared to be quite pleased with me. Her cargo chiefly consisted of cotton in bales. After filling her hold, they were obliged to lash a great number of bales on deck. The sailors, growing more and more attached to me, they proposed to me to leave, in the centre of the cotton bales on deck, a hole or place sufficiently large for me to stow away in, with my necessary provisions. Whether they then had any idea of my coming away with them or not, I cannot say; but this I can say safely, a place was left, and I occupied it during the passage, and by that means made my escape. The evening before the brig was to sail I went with a colored man (a sailor on board) up into town and procured some bread, water, dried beef, and such other necessaries that I should naturally want. It was late in the evening, and he being a Yankee sailor, I directed him to walk behind me in the capacity of a servant, (as they would consider me his master, the watch or guard being all on their posts;) he did so, and we procured every thing necessary for me, took them on board, and I stowed them away in the hole left for me, where I myself went and remained until we arrived at the Quarantine Ground, New York. I will here mention that during my passage I lay concealed as much as possible: some evenings I would crawl out and go and lie down with the sailors on deck; the night being dark, the captain could not distinguish me from the hands, having a number on board of different complexions. He, or some one, would often in the night, when there was something to be done, come on deck and call, forward, there, boys! Aye, aye, sir, was the reply; then they would be immediately at their posts, I remaining on the floor, not perceived by him. We cast off from the wharf at Savannah Saturday night, and remained in the Savannah river until Monday morning; we then crossed the bar near the light-house. After we had got into the ocean the sailors gave three hearty cheers, and gave me to understand that I was clear; we were out of sight of land, they said. Nothing more of any consequence occurred until we arrived at the Quarantine Ground, New York. I remained concealed from the captain, mate and steward until after we arrived. One morning after I left my place of concealment, and was in the forecastle of the vessel intending to change my clothes, as I was putting on a clean shirt, the mate came down, (the captain and passengers having gone before to New York;) he perceived me with my shirt half on (being so frightened that I stood motionless,) said, why, Grimes, how came you here? I could make him no answer. He then called some of the crew and inquired of them how I came there. They replied, poor fellow, he stole aboard. He then inquired if the steward knew that I was aboard. I told him that he did not. He replied, know well that you do not let him know it. He then inquired if the captain knew it. I answered him, no sir. He then said to me, let no one know anything about it; I wish that I myself knew nothing of it. Here, boys, put him over the bows, and set him ashore on Staten Island. Upon that, one of the sailors took me ashore in the boat. On landing he found another sailor with whom he was acquainted, and told him my circumstances, requesting him to assist me in getting to New York. He promised him that he would. After staying on the island a few hours, this man told me to follow him down to the river, where the packet-boat lay, as she would sail soon. There being some of the crew on board the Casket sick, it was necessary that all who passed from the island, having been on board of her, and all other persons who went from the island to New York, should be examined by a doctor stationed there for that purpose. This was what I most feared. This man had once spoken to the doctor, and his name entered on the book; the doctor stood on the wharf to receive the names of all those who passed into the packet, and none to pass without giving their names, the same to be recorded in his book, which he held in his hand. As we approached the wharf, I felt as if my heart was in my mouth, or in other words, very much afraid that I should be compelled to give my name, together with an account from where I came, and where I was going, and in what manner I came there. To all this I should not dare to answer, (fearing in one case to implicate the master of the vessel in which I came, who was perfectly innocent, and in the second, of being taken and again returned to my master, there to remain in slavery during the rest of my life;) but I followed him down to the packet-boat. I perceived the doctor had his head turned a little to the left, looking at something in that direction. He perceived the sailor who was my conductor, and recognized him as one he had examined; but not noticing me, I slipped aboard without being interrogated at all. I was in the greatest fear of being detected, so much so that I almost fainted; but when I heard the word given to push off, I rejoiced heartily. I then told the sailor, who had been my friend, that I was convinced I should meet with some person on my landing whom I had formerly known. He replied, never mind that, take hold of my chest, and come along with me. I did so, and soon after we arrived at the lodgings of this sailor, who proved to be my friend (which I made my place of abode for the present.) In the course of the afternoon I saw a colored girl in the street near the house. I inquired of her if she would walk with me a little ways, in order to see the town, and that I could again find my lodgings. I being a stranger there, was afraid of being lost.

We walked about the city some time; at length, as we were walking up Broadway, who should I see but Mr. Oliver Sturges, of Fairfield, who once had been my master in Savannah. To my great astonishment, he came up to me, and said, why, Theodore, how came you here? I lied to him, and told him I had been there about two weeks; being so frightened, I knew not what to say, never intending to tell a lie, wilfully or maliciously. He asked me how all things were going on at his yard in Savannah. I answered, all well, I just came from there, sir. After a few moments conversation, he passed on one way, and I went on towards my lodgings, where I rested that night. The next morning, after purchasing a loaf of bread and a small piece of meat, I started on foot for New Haven. I could often get an opportunity to ride; sometimes behind the stage, at others, I could sometimes persuade a teamster to take me on for a short distance. In this manner, I arrived at New Haven. After I arrived there, and even before, every carriage or person I saw coming behind me, I fancied were in pursuit of me. Lying still on board the vessel so long, made it fatiguing for me to walk far at a time without stopping to rest; my situation there being quite confined, and no opportunity for exercise. I often was obliged to go off the road and lie down for some time; and whenever I saw any person coming on, that I suspected, I took that opportunity for a resting spell, and went out of sight until they passed by. Finding my money growing short, I found that I must live prudent. I met a couple of boys on the road who had some apples. I bought them, which, together with what little provision I took with me, was all I had to subsist on until I arrived at New Haven, which was three days. I lodged the two nights I was on the road at private houses. When I arrived at New Haven, I found that all the money I had left amounted to no more than seventy-five cents. That night I lodged at a boarding house, kept by a certain Mrs. W., who took me to be a white man; and although I have lived in New Haven since that time a number of years, she never knew to this day but what it was a white man that lodged there that night. The next morning I went to work for Able Lanson, who kept a livery stable. He set me at work in a ledge of rocks, getting out stone for building. This I found to be the hardest work I had ever done, and began to repent that I had ever come away from Savannah, to this hard cold country. After I had worked at this for about three months, I got employment in taking care of a sick person, who called his name Carr, who had been a servant to Judge Clay, of Kentucky; he was then driving for Lanson. I took care of him, and took his place for some time. One day, as I was assisting Isaac (a son of Lanson) to harness a horse, to my great astonishment and surprise, master Stephen Bullock, who I have heretofore mentioned, as the relation to and superintendent of my master's office in Savannah, came up to me and said, why, John, it is as hot here as in Savannah. (I will here mention, that as it may appear strange for me to have so many names, to those who are not acquainted with the circumstance, that it is a practice among the slave holders, whenever one buys a slave of another, if the name does not suit him, or if he has one of the same name already, he gives him what name he pleases. I, for these reasons, have had three different names.) I was so much surprised to see Mr. Bullock, that I could scarce give him an answer. He spoke to me several times. I was so much afraid and astonished, that I could give him no answer. I was afraid he would ask me how I came in New Haven. Who

can express my feelings at first seeing him? I behaved so bashful and afraid
to speak, that after saying a few words he walked down Church street, and
I saw no more of him. After he had gone, Isaac said to me, why, he
appears to know you. I replied, yes, it is no wonder that he knows me. I
then went and informed my friends that I had seen my young master, and
I did not think it prudent for me to stay in New Haven long. Accordingly I
left town, and went on to a place called Southington, a few miles back in
the country, where I went to work on a farm. Here an accident befel me,
which I will mention. I one day went to assist Capt. Potter to pick up
apples, and having on a red flannel shirt, the cattle were afraid of it as I
was attempting to take them from the cart. Having stepped between them,
in order to let the tongue of the cart down, which was filled with apples,
they started and ran down a hill as fast as they possibly could. I held on to
the tongue of the cart as long as I had strength enough. They were
constantly kicking me in the face. I durst not attempt to quit my hold,
fearing I should be crushed to pieces by the loaded cart; but not being able
to hold on any longer, after they had run down the hill, and through a pair
of bars, I fell, and the cart passed over me and crushed my ancle severely.
The neighbors gathered round me, expecting every moment to see me
breathe my last. They took me up and carried me to a house, sent for a
doctor, and he came. I being so much bruised and kicked, the blood was
streaming from me in many places. The Doctor soon stopped it, and
bound up my ancle. I recovered slowly, and was obliged to crawl on my
hands and knees a great while, and supported myself on what little money
I had acquired, until I procured a pair of crutches. I then used to go
around amongst the neighbors in Southington, husking corn, and doing
such kind of work as I could do in my situation. I found it much harder at
this time to be a free man, than I had to be a slave; but finally got to be
able to earn fifty cents per day. After I had so far recovered as to be able
to walk, or rather limp without crutches, I returned to New Haven. After
staying there a short time, I was taken sick, and continued unable to work
for a week or two. I put up with Abel Lanson, and assisted him in digging
a well. I then worked about the Colleges, cutting wood, at which I earned
about one dollar a day, of which I was very saving, until I had collected
about twenty dollars. I then left New Haven and started for Providence,
where I spent the chief part of my money. I then went into partnership
with a man by the name of Boham, and kept a barber's shop. After a few
months, we dissolved partnership. I then went on to Newport, and after
waiting some time for a passage to New Bedford, at length found a packet

bound for that port; but the wind blowing very hard, I did not think it safe to go on board, so I put my trunk on board and went on, myself on foot, it being thirty miles, and arrived there before the packet. I had not money sufficient to pay for my board one week. Wishing to get a place to work as soon as I could, and hearing that Mr. John Howland wanted a servant, I applied to him for employ; we soon struck a bargain at the rate of nine dollars a month; this was in June. In the fall after, I kept shop for myself some part of the time; the rest part I worked for Mr. Howland, until it began to grow cold. I also kept a few groceries. The colored people being often in there evenings, had finally got so much habituated to take to their own heads in rioting and carousing, (which I endeavored to suppress in vain,) that Mr. Hazzet, my landlord, asked me a number of times if I had not better give up the shop. To which I replied, yes, sir, I will very gladly, for I see the colored people have imposed upon me. I being a stranger, and the only barber in the place, except white people, they would often come in with their families and dance evenings, until late; and being noisy and riotous, I would endeavor to stop them, but to no purpose; they still persisted in it, until I was obliged to give up my shop.

There was a woman who lived in the room below me: she kept house there, and was not pleased with the noise, saying she would not have it there. I suppose she complained to my landlord, and for that reason I was obliged to give up my shop. After one quarter, I did it, and paid him up my rent. After I had left the shop about two months, this woman was heard to cry murder in the night. The neighbors immediately assembled, when two sailors were seen to escape out of her window, go down on to the wharf, and go on aboard a vessel. The morning following the authority made enquiry about it. On questioning her, she said that two persons came into her room and offered her violence; she resisted as long as her strength held out, and after they had accomplished their design, they then abused and whipped her until she made the outcry. They then enquired of her if she knew who it was. She replied, no. On enquiring again if she had any reason to mistrust any one, on any account, she replied, I know of no one who owes me a grudge except William Grimes. Whilst he lived in this house, over my room, he used to have a great deal of noise there, which disturbed me; I said considerable about it, which was the means of his quitting his shop. He then threatened to be revenged for it. I can think of no other person. I was then taken before a Justice, Esq. Williams, to answer to this charge. I proved by Mr. John Howland, Jr., to whom I had hired out for the winter, for seven dollars a month, that I was in his house all that night. He knew me to go to bed, and as a light snow was then falling, he said it was impossible for me to go out of the house without his knowledge. After three days' time I was discharged, they not being able to prove anything against me. Before I left the room, I was again arrested and taken to this woman's room, where they questioned her very close. They asked her if she could or would swear to the voice of the person or persons that had been seen to come out of her window. She replied, no, I cannot. They then asked her if she was willing to swear that she was afraid of her life. She answered, yes. I was again taken back to the court for another trial; I was well convinced that the woman knew it was not me, and also knew who it was. Esq. Williams asked me if I would have a lawyer. I not knowing what to answer, never having been brought up in a court before, answered, yes, sir, I will have you for my lawyer. He replied, I am bound to do you all the good I can; I must do justice. You had better get some other attorney; but there being no one handy, they (my opponents) said, as you have no attorney, we will have none. Esq. Williams then said to me, you must be recognized together with some other person in the sum of $300, for your appearance at Taunton court, in about three months. I not being acquainted with any person to whom I wished to apply, and having no money, I therefore went to jail, where I stayed until the court set.

When the trial came on, two witnesses were brought forward, who testified that they heard me say I would injure the woman. The Judge enquired of them, was that all you heard? is that all you know? They answered, yes. He then acquitted me, cautioning me to behave myself well. I then went directly to Providence, where I remained a few days, then continued on to Norwich, where I went to work for a few weeks, for Mr. Christopher Starr. From thence I went to New London, where I purchased a set of barber's tools. Having been informed previous to this that a barber might do well at Stonington point, after crossing the river I pursued my journey, it being through woods. I had not gone more than one or two miles before I saw four or five men, who made directly towards me. I was very much frightened when I saw them, but could not tell why. I was much more so, when they came up to me and said, where are you going, boy? I answered them to Stonington Point. Where did you come from? I came from New London. What have you got there in your bundle? I have got nothing but some barber's tools. You are a barber then, are you? Yes, I was told that Stonington Point was a good place for a barber, and I purchased a set of tools in New London, with the intention of going there to establish a shop. They then replied, there has lately been a store broken open, and we are now in pursuit of the rogues; we have orders to search every person we meet with; we are therefore under the necessity of searching you. I replied, you may search me gentlemen, if you please. They then proceeded to search my bundle, and finding nothing more there than I had told them, let me go on; but advised me not to go there: that the people were not civil, but would raise the devil with any person who should undertake to establish a barber's shop there. They advised me to return back to Mr. Starr's: and after considerable conversation I resolved to return; which I did, and worked on Mr. Starr's farm about two weeks longer. I then went to New London, and took the steamboat for New Haven, where I arrived sometime in May. I then went to work about the Colleges, as I had formerly done; also, shaving, cutting hair, &c., such as waiting on the scholars in their rooms, and all other kinds of work that I could do when not employed at this. I worked about the Colleges about six or eight months. I had then accumulated about fifty dollars, and hearing that there was no barber in Litchfield, (a very pleasant town, about thirty-six miles back in the country, where the celebrated Law School, under the direction of Tapping Reeve, Esq., was kept,) and as there were between twenty and thirty law students, I thought it a good place for me. I accordingly went and established myself as a barber. I very soon had a great deal of custom, amounting to fifty or sixty dollars per month. After I had resided there for about a year with about as good success, I undertook to keep one or two horses and gigs to let. For some time I made money very fast; but at length trading horses a number of times, the horse jockies would cheat me, and to get restitution I was compelled to sue them. I would sometimes win the case; but the lawyers would alone reap the benefit of it. At other times I lost my case, fiddle and all; besides paying my Attorney.

Let it not be imagined that the poor and friendless are entirely free from oppression where slavery does not exist: this would be fully illustrated if I should give all the particulars of my life, since I have been in Connecticut. This I may do in a future edition, and when I feel less delicacy about mentioning names.

While at Litchfield I sold a wagon to a neighbor and took a note, which I was compelled to sue. My debtor lived in a house with another man, whom I had made my enemy, by dunning him in the street for cutting his hair. They out of revenge went to a Grand Juror and made complaint against me for keeping a bad girl at my house. I always kept a girl, as we took in washing, and this girl who had been living with an inhabitant there, my wife hired about ten days before. The trial was before Squire M. who got another Esq. to sit with him, and a great court it was too. They asked me if I had a lawyer. I said I would plead my own case, as I was sure they had nothing againt me. I however told one of Judge G.'s sons that he might answer for me is he was a mind to. There were a great many of the inhabitants summoned to testify, and all of them testified in my favor except *two*. The jail-keeper who lived second door from me, said he knew nor heard nothing against me; and he was no friend of mine. Trowbridge and Hungerford said they had heard thus and so: but were not questioned where they got their information. If I had plead my own case, I could have done better than any lawyer or rather student. M. Smith managed the case against me. Esq., one of the court as before mentioned by invitation, in giving his opinion, made a long speech against me; or rather, he said there was proof enough that such report was enough to convict me; he said more than the lawyer against me. I had got most of my business by activity, from his servant, who, before I went to Litchfield, was the principal waiter, &c., for the students. I thought this trial showed his master, and some others thought as much of this as of the crime of which I was accused; particularly as it was one at which they were not likely to feel much indignation in their hearts. The girl was of a bad character; but I did not know it. She was white. I sent her away as soon as I heard anything against her. I asked my lawyer why he did not question the witness against me, where they heard reports; and he said there was nothing proved against me. The court, he said, did as they was a mind to. I being a negro, I suppose they thought no one would ever notice it. I had money, and if I had not, the town *would* have to pay the cost. I say before my God, that I was convicted of keeping a bad house when I had only kept this girl in my house ten days, and knew nothing but that she was virtuous.

I was warned out of town shortly after I went to Litchfield by one of the Selectmen, and through the influence of this servant before mentioned or his friends. But I went to Esq. B. who told them to let me stay, and I heard no more about it. After I was put under bonds, I was obliged to give a mortgage of my house; and this same trial was five hundred dollars damage to me; it injured my character of course, and those who suppose I have no feelings are mistaken.

A few days after my trial I went down to cut the Governor's hair, and he said to me, Grimes, I am sorry that you got in such a scrape. I suppose his since Secretary would persuade him that I was guilty. I only said I was not guilty; and I do wish that the Governor only did know the truth about it. I after this met Esq. B. in the street, and he said, William, they did not do you justice at the trial. I talked with him, and he told me when the county court set, he would get the bonds taken off if the State's Attorney did not object; but the Attorney did object at the instigation of———.

This servant had been tried for the same offence which I had, and was convicted; but found friends. I presume if I had been actually guilty, I should have met with different treatment.

It has been my fortune most always to be suspected by the good, and to be cheated and abused by the vicious. An instance of rascality I will now mention, which took place at Litchfield: one J. swapped horses with me, and by fraud induced me to give twenty dollars to boot. The horse I swapped cost me five. I sold the horse I had of him for fifteen dollars. I sued him though, and recovered, I believe thirty dollars. I bought a mare of one P. and paid him good money. Afterwards he came to me with a counterfeit bill, and said I paid it to him. I knew I did not, for it was torn and ragged. He threatened me and I took it, being ignorant of the law. But I understand the law now, pretty well, at least that part which consists in paying *fees*. My case with the horse jockey cost me a great deal of money. It was curious to hear his witnesses testify: some who knew nothing about the horse or the bargain, swore just as if they were reciting their catechism. God help them! One of my children was sick, and I sold a buffalo skin to the physician while he was visiting the child, for which he gave me six dollars. Before I left Litchfield I could not get him to make out his bill: but after I went to New Haven, this doctor sent his bill down there for collection. I thought I had paid enough, and refused paying any more than the six dollars, unless he swore to his account. This he did, but what was strange, he went up into Tolland County, about forty miles off, to do it. I was in as good credit as any man in Litchfield, and as good a paymaster. Quackery and extortion generally go together.

I used to carry to the students' rooms their meals when they wanted. One of them from Charleston, a graduate of Yale College, sent for his dinner one day. I carried a variety of dishes, a very large dinner, and a plenty of wine and brandy. He had several gentlemen in the room with him that day, and they did all sit down at the table, and they would have me sit down to the table too. One of them would say, Mr. Grimes, a glass of wine with you, sir; and the next gentleman would say the same, and so they kept on, until I had got two glasses to their one all round the table. I began to feel myself on a footing with them, and made as free with them as they did with me, and drank to them, and they would set me to making speeches. They not only drank with me themselves, until they got me as drunk as a fool, but they called in Peter Hamden, who was going along, and made him drink a glass of brandy and water with me. At last I took the floor and lay there speechless some hours. I had two or three apprentice boys; towards night, they came after me and led me home. I never was so drunk in my life before. I looked so like death, my wife was shocked at the sight of me.

Harry, the servant I have mentioned before, as my great rival and enemy, I knew kept a lewd house. His protector had been so active in the prosecution against me, that I thought I would retaliate a little. I went to a grand juror therefore, and made a complaint against Harry. The grand juror did not understand managing the case at all, as he was just appointed. The trial was before Esquire B. Mr. Beers managed the case for Harry, and got him clear; the witnesses being all Harry's friends. And when a lawyer makes a justice, the justice sometimes is very apt to remember his creator. Harry then turned round and sued me for damages in getting him complained of. He employed two lawyers. Mr. Sanford and Mr. Beers, and I employed two. Before I made complaint against Harry, I was riding in the stage with a man to New Haven, who told me all about Harry's house. I now went to New Haven, and took this man's deposition before Esquire Dennison. At the trial, which made some noise in Litchfield, we called on Harry's lawyers to give bonds, which they did, and at it they went until dinner, when the court adjourned. Only one of Harry's lawyers returned after dinner, and all he did was to pay the cost and be off. So I came off triumphant.

At one time while I was living in New Haven, I applied to the jail keeper in Litchfield, to borrow two hundred dollars. He said if I would buy his horse and cutter, he would let me have fifty dollars cash, and I must give my note for two hundred dollars, with a mortgage on my place for security. I did so. The horse and cutter I suppose was worth seventy-five dollars. But while my ignorance thus exposed me to imposition, it was perhaps the only way in which I could learn wisdom; indeed, those to whom I have done kindness, have often proved ungrateful. One Barnes I recollect was confined in Litchfield jail for the fine and cost which had been imposed for a fighting scrape. He told me if I would pay it, which was twelve dollars, he would let me have his cow to get my pay. I paid it, give him some change after I had taken him out, and shaved him, so that he might go home and see his wife. But I found the cow was not his. His brother is a cabinet maker and rich, but would not help him, I believe.

I got into a quarrel with a student. He struck me in a passion and I sued. He gave me twenty dollars, and I settled it; and having about this time an opportunity to let my place, I did so. The rent was seventy dollars a year. My object was to go to New Haven, which I now did. I hired a place of Esquire Daggett in New Haven, close by the Colleges, and gave him one hundred dollars rent. I kept a victualing shop, and waited on the students. I kept money to let, and soon got into full business. I bought furniture too of the students; in this my business interfered with Mr. E. my next neighbor, which brought upon me his displeasure. In fact, I had such a run of custom, that all the shop keepers, that is of the huckster shops about college, and who get their living out of the students, fell upon me, to injure me in every possible manner; they had more sense than I had about keeping in with the Faculty, and others about there, but I can swear they were not more honest in my opinion. They took pains to prejudice the college steward against me. When I wanted wood, I used to get some student who owed me, to sign a bill and then get the wood delivered at my house; the wood is furnished by college to the students. This was the only way in which I could get my pay often. I had got a load at my house, which had been delivered in this manner. The carman had thrown it part off, when the steward came up and ordered him to carry it back. I ordered him to unload. He began to put the wood back, when I seized him and stopped it. The steward says you rascal, this is my wood, and are you not going to give up? I said I am not, it is in my possession. He took back, however, what was not thrown off. But I went immediately up to the steward's office and demanded it again, and told him I would sue him if he did not restore it; and he gave it up. I told him that it was all I could get from the student. The steward knew if I sued him it would make a great noise and laugh about town, and he knew, (being a lawyer,) that I could recover. Being in opposition to all these fellows who get their living about college, they all hated me, and would go to the Tutors and throw out insinuations against me, would tell the students if they had me in their rooms, they would be suspected. But notwithstanding their efforts, I did a mighty good business.

As I have spoken of a wife, it may seem strange that I have not related the tale of love which must have preceded matrimony. It would be indelicate to relate many thing, necessary to a full understanding of a courtship, from beginning to end. One might tell how he got acquainted; whether he was welcomed or repulsed at first. Praise his wife's beauty, or comment her temper before the die is cast. Somehow I did not like, did not know how to tell it. I got married. Though before I went to Litchfield to live, and shortly after I returned to New Haven from Taunton, as is mentioned before, I used to hear students say something about taking Yankee girls for wives, and I thought I would look round and see if I could not find one. I had a great many clothes from the students, and I could rig myself up mighty well. And I have always seen that the girls seemed to like those best who dressed the finest. Yet I do reckon the generality of girls are sluttish, though my wife is not. When a servant, and since too, I have seen so much behind the curtain, that I don't want told. I recollect one student telling a story of this sort, when I was in the room. An acquaintance of his had been courting a lady some time, and I forget how it was exactly, but after he married her, come to see her in the morning, with all the curls, ribbons, combs, caps, earrings, wreaths, &c. &. stripped off, he did not knew her. While I was looking round, I found a plain looking girl in New Haven, and I found she was the very one Providence had provided for me; though her beauty, before it faded, and her figure before it was spoiled, as it always must be soon, were such as a fine Virginian like myself, might be proud to embrace. I paid my attention to her. I loved her into an engagement. After a while I got one of the students to write a publishment, and sent it to the Rev. Mr. M.; he did not read it the next Sabbath, as was customary, and I went to see him. He said he would read it next Sunday, though he thought it was a hoax. So next Sunday he made proclamation. I was then married in the Episcopal manner. I reckon my wife did belong, originally, at Middlebury, twenty miles from New Haven. I had at that time become much alarmed about being taken up and carried back to my master, which was one reason why I left New Haven for Litchfield. My wife's mother came down to see her, and she went home with her, and came down in a wagon after me, and as I was walking in the street that evening she came, I though I heard the constable after me, and Mr. Sturges, who formerly owned me. I heard them say, the constable and another, that fellow ran away from Savannah. I was so frightened, my strength left me. But I began to run. I stopped at Lanson's, and left word for my wife, and then went on as swift as a deer, over the fences. I never thought where I was going. I traveled until two or three o'clock. Oh, how the sweat did run off me! I crept into a barn and slept; and the next day I arrived at Middlebury. Here I went to work among the farmers, until I left for Litchfield, as aforementioned, and commenced my barber shop and waiting. I suppose I staid at Litchfield four years, until when I rented my house, and came to New Haven, as above stated.

While living in New Haven, one C. a student, gave me a room in the house where he roomed, and I waited on him. He sent me to the College Hall after his breakfast. Mr. Kennedy, one of the cooks, ordered me out, and we had considerable of a scrumage in the Hall, but I got the breakfast. I told Corbett, and he advised me to sue him. I went to lawyer Thomas, and got a writ drawn, and had it served that day. Mr. Kennedy got Mr. Twining for his attorney; indeed I think he had two lawyers. I lost my case. They had President Dwight's deposition, who stated that he put these men in the hall to do for him as they would in their own houses. Therefore, Kennedy had according to law, a right to put me out. I was at this time a stranger in New Haven, but I knew a great many of the students, and they were very good to me. They paid the cost of this case, or gave me clothes and money, so that I made money, if anything by the suit.

My acquaintance among the black people were friendly to me in New Haven, and it is no more than just that I should preserve the name of one of them, who is now dead, from oblivion, particularly as he was a runaway slave, like myself and very distinguished in his profession. As soon as I came from New Bedford to New Haven, I went up to College to see Barber Thompson, and to see how he came on; and I found him very sick. He was very glad to see me, and gave the shop into my possession, to keep for him. Barber Thompson, for that was the name he went by in New Haven, was a slave to Mr. Benly, of Port Royal, Va. He came on to the north with a gentleman, to wait on him, and ran away during the last war. He was honest and clever, was called the greatest barber in America, kept shop by the College, and was often called to officiate at parties and weddings, being the politest servant in town. He died last winter, and I had him buried in my burying ground.

That poverty which oftens leaves my wife and children without a supper, may well excuse me for leaving his grave nameless. A stone I intended to erect with this epitaph:

> Here lies old Thompson! and now he is dead
> I think some one should tell his story;
> For while men's faces must be shaved,
> His name should live in glory.

But I have not for the reason above, put up a stone.

The enmity of some of my rivals in business, led them to make misrepresentations about town against my character, and one of them had some authority in town affairs. My conduct was good, and the strict laws of Connecticut could find nothing to punish; but the selectmen have power to warn any man out of town who has not gained a settlement, which is a difficult thing for a poor man. This was the only course my enemies could take with me. There was certainly no danger of my coming upon the town, which is all the object of the law to prevent. It is very mean and cruel to drive a man out of town because he is suspected of some crime, or breach of law. If he is guilty, punish him, but not set him adrift on suspicion, or from mere tyranny, because his poverty exposes him to it. If I was a pimp why not punish me for it, not warn a man out of town, because his enemies accuse him of crime. Such was the fact though. They then brought a suit for the penalty, one dollar and sixty-seven cents a week. The suit was before a justice in Woodbridge. I saw him in town and told him I wished to have the case adjorned to New Haven. They got judgment against me, as I did not appear. I was then in this predicament, liable to be whipped at the post, if I did not pay the fine or depart in ten days. I think I should not have left, but paid my dollar and sixty-seven cents a week and staid, if I had not at this time become alarmed about being taken up by my old master in Savannah. I was often recognized by students and others from the South; and my master knew where I was. I thought if I went back in the country, if I was taken up I should have more chance to buy myself free; I therefore returned to Litchfield.

After I returned to Litchfield, Mr. Thompson came on as I anticipated, with power from my master to free me or take me back. He said he would put me in irons and sent me down to New York, and then on to Savannah, if I did not buy myself. I instantly offered to give up my house and land, all I had. The house was under a mortgage to Dr. Cottin. A Mr. Burrows from the South had before this seen me in New Haven, and said my master would send on for me. I got a gentleman in Litchfield to write to my master, to know what he would do, and he wrote back he would take five hundred dollars for me, though I was worth eight. Mr. Thompson had now come on with discretionary power. My house would sell for only $425, under the incumbrance. Mr. T. wished me to give my note for fifty dollars in addition. I went to the Governor and told him the whole story; and the Governor said, not so, Grimes; you must have what you get hereafter, for yourself. The Governor did pity my case, and was willing to assist me, for such is his feeling to the poor.

To be put in irons and dragged back to a state of slavery, and either leave my wife and children in the street, or take them into servitude, was a situation in which my soul now shudders at the thought of having been placed. It would have exhibited an awful spectacle of the conduct and inconsistency of men, to have done it; yet I was undoubtedly the lawful property of my master, according to the laws of the country, and though many would justify him, perhaps aid in taking me back, yet if there is any man in God's whole creation, who will say, with respect to himself, (only bring the case home,) that there are any possible circumstances in which it is just that he should be at the capricious disposal of a fellow being, if he will say, that nature within him, that feeling, that reason tells him so, or can convince him so, that man lies! The soul of man cannot be made to feel it, to think it, to own it, or believe it. I may give my life for the good or the safety of others. But no law, no consequences, not the lives of millions, can authorize them to take my life or liberty from me while innocent of any crime.

I have to thank my master, however, that he took what I had, and freed me. I gave a deed of my house to a gentleman in Litchfield. He paid the money for it to Mr. T., who then gave me my free papers. Oh! how my heart did rejoice and thank God. From what anxiety, what pain and heartache did it relieve me! For even though I might have fared better the rest of life under my master, yet the thought of being snatched up and taken back, was awful. Accustomed as I had been to freedom for years, the miseries of slavery which I had felt, and knew, and tasted, were presented to my mind in no faint image. To say that a man is better off in one situation than another, if in the one he is better clothed and better fed, and has less care than in the other, is false. It is true, if you regard him as a brute, as destitute of the feelings of human nature. But I will not speak on the subject more. Those slaves who have kind masters are, perhaps, as happy as the generality of mankind. They are not aware that their condition can be better, and I don't know as it can: indeed it cannot, except by their own exertions. I would advise no slave to leave his master. If he runs away, he is most sure to be taken: if he is not, he will ever be in the apprehension of it; and I do think there is no inducement for a slave to leave his master and be set free in the Northern States. I have had to work hard; I have been often cheated, insulted, abused and injured; yet a black man, if he will be industrious and honest, can get along here as well as any one who is poor and in a situation to be imposed on. I have been very unfortunate in life in this respect. Notwithstanding all my struggles, and sufferings, and injuries, I have been an honest man. There is no one who can come forward and say he knows anything against Grimes. This I know, that I have been punished for being suspected of things of which some of those who were loudest against me were actually guilty. The practice of warning poor people out of town is very cruel. It may be necessary that towns should have that power, otherwise some might be overrun with paupers. But it is mighty apt to be abused. A poor man just gets agoing in business, and is then warned to depart; perhaps he has a family, and don't know where to go, or what to do. I am a poor man, and ignorant; but I am a man of sense. I have seen them contributing at church for the heathen, to build churches, and send preachers to them, yet there was no place where I could get a seat in the church. I knew in New Haven indians and negroes, come from a great many thousand miles, sent to be educated, while there were people I knew in the town cold and hungry, and ignorant. They have kind of societies to make clothes for those who, they say, go naked in their own countries. The ladies sometimes do this at one end of a town, while their fathers, who may happen to be selectmen, may be warning a poor man and his family out at the other end, for fear they may have to be buried at the town expense. It sounds rather strange upon a man's ear who feels that he is friendless and abused in society, to hear so many speeches about charity; for I was always inclined to be observing.

I have forebore to mention names in my history where it might give the least pain; in this I have made it less interesting, and injured myself.

I may sometimes be a little mistaken, as I have to write from memory, and there is a great deal I have omitted from want of recollection at the time of writing. I cannot speak as I feel on some subjects. If those who read my history think I have not led a life of trial, I have failed to give a correct representation. I think I must be forty years of age, but don't know; I could not tell my wife my age. I have learned to read and write pretty well; if I had an opportunity I could learn very fast. My wife has had a tolerable good education, which has been a help to me.

I hope some will buy my books from charity; but I am no beggar. I am now entirely destitute of property; where and how I shall live I don't know; where and how I shall die I don't know; but I hope I may be prepared. If it were not for the stripes on my back which were made while I was a slave, I would in my will leave my skin as a legacy to the government, desiring that it might be taken off and made into parchment, and then bind the constitution of glorious, happy, and *free* America. Let the skin of an American slave bind the charter of American liberty!

WILLIAM GRIMES.

CONCLUSION.

IT is now more than thirty years since the foregoing true and eventful Life was written and published. Although a large edition was printed, a very few copies are now in existence; and it was only when I advertised in the public papers, that I was myself enabled to procure a perfect one. By the kindness of a gentleman, who will long be held in grateful remembrance, a copy was put in my hands. A large number of my intimate friends have urgently requested me to print another edition of my Life, with such additions as I can find time to add in this my old age. I am greatly indebted to many distinguished men of New Haven, and the obligations I owe them, I hope in a measure to repay, by presenting to them this second edition of the Life of one who has often been called one of the most remarkable personages of modern times. I comply with the request, for the purpose, in the first place, of raising, if possible, a small amount of money, for I believe almost everybody will purchase a copy of my Life; and in the second place, to gratify the laudable curiosity which so many of my friends have exhibited to procure a true and perfect Life of "Old Grimes."

In presenting this account to my fellow citizens of New Haven, "and the rest of mankind," I do not think it necessary to enter into all the particulars of my life, since I have lived in New Haven, as, after a residence here of nearly thirty years, I have become, as the newspapers say, "a fixed institution," and have also become pretty generally known. I shall therefore add but little to the preceding account of one who has tasted the bitter dregs of slavery—having been the slave of *ten* masters—but who has yet been permitted, through a kind Providence, to drink at the fountain of Liberty, although many of his best years were spent in degradation and misery.

I am now an old man—"Old Grimes"—being more than seventy years of age, and the father of eighteen lovely and beautiful children, of whom only twelve, I believe, are living. The youngest child, now eight years old, a smart and active lad, is the only one now with me. The other children that are living are scattered all over the world, one son being now in Australia, digging for gold.

My wife, who at the time we were married, was called in the papers, "the lovely and all-accomplished Miss Clarissa Caesar," has also grown old, since I introduced her to the reader, as may well be supposed; but she is yet very smart, for so fruitful a vine, and I don't think there are many to be compared to her. Like her noble son, she too is seeking for gold, having been for some time in California.

But I must now give my readers a short account of myself from the time I left them in the first part of my book. I then lived in Litchfield, but since that time I have lived in a great many places, some of which I will mention. When I left Litchfield, I went with my family to Bridgeport, and set up a barber shop. I was called a good barber, and had a great many customers. I made money quite fast, and ought to have been satisfied; but somehow I was not, and had to be on the move. So I pulled up stakes, packed up my things, and off we started for Stratford.

But here I should tell what a narrow escape I had from drowning, while I lived in Bridgeport, There was a camp meeting at Saugatuck, and being a good Methodist, I thought I would attend. About five hundred persons got on board the steamboat Lafayette, at Bridgeport, but before we arrived at the camp ground there came up a most dreadful storm of rain, and the wind blew like a hurricane. All the people were almost frightened to death, and expected that the steamboat would sink, and all go to the bottom of the Sound. I never was so scared before, and never expected to feel so awful as I did then; but I came very near being drowned after that time, when I lived in New Haven, which I will tell all about soon. Although all expected to be lost, we were spared, and at last arrived safe at the camp meeting, and had a good time.

I lived in Stratford some time, but didn't make much by the operation of moving, and so went back to Bridgeport, where I stayed a little while and then went to Norwalk. Here I carried on my old business of a barber, and cleaning old clothes, and made out to live very comfortable. But as at this time I happened to get into trouble, I didn't stay long in Norwalk. The trouble I got into was, that a large butcher one day insulted me and I knocked him down. I was then younger than I am now, and if anybody meddled with Grimes, he was sure to be punished, if he wasn't stronger and a better man than I was. I did no more than any one would do when abused, but I being a *negro*, as they called me, and the butcher a *white* man, although his skin was a great deal blacker than mine, I was put under

$500 bonds. No one would go bail for poor Grimes, so he had to go to jail. I didn't mind that much, as I had before been in such places; but at last I found a friend in Lawyer Fitch Wheeler, of Monroe, and after I had been in jail about a week, he gave bonds for me, and once more I was enjoying my liberty. When the trial came on, the butcher paid the cost of court, and I was discharged. Afterwards I sued the butcher before a Justice in Bridgeport, got my case, and the butcher had to pay one dollar and the costs of court.

From Norwalk I went to Fairfield. Here I did a good business, shaving and powdering my friends Judge Daggett and Lawyer Nathan Smith, when they came there to attend court. Sometimes I made more than three dollars a day. I had a great run of custom—all the first men of Fairfield came to Grimes to have their hair trimmed and to be shaved. I ought to have been contented, but I wasn't, and again was on the move.

When I say I *shaved* my friends, I want my readers to understand what I mean, for I wasn't then in the brokerage business, which I afterwards followed very successfully, and of which I shall speak soon. Being a barber and being a broker, is quite different, and I hope no one will confound the one with the other.

From Fairfield I went to Stratford Point. I made out tolerable well there, but after I had been in the place about a year, we packed up all our things, put them on board a sloop, and started for New Haven,

When I got to New Haven, I set up a barber shop and clothes cleaning establishment, in Chapel street. I hired my shop of Esquire Daggett, who was always a good friend to Grimes. Chapel street then wasn't much like what it is now. One could then hire a store cheap, now it takes a great deal of money, and if Grimes could hire a shop anywhere, he would have to go to some old place where the gentlemen wouldn't come. When I got to New Haven, I thought I would let my old friends know what I intended to do, so I put an advertisement in the paper, headed with these lines:

Old Grimes is not dead,
   But you may see him more,
Cleaning coats and shaving heads,
   Just as before.

Though long old Grimes has slept,
   He only sleeps to wake;
And those who thought him dead and gone,
   Now laugh at their mistake.

Here I did a good business, shaving for only three cents, and trimming heads cheap. I also cleaned clothes and did almost everything to get an honest living. I have worked at the Colleges, and have always been an industrious man, and have endeavored to get an honest living, and if I could not do it one way I have tried another. That my readers may see what a variety of callings I have been engaged in, I here copy the truthful and interesting lines, written by a gentleman of New Haven, who has long been acquainted with me, and whom I have always considered one of my best friends. I don't know whether I ought to give the name of the author of this poem, and therefore I omit to do so; but any one whose curiosity is excited, can learn my friend's name by calling on me.

OLD GRIMES' SON.

Old Grimes' boy lives in our town,
    A clever lad is he,—
He's long enough, if cut in half,
    To make two men like me.

He has a sort of waggish look,
    And cracks a harmless jest;
His clothes are rather worse for wear,
    Except his Sunday's best.

He is a man of many parts,
    As all who know can tell;
He sometimes reads the list of goods,
    And rings the auction bell.

He's kind and lib'ral to the poor,
    That is, to number one;
He sometimes saws a load of wood,
    And piles it when he's done.

He's always ready for a job—
    (When paid)—whate'er you choose;
He's often at the Colleges,
    And brushes boots and shoes.

Like honest men, he pays his debts,
    No fears has he of duns;
At leisure he prefers to walk,
    And when in haste, he runs.

In all his intercourse with folks,
　　His object is to please;
His pantaloons curve out before,
　　Just where he bends his knees.

His life was written sometime since,
　　And many read it through;
He makes a racket when he snores,
　　As other people do.

When once oppressed he prov'd his blood
　　Not covered with the yoke;
But now he sports a freeman's cap,
　　And when it rains, a cloak!

He's drooped beneath the southern skies,
　　And tread on northern snows;
He's taller by a foot or more,
　　When standing on his toes.

In Church he credits all that's said,
　　Whatever preacher rise;
They say he has been seen in tears,
　　When dust got in his eyes.

A man remarkable as this,
　　Must sure immortal be,
And more than all, because he is
　　Old Grimes' posterity!

After I had been in New Haven several years—I don't know how many, for I can't keep the run of dates—I went into the brokerage business, and have continued it more or less to the present time. I wasn't exactly at the head of the concern, but still I was considered an indispensable part of the establishment, and although I didn't get *rich* by becoming a broker, others made a great deal of money by my exertions. I would often have dreams, and of course I told my friends of them, and then they would greedily seize the lucky numbers, and be *almost* sure to get a prize.

Some people used to say it wasn't right to sell lottery tickets, but as a great many better people than myself sold tickets, I din't think I was doing wrong.

About this time I joined the Methodist Church, in this city. After I became a broker, some of my brethren thought I wasn't doing right by

selling lottery tickets, and they brought me up before the Church, and
turned me out. Thus Grimes got into trouble again; but not despairing, I
applied to Dr. Croswell, and was confirmed by the Bishop, and I am now a
member in full communion in Dr. Croswell's Church. There were a great
many confirmed when I was. While the Bishop put only one hand on the
heads of the others, I being the last, he put both hands on mine—thus
doubly blessing me.

I now sometimes attend Dr. Stiles' Church, because the Doctor is an old
friend of mine. When the Doctor was a student I used to work for
him—make his fires and sometimes shave him and dress his hair; and when
he went to Litchfield to study law, I also was there, and waited on him.

And now I ought to tell about the other narrow escape from drowning. I
don't know what year it was, but it was the same year that the steamer
Lexington was burnt in the Sound, and so many lives lost. That was a
dreadful accident; but the danger I was in, was almost equal to those
unfortunate beings on board of the Lexington.

At this time I lived over on what is called the Dyke, and there came on a
most powerful rain storm, and the water rose so fast that before we were
aware of it, my house was all surrounded with water, and we found it
impossible to escape. The water came into the first story and we went to
the second, and from the second to the third, and then it was that we all
expected to be drowned. This was in the night. At last I got my head out
of the garret window, and with a speaking trumpet, cried out most all
night, "Oh for a cannon to wake those sleepy men." Finally I waked up a
man and he went and got Rev. Mr. Jewett's *horse* out of the water, and
saved *his* life. He too had a narrow escape, his head being only out of the
water. After they had got the horse out, the water began to lower, and in a
little time we were all left safe from harm.

Now I might as well tell about that witch that I mentioned in the book,
riding me. Some persons think it isn't true, but it is, every word of it, and I
might tell a great deal more about it. To convince my readers that it is true
I must say that I have heard from my old master, and he says that Frankee
is dead. He also says that when he thought Frankee was agoing to die he
told her that she had been a good slave, and asked her what he could do
for her. He asked her what he should do with her things after she was
dead; if she wanted any of them given to any of her fellow slaves. No,
massa, said she, I don't care about any body. Bury them all with me. And
when she died my old massa dug a trench beside of her grave, and put in

everything—bed and bed-clothes, tables, chairs, frying-pan, dishes, &c. &c., and buried them all up with her.

I must mention one thing more. Many years ago I bought a burying ground lot, among the rich folks' lot, and had some of my children buried in it, and now they want to get it away, saying they can't find my land. My land was recorded, but yet the new surveyor says he can't find it, and says that there is not any left after others have got their share. I am a poor man, and perhaps because I am, I shall not have a place to put my old worn out body, but I know I bought and paid for a lot in the burying ground.

I have now been in New Haven more than thirty years, and have always meant to be an honest man and deal justly with all. I have always tried to pay my debts and keep out of jail; but I have been in jail twice in New Haven—once because I didn't pay Mr. Bradley for breaking his carriage—amounting to twenty dollars, and once because I hadn't the money to pay two or three dollars for rent. My friends, however, raised the money, and I was again free, and hope to remain so.

I said in the former part of my book, that the poor and friendless are not entirely free from apprehension, even in this land of liberty, and that this could be illustrated if I should give all the particulars of my life, since I have been in Connecticut, and that I might do so in a future edition. But on reflection I have concluded not to rake up old affairs, and as all the wrongs which I have met with in my eventful life have no doubt been ordered wisely, I have forgiven all, and hope, if possible, to forget them. But when they are called to mind, I think those persons who have oppressed poor Grimes, should recollect that although his skin is perhaps a little darker than theirs, he yet has the feelings of a man, and knows when he is abused.

And now, as I have brought my narrative to a close, I wish only to add a few lines to say that I hope all my friends and acquaintances will purchase a copy of my book, and thus help "Old Grimes" to pay the printer, and have a small amount left to carry him safely through the coming year. As before remarked, I am now an old man, and am almost wholly dependent on my acquaintances for the means of support; and while the purchasers of my book benefit me by so doing, I hope and believe they will find themselves abundantly repaid by the perusal of it. The book, as will be seen, is *illustrated* by a likeness of "Old Grimes," engraved by Sanford from a Photograph by Wells, Daguerreian Artist, Nos. 10 and 11, Mitchell's

Building. I am indebted to the generosity of Mr. Wells for this likeness of myself, and I here return him my thanks, and would recommend all my readers to visit his rooms, examine his specimens of Photograph and Daguerreotype likenesses, and then have their own taken.

Here I part with my readers. It is not likely that I shall ever again appear before the public as an author. I hope, however, long to enjoy the kind regards of the good people of New Haven, and when this old, weary, worn out body is lain in that place prepared for all living, the silent tear may be dropped for "poor Old Grimes," and his frailties, whatever they be, forgotten. To all I now bid FAREWELL!

A NARRATIVE

LIFE AND LABORS

REV. G. W. OFFLEY,

A COLORED MAN,

AND LOCAL PREACHER,

Who lived twenty-seven years at the South and twenty-four at the North; who never went to school a day in his life, and only commenced to learn his letters when nineteen years and eight months old; the emancipation of his mother and her three children; how he learned to read while living in a slave state, and supported himself from the time he was nine years old until he was twenty-one.

An interesting story of a slave woman, Jane Brown—her dream fulfilled—the separation of her husband and two children.

The escape of D. Green, a slave woman and her infant, in one night, by the aid of a white woman and three colored men.

Proposition of a slaveholder to G. W. Offley to marry his slave girl.

The slave girl runaway and got married on Saturday night and came home Sunday morning.

HARTFORD, CONN.

1860.

NAMES OF GENTLEMEN WHO SPEAK IN HIGH
TERMS OF HIS MORAL WORTH

Ware, Mass., Feb., 1852.
REV. W. WARD.

Hartford, Conn., 1854.
REV. DR. J. HAWES.
    "   DR. H. BUSHNELL.

Worcester, Mass., 1854.
REV. O. SWEETSER.
    "   E. SMALLEY.
    "   GEO. BUSHNELL.
    "   DR. A. HILL.
HON. JOHN DAVIS.
REV. O. H. TILLOTSON.

Boston, Mass., 1859.
REV. JOHN W. DADMAN.
REV. E. E. HALL.

NARRATIVE

OF THE LIFE OF

REV. G. W. OFFLEY.

MY mother was born a slave in the State of Virginia, and sold in the State of Maryland, and there remained until married, and became the mother of three children. She was willed free at the death of her master; her three children were also willed free at the age of twenty-five. But my youngest brother was put on a second will, which was destroyed by the widow and the children, and he was subjected to bondage for life. My father was a free man, and therefore bought him as a slave for life and give him his freedom at the age of twenty years. He also bought my sister for a term of years, say until she was twenty-five years old. He gave her her freedom at the age of sixteen years. He bought my grand-mother, who was too old to set free, that she might be exempted from hard servitude in her old age.

Previous to the sale of this family, my mother was living with her master's children, and they persuaded mother to not consent to father's buying the children, and told father if he attempted to buy one of them they would shoot him dead on the auction ground; that they would buy the children themselves, and they should have their freedom according to their father's will. Mother told them they might buy them and welcome, but you had better throw your money in the fire, for if you buy one of my children I will cut all three of their throats while they are asleep, and your money will do you no good. Her young masters were afraid that she meant what she said, and they concluded that it would bring a disgrace upon the family to prohibit a man from buying his own children, though mother had no intention of doing as she said.

The auctioneer was a true friend to father, and used great deception in making the purchaser believe that the two children would die unless they could have their mother's care, so that father bought them at his own price, as no person bid against him. They wanted to have mother and father to work for them, and they would bring up the two children as mother had; neither had any care of a family, and they was afraid the children would suffer. Mother said if they did suffer they would not be accountable for it,—that she had two hands, and she could work and take care of her own children without their help. But when she became the mother of eight children, and father working for twenty-five or fifty cents per day, she often would think of her old master's kitchen and wish for some of the good victuals she had given to the poor whites, and the field slaves. But little did they think they would ever be poor. One of her young mistresses married a miserable young man and she went blind and died heart-broken. Her young master's daughter married a similar kind of wretch, and died young, as thousands of the wicked do.

I was born Dec. 18th, 1808, in the State of Maryland, Queen Ann's County, Centerville. My mother and father were illiterate, and kept no record of their children's births, only refering to circumstances. But when I was seven years old I heard mother say that her young master's daughter Ann was two weeks older than myself, and I got a stick, or piece of wood, and made 1111111 notches, and at the end of every year would add another 1 notch until I was twenty-one years old. At that time there was a dispute between mother and father about my age. Mother said I was twenty-one, and father thought I was only twenty, and I went to Centerville and saw Miss Ann, who was born two weeks before me. I asked her if she was twenty-one, and she said yes she was just twenty-one years old, and I returned from my ten miles walk, but dare not name it to father until he mentioned it, and I told him I had been to see Miss Ann and she said I was twenty-one years old; then said he you are free from me. During my boyhood father hired me to a slaveholder for a term of four years to pay his house rent. From the time I was nine years old I worked and supported myself until I was twenty-one years old, and never received one dollar of my wages. When I was ten years old I sat down and taking an old basket to pieces, learned myself to make baskets. After that I learned to make foot mats and horse collars, not of leather but of corn husks; also two kinds of brooms. These articles I used to make nights and sell to get money for myself. When I was sixteen years old I commenced taking contracts of wood-chopping, at fifty cents per cord, and hired slaves to chop for me nights, when the moon shone bright. In the fall and winter we would make our fire and chop until eleven or twelve at night. We used to catch oysters and fish nights, and hire other slaves to peddle them out on Sunday mornings. By this way I have helped some to get their freedom.

EXODUS 20 — 12: Honor thy father and thy mother, that thy days may be long upon the land which the Lord thy God giveth thee.

When I was twenty-one years old I gave my father one year's work to buy him a horse. One year's wages for an able bodied man $50, or $60, fifty or sixty dollars per year, and two holidays at Easter,—two in June, two in harvest, and six at the end of the year; one pair of shoes, one pair stockings, one pair woolen pants, one coat, two pairs coarse tow linen pants, two shirts, and board, is the law of the State of Maryland allows a man, free or slave, black or white, who hires for one year.

My friends who may read this little work, will make due allowance when they see that I never possessed the advantage of one day's schooling in my life, and only commenced to learn my letters when nineteen years and eight months old.

At one time, when going to my work, I found a piece of a chapter of an old Bible, Genesis 25, concerning Isaac, Jacob, and Esau. At this time there was an old colored man working for my father. He, taking the piece of Bible, and read it to me; I do not remember ever hearing that much of the Bible read before. I told him I would like to learn to read; he told me to get a book and he would learn me, while he stayed with us. I bought a little primer, and Sunday morning he commenced learning me my letters. By Monday morning I could say them all. He would give me lessons nights and Sabbath mornings. He said when he used to take his master's children to school, he would carry his book in his hat and get the children to give him a lesson in the interval of the school. He grew up to be a young man, experienced religion, and joined the M. E. church, and was authorized to preach among his colored brethren, free and slave, and was set free some time before he worked for my father.

After he left our house I was without a teacher, and there was an old man about seventy-five or eighty years old, a slaveholder, owned a small farm and one slave woman married to a slave belonging to another slaveholder. This woman was the mother of two small children. Her old master had five daughters, one son eighteen years of age, a family of ten in number, to be supported from this little farm,—no one to work except this son and the slave woman, only as I would go and help them occasionally. By this the young man and I became very intimate, and I learned him the art of wrestling, boxing and fighting, and he learned me to read. After that I went to work on a rail road; then I taught boxing school, and learned to write. After that I went to St. George, Del., to work at a hotel. One day a white boy came to me and said that he was hungry; his father gambled away his money, and if I would give him and his little sister something to eat occasionally, he would come three nights in the week and set copies for me to write, and learn me to cypher. The landlady was very glad of the opportunity, and gave me the privilege of giving them as much as I pleased, and I used to take them in the kitchen and give them what they could eat, and fill their little basket to take home. He would stay with me sometimes until 2 or 3 o'clock P.M., and learn me to cypher to the single rule of three.

I arrived at Hartford on the 15th of Nov., 1835. Since that time some of my good white friends have assisted me by referring me to good books, and giving good instruction, of which I have reason to believe some of them are in heaven, and others on earth doing good.

My mother's and father's theology, or the way we children were taught by our parents, neither of them could read; but as mother's master was a member of the M. E. church, and used to read the Bible to his slaves—not learn nor teach them to read, but read the Bible to them.

First, man is a compound being, possessing two natures, a soul and a body; the body is of the earth, and must die and return to the dust from whence it came; but the soul is immortal; that is, will never die, but will live forever in happiness with God, or exist in hell for ever. This theology teaches of two places for the souls of the human family after death, and the condition by which they must go first. If children were obedient to their parents or their owners, and prayed to the Lord to forgive them of their sins and make them good children, and keep them from telling lies, from stealing, from taking the Lord's name in vain, and to keep the Sabbath holy. But above all, never to be saucy to old people, lest our case should be like the forty-two children destroyed by the two she bears—II KINGS, chap. 2—23: and he went up from thence unto Bethel, and as he was going up by the way there came forth little children out of the city and mocked him, and said unto him, Go up, thou bald head, go up thou bald head. Verse 24: and he turned back and looked on them and cursed them in the name of the Lord; and there came forth two she-bears out of the wood and tore forty and two children of them. And I am glad to know that even from the most oppressed slave to the most refined white family's children at the south, are taught to respect the old, white or black. Their children call old colored people aunt and uncle by way of respect. None use the word 'nigger' but the low and vulgar.

Our family theology teaches that God is no respecter of persons, but gave his son to die for all, bond or free, black or white, rich or poor. If we keep his commandments, we will be happy after death. It also teaches that if God calls and sanctifies a person to do some great work, that person is immortal until his work is done; that God is able and will protect him from all danger or accident in life if he is faithful to his calling or charge committed by the Lord. This is a borrowed idea from circumstances too numerous to mention. Here is one man we present as a proof of the immortality of man, while in the flesh: Praying Jacob. This man was a slave in the State of Maryland. His master was very cruel to his slaves. Jacob's rule was to pray three times a day, at just such an hour of the day; no matter what his work was or where he might be, he would stop and go and pray. His master has been to him and pointed his gun at him, and told him if he did not cease praying he would blow out his brains. Jacob would finish his prayer and then tell his master to shoot in welcome—your loss will be my gain—I have two masters, one on earth and one in heaven—master Jesus in heaven, and master Saunders on earth. I have a soul and a body; the body belongs to you, master Saunders, and the soul to master Jesus. Jesus says men ought always to pray, but you will not pray, neither do you want to have me pray. This man said in private conversation that several times he went home and drank an unusual quantity of brandy to harden his heart that he might kill him; but he never had power to strike nor shoot him, and he would freely give the world, if he had it in his possession for what he believed his Jacob to possess. He also thought that Jacob was as sure of Heaven as the apostle Paul or Peter. Sometimes Mr. S. would be in the field about half drunk, raging like a madman, whipping the other slaves; and when Jacob's hour would come for prayer, he would stop his horses and plough and kneel down and pray; but he could not strike the man of God.

The first Methodist minister that ever preached in a certain town in Queen Ann's county, there was a great revival of religion among the rich and poor, black and white, free and slaves. When many of them experienced religion they would disobey their ungodly masters and would go to meetings nights and Sundays. Two rich slaveholders waylaid the minister at night, and taking him off from his horse and beat him until they thought he was dead. But the Lord saved his life to preach his Word, and many were converted in the same town through his preaching, and many masters, when converted, set their slaves free.

My grandmother died at ninety years of age; my mother at seventy, and my father at eighty years of age. These three friends died in the strongest triumph of faith in Jesus, who when on earth said he would be with his people to the end of the world. Amen.

Perhaps some person will ask why did I teach the art of wrestling, boxing and fighting, when desirous to learn to read the Bible? I answer because no one is so contemptible as a coward. With us a coward is looked upon as the most degraded wretch on earth, and is only worthy to be a slave. My brother's master, Governor R. Right, of Maryland, taught his children never to take an insult from one of their equals—that is, from the rich and educated. Their domestic slaves were taught not to take an insult from another rich man's domestic slave under any consideration. By this, you perceive, I was trying to be respectable by doing like the rich. Those who read the lives of our great statesmen, know they were duellists. Then I thought he who could control his antagonist by the art of his physical power was a great man. But I thank the Lord, since the 21st of Feb., 1836, I have been enabled to see things in a different light, and believe the man is greater who can overcome his foes by his Christlike example.

A word to my colored friends. It is often said that we are a degraded people in this country as well as in Africa. Before we consent to the charge, let us look at the word degradation. Walker says it means "deprivation of office or dignity, degeneracy, to lessen, to diminish." I cannot see that his explanation has anything to do with the charge against us in a moral sense of the term. When properly taken into consideration, if we only number one-sixth part of the population of the United States. Because we have six men against one to vote us out of office; that is not degrading us, it is oppressing us. If six colored men should take a white child from its parents, and teach it that its highest obligations belong to us, we six men, that we stand in the place of God—this is the kind of education many of our people have at the south. Now I ask if this child should become a sabbath-breaker, or a liar, a thief, or a drunkard, or an adulterer, not having the advantage to know better, I ask who is the degraded man? Paul says, Romans 4;15: For where there is no law there is no transgression. Then the moral guilt rests on the oppressor and not on the oppressed. We must not feel that we are degraded. The true meaning of the word degrade, is to be low, mean, contemptible, willing to do a mean act that we know is displeasing in the sight of God and man. Therefore we may be oppressed by man, but never morally degraded, only as we are made willing subjects to do sinful acts against what we know or have the power to know is wrong in the sight of God and man.

No difference how poor we are, if we are respectable, honest, and upright, with God, ourselves, and our fellow man. For St. Peter declares, Acts 10, 34–35, that God is no respecter of persons. But in every nation, he that feareth him, and worketh righteousness, is accepted with him. And if any man is accepted with his God, then oppression, nor prejudice, or prisons, or chains, or whips, or anything formed by man, cannot degrade us. No, we must voluntarily subscribe to some mean act before we can be mean or low in the sight of our dear Lord and Master.

My dear and much beloved friends, allow me to say to one and all, be sure to send your children to the day and sabbath school.

Yours in love,

G. W. OFFLEY.

AUTOBIOGRAPHY

OF

JAMES L. SMITH,

INCLUDING, ALSO,

REMINISCENCES OF SLAVE LIFE. RECOLLECTIONS
OF THE WAR, EDUCATION OF FREEDMEN,
CAUSES OF THE EXODUS, ETC.

NORWICH:
PRESS OF THE BULLETIN COMPANY.
1881.

TO THE MEMORY OF
MY FATHER,
CHARLES PAYNE,
WHO LIES IN A NAMELESS,
UNKNOWN GRAVE,
THIS VOLUME
IS DEDICATED.

PREFACE

THE writer would bring before the public the narrative of his life while in bondage, which is substantially true in all its details. The painful wrongs inflicted then and now have caused the writer, though many years have passed, to take up the publication of this narrative of himself. There are many incidents and characters described in this narrative personally known to the writer, which make him anxious to put forth some effort, however humble it may be, to ameliorate the condition of his now suffering people, in order that the facts may confirm the truthful saying: "My people will be styled a nation yet, and also claim their nationality." For this they have fought and suffered hundreds of years in servitude and bondage. It is a fact which ought to thrill the heart of every American citizen to see the interest they take in learning; the untiring exertions they make to overcome every obstacle, even death itself to acquire it. It is what God has promised: "To be a God to the faithful and to their seed after them."

The writer hopes not to weary your patience in reviewing his narrative, which is fraught with so many exciting scenes. It is the duty of men to occupy places of power and trust, therefore our rulers, above all others, ought to be holy and devoted men. There are, however, some found in every age of the world who believe in freedom of thought and speech; and many who are untiring in their efforts to secure the future well-being of those intrusted to their care; it affords the most powerful argument to influence the minds of some. It is believed that no one who reads attentively, and reflects seriously, will doubt that the time is near at hand, which is spoken of by God: "Ye shall let my people go free." Now the great revolution seems to me to have come; now is the time for us to act in trying to save that which was lost; in stimulating them to education; and in building homes and schoolhouses for their children, that they may become honorable and respectable citizens of the States to which they have acceded. We want earnest laborers amongst us, for those who are instructing my people are few and far between; and we have been deprived of education by the hand of slavery and servitude, which has been brought upon us by the slave-holder. I feel it is the duty of the people to take up our cause, and instruct wherever they can.

Our ignorance, which is often spoken of, and for which we are not to blame, is caused by this ill, slavery; and the whipping post was resorted to if any attempt was made to learn the alphabet. I can say in the fullness of my heart that there is no darkness equal to this, not even the Egyptian darkness which is spoken of by missionaries now laboring in foreign lands. I only pray to hope on, and on, that God may appear in our behalf, and let the sun of civilization and education be extended among my people until it shall reach from sea to sea, and from land to land. Then shall Ethiopia stretch forth her hand unto God and call you blessed. I thank God for what I have seen and experienced so far in regard to the amelioration of our condition as a people. I hardly expect to see the completion of the act of liberty which was commenced by our most earnest friend, Senator Sumner. "See to the Civil Rights Bill; do n't let it fail," were among his last words to his associate who stood beside the dying senator.

This volume speaks of our earnest desire for more liberty and rights as a free people, and that our children may enjoy that of which we have been deprived. Never was the effectiveness of our Christian instrumentalities in other lands more dependent than now upon the vigorous and progressive development of Christian principles at home.

As we are entering upon a new decade our thoughts go back to 1861; and what a period is this to review! Could we have held the glass to our vision and seen what the nation would accomplish in its terrible struggle for existence, who would not have shrunk from the almost miraculous undertaking? But God had the blank years before Him, and as they passed, He proceeded to fill out the record. Nineteen years ago we were rocking in the swell of the gathering storm which was so soon and unexpectedly to break in its fury, and who could tell how many were to perish and go down ere its fury should be spent. In the strike which slavery made for the ascendancy, how little did we know through what terrible revulsions it would pass on its way to destruction. The cry was, "slavery must go down." How many mighty obstacles must fall before the march of the avalanche. How many disputed the question at the time, as to how this should be accomplished. But like the great iceberg when soft winds blow, and gentle rays fall on it, whether God would prostrate it as he does great cities when earthquakes rock them, was the question to be considered. Such was our uncertainty then; but these counsels were made known to us more speedily than we dreamed.

We have seen how the system of slavery was to be destroyed; and there is work for the Christian Church, there are responsibilities on Christian hearts which we did not anticipate nineteen years ago. National politics have brought about many incidental questions; but there is a period of new and aggressive work in which we are led to go forward and possess the land. Such a burden of duty as it bears upon us at this time, to remember that we are hourly approaching opportunities and responsibilities greater than we have hitherto known. In this spirit we have labored for the grand conquests which to-day are calling us onward. In this spirit we must toil now. How much we ask, bringing to you our pressing wants—come over and help us, for my people are in need of instruction, both spiritual and educational; and in thus aiding us you will accomplish a work of far reaching power, of which you have now no comprehension. "If God be for us, who can be against us?"

May this narrative awaken some to still greater earnestness in working for Christ, and freedom through the land. "Be not weary in well doing, for in due season ye shall reap if ye faint not." It is my privilege to speak about the impoverished people of the South, and those main pillars of our Republic, the Church and the School: thus following up the victories of our arms with the sublimer victories of Christian love. What tremendous agencies God has employed within these few years, and what He has caused to be exerted for all generations to come; and if there is one scripture which is most forcibly illustrated and impressed upon me than any other, it is this: "Whereas ye know not what shall be on the morrow." Who could have foreseen how much God would bring to pass in these nineteen years? Could the author have held the glass to his vision, and seen what the nation would accomplish in its terrible struggle for existence, he would have despaired; but as the period has arrived, my people are determined to go forward and possess the land which will bring our children within the pale of intellectual training in the institutions of education and religion; for we all know that without this education we must expect to be defrauded of our homes, our earnings, and our lands. Many only make their mark in signing their names, for they cannot read or write.

This is the secret of their not having any thing to-day, and the responsibility rests on you, Christian people of these United States of America; and the cry is for help now. There is not a nation under heaven that needs more sympathy and pity from the people of the United States than my people; for they are maltreated every way in the higher educational schools, while endeavoring to obtain an education.

During the most eventful period in our history, the little stream of light that began to flow in Virginia and the Mississippi Valley has from year to year widened and deepened, and rolled with mighty healing power. It has passed the dividing mountains, and carried a flood of Divine blessings to many of my people. "But blessed are your eyes, for they see, and your ears, for they hear: for verily I say unto you, that many prophets and righteous men have desired to see these things which ye see, and have not seen them, and to hear these things which ye hear, and have not heard them." We still have hope of saving our beloved people, and of seeing prosperity in the future. Many of the colored people deserve much of this country for what they did and suffered in the great national struggle. When the Rebels appeared in their strength, and defeat followed defeat in quick succession, while the government was bleeding at every pore, and there appeared to be no help or power to save the Union, then our colored soldiers came to its timely aid and fought like brave men. The rebel lion struck at the very heart of our country. Many of them were ill-treated by the Union soldiers—many a colored soldier was knocked down by them, and maltreated in every way. The treatment the colored soldiers received from the hands of the white soldiers was equal to slavery. All this was because the white soldiers did not want to stand side by side with them—did not want the negro in the ranks. Pen can not begin to describe the extreme sufferings of the colored men in this respect. The Yankee soldiers were eager for glory; the idea of having a colored man in the ranks caused many of them to be angry. "I will never die by the side of a nigger," was uttered from the lips of many.

I hope this work may find its way into the homes and hearts of those who are endeavoring still to help us in our efforts for liberty; if I succeed in this, it is all I desire. That I may have the prayers of all who are interested in my behalf, is the earnest desire of the writer.

In purchasing this narrative you will be assisting one who has been held in the chattels of slavery: who is now broken down by the infirmities of age, and asks your help to aid him in this, his means of support in his declining years.

CONTENTS.

CHAPTER I.
BIRTH AND CHILDHOOD.

CHAPTER II.
YOUTH AND EARLY MANHOOD.

CHAPTER III.
LIFE IN HEATHSVILLE.

CHAPTER IV.
ESCAPE FROM SLAVERY.

CHAPTER V.
LIFE IN FREEDOM.

AUTOBIOGRAPHY

OF

JAMES L. SMITH.

CHAPTER I.

BIRTH AND CHILDHOOD.

Birthplace–Parentage–Accident from disobedience–Sickness–Crippled for life–
Death of master, and change of situation–Cecilia–Jealousy, and attempt to take
the life of my father by poisoning–Discovery and punishment–Removal to
Northern Neck–Mode of living in old Virginia–Experiences of slave life–A cruel
mistress–Work on plantation–Feigning sickness–Death of father and mother–
Bound out to a trade–A brutal master.

MY birthplace was in Northern Neck, Northumberland Country, Virginia.
My mother's name was Rachel, and my father's was Charles. Our cabin
home was just across the creek. This creek formed the head of the
Wycomco River. Thomas Langsdon, my master, lived on one side of the
creek, and my mother's family–which was very large–on the opposite
side. Every year a new comer was added to our humble cabin home, till
she gave birth to the eleventh child. My mother had just so much cotton to
spin every day as her stint. I lived here till I was quite a lad.

There was a man who lived near us whose name was Haney, a coach
maker by trade. He always had his timber brought up to the creek. One
day he ordered one of his slave women to go down and bring up some of
the timber. She took with her a small lad, about my size, to assist her. She
came along by our cabin, as it was near the place where the timber was,
and asked me to go along with her to help her. I asked mother if I could
go. She decidedly said "No!" As my mother was sick, and confined to her
bed at that time, I took this opportunity to steal away, unknown to her.
We endeavored, at first, to carry a large piece of timber–the woman
holding one end, I the other, and the boy in the middle. Before we had

gone far her foot struck something that caused her to fall, so that it jarred my end, causing it to drop on my knee. The boy being in the middle, the full weight of the timber fell on his foot, crushing and mangling it in a most shocking manner. After this accident, the woman and boy started for home, carrying some smaller pieces of timber with them.

After a few days of painful sickness, mortification took place in the little boy's foot, and death claimed him for his own. My grandmother hearing my voice of distress came after me and brought me home. At the time she did not think I was hurt very seriously. My mother called me to her bedside and punished me for disobeying her. After a day or two my knee began to contract, to shrink. This caused my mother to feel that there was something very serious about it, and as soon as she was able to get around, she went to the "great house," the home of Thos. Langsdon, and told him that I was badly hurt, and that something must be done for me. He asked her what was the matter. She told him what had happened to me, and how seriously I was hurt with the timber. After hearing this sad news, he said he had niggers enough without me; I was not worth much any how, and he did not care if I did die. He positively declared that he should not employ a physician for me. As there was no medical remedy applied to my knee, it grew worse and worse until I could not touch my foot to the ground without the most intense pain. There was a doctor in the neighborhood at this time, and mother knowing it sent me to see him, unknowingly to my master. He examined my knee and said, as it had been out of joint so long it would be a difficult matter to break it over again and then set it. He told my mother to take me home and bathe it in cold spring water to prevent it from ulcerating, for if it should it would kill me.

When I was able to walk around with my lameness, Thomas Langsdon took me across the creek to his house to do chores. I was then quite a boy. After a while my leg commenced swelling, and after that ulcerating. It broke in seven places. I was flat on my back for seven or eight weeks before I could raise myself without help. I suffered every thing but death itself, and would have died if it had not been for Miss Ayers, who was house-keeper in the "great house." She came into the kitchen every day to dress my knee, till I could get around. Not having any shoes, and being exposed to the weather, I took a heavy cold which caused my knee to ulcerate. When I was able to get around, the father of my young master was taken sick, and was confined to his bed for months. I, with another boy about my size and age—six or seven years—sat by his bedside. We took our turns alternately, the boy so many hours and I so many, to keep the flies off from him. After a while the old man died, then I was relieved from fighting or contending with flies.

After this I went across the creek to help my mother, as I was not large enough to be of any service on the plantation. In the course of time my young master died, also his wife, leaving two sons, Thomas and John Langsdon. My young master chose for us (slaves) a guardian, who hired us all out. As my mother gave birth to so many children, it made her not very profitable as a servant, and instead of being let out to the highest bidder, was led out to the lowest one that would support her for the least money. Hence my father, though a slave, agreed to take her and the children, and support them for so much money.

My father's master had a brother by the name of Thad. Guttridge, who lived in Lancaster County, who died, leaving his plantation to his brother, (my father's master). My father was then sent to take charge of this new plantation, and moved my mother and the children with him into the "great house;" my mother as mistress of the house.

This Thad. Guttridge had a woman by the name of Cecilia, or Cella, as she was called, whom he kept as house-keeper and mistress, by whom he had one child, a beautiful girl almost white. After this new arrangement was made for my father to take charge of the new plantation, this woman Cella, was turned out of her position as house-keeper to a field hand, to work on the plantation in exchange with my mother.

This was not very agreeable to Cella, so she sought or contrived some plan to avenge herself. So one Saturday night Cella went off, and did not return till Sunday night. When she did return she brought with her some whisky, in two bottles. She asked father if he would like to take a dram; and, not thinking there would be any trouble resulting from it, he replied: "Yes." Giving him the bottle, he took a drink. She then gave the other bottle to my mother, and she took a drink. Afterwards, Cella gave us children some out of the same bottle that my mother drank from. Father went to bed that night, complaining of not feeling very well. The next morning he was worse, and continued to grow worse until he was very low. His master was immediately sent for, who came in great haste. On his arrival he found father very low, not able to speak aloud. My master, seeing in what a critical condition he was, sent for a white doctor, who came, and gave father some medicine. He grew worse every time he took the medicine. There was an old colored doctor who lived some ten miles off. Some one told Bill Guttridge that he had better see him, and, perhaps he could tell what was the matter with my father. Bill Guttridge went to see this colored doctor.

The doctor looked at his cards, and told him that his Charles was poisoned, and even told him who did it, and her motive for doing it. Her intention was to get father and mother out of their place, so that she could get back again. Little did she think that the course she took would prove a failure. The doctor gave Guttridge a bottle of medicine, and told him to return in haste, and give father a dose of it. He did so. I saw him coming down the lane towards the house, at full speed. He jumped off his horse, took his saddle-bags and ran into the house. He called my mother to give him a cup, so he could pour out some of the medicine. He then raised my father up, and gave him some of it out of the cup. After he had laid him down, and replaced the covering over him again, he took his hickory cane and went out into the kitchen—Cella sat here with her work—with an oath told her: "You have poisoned my Charles." He had no sooner uttered these words, when he flew at her with his cane. As he was very much enraged, he commenced beating her over the head and shoulders till he had worn the cane out. After he had stopped beating her in this brutal manner her head was swollen or puffed to such size that it was impossible to recognize who she was; she did not look like the same woman. Not being satisfied with this punishment, he told her that he intended repeating it in the morning. In the morning, when he went to look for her, she was gone. He stayed with father till he was able to sit up. When he returned home—which was about ten miles—he left word with father that if Cella came home, to bind her and send her down to him.

This was in the fall of the year. Some months passed before we saw Cella again. The following spring, while the men were cleaning up the new land, Cella came to them; they took and brought her to the house. Father was then able to walk about the house, but was unable to work much. He had her tied, and put behind a man on horseback and carried down to his master, who took her and put her on board a vessel to be sent to Norfolk. He sold her to some one there. This was the last time we ever saw, or heard from her.

We lived here quite a number of years on Lancaster plantation. Finally my father's master sold it, and also his brother's daughter, Cella's child. We then returned from Lancaster plantation to Northern Neck, Va., and lived nearly in the same place, called Hog Point; we lived here quite a number of years. Mr. Dick Mitchell, my master's guardian, took me away from my mother to Lancaster County, on his plantation, where I lived about six months. I used to do chores about the house, and card rolls for the women. Being lame unfitted me for a field hand, so I had to do work about the house, to help the women.

Our dress was made of tow cloth; for the children, nothing was furnished them but a shirt; for the older ones, a pair of pantaloons or a gown, in addition, according to the sex. Besides these, in the winter season an overcoat, or a round jacket; a wool hat once in two or three years for the men, and a pair of coarse brogan shoes once a year. We dwelt in log cabins, and on the bare ground. Wooden floors were an unknown luxury to the slave. There were neither furniture nor bedsteads of any description; our beds were collections of straw and old rags, thrown down in the corners; some were boxed in with boards, while others were old ticks filled with straw. All ideas of decency and refinement were, of course, out of the question.

Our mode of living in Virginia was not unlike all other slave states. At night, each slept rolled up in a coarse blanket; one partition, which was an old quilt or blanket, or something else that answered the purpose, was extended across the hut; wood partitions were unknown to the doomed slave. A water pail, a boiling pot, and a few gourds made up the furniture. When the corn had been ground in a hand-mill, and then boiled, the pot was swung from the fire and the children squatted around it, with oyster shells for spoons. Sweet potatoes, oysters and crabs varied the diet. Early in the morning the mothers went off to the fields in companies, while some women too old to do anything but wield a stick were left in charge of the strangely silent and quiet babies. The field hands having no time to prepare any thing for their morning meals, took up hastily a piece of hoe-cake and bacon, or any thing that was near at hand, and then, with rakes or hoes in the hand, hurried off to the fields at early dawn, for the loud horn called them to their labors. Heavy were their hearts as they daily traversed the long cotton rows. The overseer's whip took no note of aching hearts.

The allowance for the slave men for the week was a peck-and-a-half of corn meal, and two pounds of bacon. The women's allowance was a peck of meal, and from one pound-and-a-half to two pounds of bacon; and so much for each child, varying from one-half to a peck a week, and of bacon, from one-half to a pound a week. In order to make our allowance hold out, we went crabbing or fishing. In the winter season we used to go hunting nights, catching oysters, coons and possums. When I was home, the slaves used to bake their hoe-cakes on hoes; these hoes were larger than those used in the northern states. Another way for cooking them was to rake the ashes and then put the meal cake between the ashes and the fire—this was called ash pone; and still another way was to bake the bare cake in a Dutch oven, heated for the purpose—that was called oven pone. This latter way of baking them was much practiced, or customary at the home of the slave-holders.

The "great house," so called by the plantation hands, was the home where the master and his family lived. The kitchen was an apartment by itself in the yard, a little distance from the "great house," so as to face the front part of the house; others were built in the back yard. The kitchens had one bed-room attached to them.

One night I went crabbing, and was up most all night; a boy accompanied me. We caught a large mess of crabs, and took them home with us. The next day I had to card for one of the women to spin, and, being up all night, I could hardly keep my eyes open; every once in a while I would fall asleep. Mrs. Mitchell could look through her window into the kitchen, it being in front of the "great house." She placed herself in the portico, to see that I worked. When I fell into a quiet slumber she would halloo out and threaten to cowhide me; but, for all that, I could not keep awake. Seeing that I did not heed her threatenings, she took her rawhide and sewing and seated herself close by me, saying she would see if she could keep me awake. She asked me what was the matter; I told her I felt sick. (I was a great hand to feign sickness). She asked me what kind of sickness; I told her I had the stomach ache and could not work. Thinking that something did ail me, she sent Alfred, the slave boy, into the house after her medicine chest; she also told him to bring her the decanter of whisky. She then poured out a tumbler most full of whisky and then made me drink all of it. After drinking it I was worse than I was before, for I was so drunk I could not see what I was doing. Every once in a while when I fell asleep she would give me a cut with the rawhide. At last, night came and I was relieved from working so steady. When I was not carding I was obliged to knit; I disliked it very much; I was very slow; it used to take me two or three weeks to knit one stocking, and when I had finished it you could not tell what the color was.

I had also to drive the calves for the milk-woman to milk. One afternoon, towards night, I stopped my other work to hunt up the calves and have them at the cow-pen by the time the milk-woman came, with the cows; I went in one of the quarters, and being tired, I sat down on a bench, and before I knew it I fell asleep and slept till after dark. The milk-woman came with the cows, but there were no calves there. She hallooed for me, but I was not within hearing. As the cow-pen was not far from the "great house" the mistress heard her. At last the milk-woman came to the "great house" to see what had become of me, but no Lindsey could be found. She went to the kitchen where the milk pails were kept, took them, and then drove the calves up herself and went to milking. Before she had finished, I awoke and started for the kitchen for the pails. When I got there, Mrs. Mitchell was standing up in the middle of the kitchen floor. She asked me where I had been; I told her I fell asleep in the quarters' and forgot myself. She said she would learn me how to attend to my business, so she told Alfred to go into the "great house" and bring her the rawhide. I stood there trembling about mid-way of the floor. Taking the cow-hide, and lifting her large arms as high as she could, applied it to my back. The sharp twang of the rawhide, as it struck my shoulders, raised me from the floor.

Jinny (the cook) told me afterwards, that when Mrs. Mitchell struck me I jumped about four feet, and did not touch the floor again till I was out doors. She followed me to the door and just had time to see me turn the corner of the "great house." I then ran down towards the cow-pen. The cook told me the way I was running as I turned the corner, that she did not believe that there was a dog or horse on the plantation that could have caught me. I went to the cow-pen and helped the woman to finish milking, and stayed around till I thought that Mrs. Mitchell had gone into the "great house." But to my astonishment when I went to the kitchen again, behold, there she was still waiting for me. She asked me why I ran from her; I told her that it hurt me so bad when she struck me, that I did not know that I was running. She said the next time she whipped me that she would have me tied, then she guessed I would not run. She let me off that night by promising her that I would do better, and never run from her again.

Mrs. Mitchell was a very cruel woman; I have seen her whip Jinny in a very brutal manner. There was a large shade tree that stood in the yard; she would make Jinny come out under this tree, and strip her shoulders all bare; then she would apply the rawhide to her bare back until she had exhausted her own strength, and was obliged to call some of the house servants to being her a chair. While she was resting, she would keep Jinny still standing. After resting her weary arms, she commenced again. Thus she whipped and rested, till she had applied fifty blows upon her suffering back. There was not a spot upon her naked back to lay a finger but there would be a gash, gushing forth the blood; every cut of the rawhide forced an extraordinary groan from the suffering victim; she then sent her back to the kitchen, with her back sore and bleeding, to her work. We slaves often talked the matter over amongst ourselves, and wondered why God suffered such a cruel woman to live. One night, as we were talking the matter over, Jinny exclaimed: "De Lord bless me, chile, I do not believe dat dat devil will ever die, but live to torment us."

After a while I left there for Hog Point, to live with my mother. In the course of a year or two old Mrs. Mitchell sickened, and died.

After she died, I went down to see the folks on the plantation. After my arrival, they told me that just before she breathed her last, she sent for Jinny to come to her bedroom. As she entered, she looked up and said: "Jinny, I am going to die, and I suppose you are glad of it." Jinny replied: "No, I am not." After pretending to cry, she came back to the kitchen and exclaimed: "Dat old devil is going to die, and I am glad of it." When her mistress died her poor back had a brief respite for a while. I do not know what took place upon the plantation after this.

As my young master became of age about this time, Mr. Mitchell gave the guardianship to him. During this time my mother died; then I was bound out to his uncle, John Langsdon, to learn the shoe-maker's trade. John Langsdon was a very kind man, and struck me but once the whole time I was with him in Fairfield, and then it was my own fault. One day, while I was at work in the shop, I put my work down and went out; while I was out, I stepped into the "great house." His two sons were in the house shelling corn; some words passed between his eldest son and me, which resulted in a fight. Mr. Langsdon was looking out of the shop window and saw us fighting; so he caught up a stick and struck me three or four times, and then drove me off to the shop to my work. I took hold of shoe-making very readily; I had not been there a great while when I could make a shoe, or a boot—this I acquired by untiring industry. He used to give me my stint, a pair of shoes a day. I remained with him four years.

The first cruel act of my master, as soon as he became of age, and took his slaves home, was to sell one of my mother's children, whose name was Cella, who was carried off by a trader. We never saw or heard from her again. Oh! how it rent my mother's heart; although her heart was almost broken by grief and despair, she bore this shock in silent but bitter agony. Her countenance exhibited an anxious and sorrowful expression, and her manner gave evidence of a deep settled melancholy. This, and other troubles which she was compelled to pass through, and constant toil and exposure so shattered her physical frame that disease soon preyed upon her, that hastened her to the grave. Ah! I saw not the death-angel, as with white wings he approached. When the hour came for her departure from earth there was but a slight struggle, a faint gasp, and the freed spirit went to its final home. Gone where there are neither bonds nor tortures, sorrow and weeping are unknown.

My mother was buried in a field where there was no other dead deposited; no stone marks her resting place; no fragrant flowers adorn the sod that covers her silent house.

My father soon followed my mother to the grave; then we children were left fatherless and motherless in the cold world. My father's death was very much felt as a good servant, being quick and energetic, rendered him a favorite with his master. When my father was about to die, he called his children, those who were at home around him, as no medicine could now retard the steady approach of the death-angel. When we assembled about him he bade us all farewell, saying, there was but one thing that troubled him, and that was, not one of us professed religion. When I heard that, and saw his sunken eye and hollow cheek, my heart sank within me. Oh! how those words did cut me, like a two-edged sword. From that day I commenced to seek the Lord with all my heart, and never stopped till I found Him. After my father's death, my eldest sister took charge of the younger children, until her master took her home.

One cold morning, while I lived at Hog Point, we looked out and saw three men coming towards the house. One was Mr. Haney, the other one was one of his neighbors, and the last one was his slave. Near our cabin home was a large oak tree; they took this doomed slave down to this tree, and stripped him entirely naked; then they threw a rope across a limb and tied him by his wrists, and drew him up so that his feet cleared the ground. They then applied the lash to his bare back till the blood streamed and reddened the ground underneath where he hung. After whipping him to their satisfaction, they took him down, and led him bound through our yard. I looked at him as he passed, and saw the great ridges in his back as the blood was pouring out of them, and it was as a dagger to my heart. They took him and forced him to work, with his back sore and bleeding. He came to our cabin, a night or two afterwards; my mother asked him what Mr. Haney beat him for; he said it was for nothing only because he did not work enough for him; he did all he could, but the unreasonable master demanded more. I never saw him any more, for shortly after this we moved away.

CHAPTER II.

YOUTH AND EARLY MANHOOD.

Cook on board a ship—A heartless master—An unsavory breakfast, and punishment—
A difficult voyage—Tired of life, and attempt at suicide—Escape—Life on
plantation—A successful ruse—Removal to Heathsville.

WHEN I lived at Mrs. Mitchell's there was a man who owned a vessel, who
came there and took our grain. He told Mr. Mitchell he would like to take
me and make a sailor of me. He liked the looks of my countenance very
much, so they struck a bargain. The captain took me on board his vessel
and made a cook of me. I stayed with him about two years, and most of
the time he treated me very cruelly. He used to strip and whip me with the
cat-o'-nine-tails. [This cat-o'-nine-tails was a rope having nine long ends
and at each end a hard knot.]

One day as we lay at the dock in Richmond, Va., he rose very early one
morning, and told me that he was going up town, advising me to have
breakfast ready by the time he arrived. The weather was very cold. As it
stormed that morning very hard, I asked him if I could cook down in the
cabin. His reply was "No;" and that I must cook in the caboose. [This
caboose was a large black kettle set on the deck, all open to the weather,
to make fire in, and supported by bricks to prevent it burning the deck.]
Seeing I had to be reconciled to my situation, I made my fire the best I
could. The rain and wind extinguished the fire, so that I could not fry the
fish; hence I could not turn them, for they cleaved to the frying pan; so I
thought I would stir them up in a mess and make poached fish of them; I
then poured them out into a dish, and placed them on the table.

Very soon the captain came aboard drunk, and asked me if breakfast was
ready; I told him: "Yes." When he went down into the cabin and sat at the
table, I crept off and peeped through the cabin window, to see what effect
the breakfast would have upon him. While he sat there, I beheld that he
looked at the poached fish with a great deal of dissatisfaction and disgust.
He called me "doctor," and commanded me to come down into the cabin.
I replied promptly. When I got there, he pointed to the fish, and asked me

if I could tell which parts of those fish belonged to each other; I told him I could not tell. As the cooking devolved on me that morning, I tried to justify myself by telling him that the rain and wind cooled my pan so that I could not fry the fish, and that I had done the best I could.

After hearing this, he told me to strip myself, and then go and stand on deck till he had eaten his breakfast. I suffered intensely with the cold. Some of the people on the dock laughed at me, while others pitied me. There I was, divested of my clothing! He turned his fiery eyes on me when he came on deck; and, with a look of fierce decision on his face, (for now all the fierceness of his nature was roused), he took a rope's end and applied it vigorously to my naked back until he deemed that I had atoned for my offence. The blows fell hard and fast, raising the skin at every stroke; by the time he was through whipping me I was warm enough. I then went down into the cabin to remove the breakfast things. I did not eat anything, for I had lost all appetite for food. In the course of the day we got under way, and started for home.

We then proceeded down the James River, and thence to a place called Carter's Creek. Here we took in a haul of oysters, and then started for Alexandria. The wind headed us off for several days, and the weather was very cold. At last the wind favored us, enabling us to continue our voyage till we arrived at Chesapeake Bay; just at this time the wind came in contact with our vessel and headed us off again. It was now in the stillness of the night (mid-night) when the mate in the cabin was far under the influence of liquor; he was so beastly drunk that he could not get out to give any assistance whatever. Hence I had to manage the sails the best I could, while the captain stood at the helm. We strove all night endeavoring to get up the bay. About two o'clock in the morning the captain told me to bring up the jug of whisky to him. Just at this time the vessel sprung a leak. I did all I could to stop the leakage: the captain told me to go to the pump and do the best I could till morning. Both of us tried to get the mate out, but did not succeed. We then turned the vessel around and put back, reaching about day the place from whence we first started. By this time the mate was nearly over his drunken spell and was somewhat more sober, seeing what peril we were in, went with us to the pump to free the vessel. On account of the cold weather, we lay in Carter's Creek several days; our oysters spoiled and we were obliged to throw them overboard. We then took in a freight of merchandise and started for Fredericksburg; here we discharged our freight and returned, going down the Rappahannock we stopped to take in a freight of corn for Fredericksburg. One morning the captain and mate went ashore after a load of corn, leaving me on board to get breakfast and to have it ready by the time they returned. I had it ready as he requested. When they had nearly finished their meal the captain asked me for more tea; I told him it was all out; he wanted to know why I did not make more tea; I told him I thought there was a plenty, it was as much as I generally made. He challenged me for daring to think; he told me to go forward and divest myself of every article of clothing, and wait till he came. When he did come he put my head between his legs, and while I was in this position I thought my last days had come; I thought while he was using the cat-o'-nine-tails to my naked back, and hearing the whizzing of the rope, that if ever I got away I would throw myself overboard and put an end to my life. The captain had punished me so much that I was tired of life, for it became a burden to me.

The cat-o'-nine-tails had no rest, for so dearly did he love its music that a day seldom passed on which he could find no occasion for its use. On the impulse of the moment, I gave a sudden spring, and struck the water some distance from the vessel, and as I could not swim I began to sink. I found that unless I was helped soon I would drown. I began to repent of what I had done, and wished that I had not committed such a rash act. When I attempted to bring myself up to the surface of the water with success, I looked towards the vessel to see if the captain was coming to help me, and at this moment of my peril, instead of rendering any assistance he sat perfectly at ease, or composed on the deck looking at me, but making no effort to help me. I said to myself, I wonder if that old devil intends to let me drown, and not try to save me. All that I could do I was not able to keep myself on the surface of the water. Before I was out of reach and began to sink for the last time, I felt something grasp me; I found that it was the captain, who finally consented to draw me up to the surface of the water and throw me in the boat. I was so exhausted that I could neither stand up or sit down, but was obliged to lay on the bottom of the boat. While I was lying down he commenced beating me with the cat-o'-nine-tails very unmercifully; the more he beat me, the more the water poured out of my mouth. The mate told me afterwards that the water flowing out of my mouth reminded him of a whale spouting water.

We then pursued our course to Fredericksburg; when reaching there we discharged our merchandise—the vessel made water very fast, so we returned to Carter's Creek to undergo repairs. Here it lay for a number of days, for the ship-carpenters were not ready to take care of her: hence I had to stay by the vessel while the captain and mate went home. After I had been there a few weeks, I sought an opportunity to run away. I saw a vessel one day going to my former home, Mr. Dick. Mitchell's, I got on board this vessel for home, having been gone for two years. I remained at this home about a year and did chores about the house while I did stay, and during the cotton season I had just so much cotton to pick out during the day.

One spring Mr. Mitchell put me in the field to attend to the crows, to prevent them pulling up the corn. This was three or four years before Mrs. Mitchell's death. This exercise did very well during the week days, but when the Sabbath day came I desired a respite from this monotonous work. The Sabbath day was a lonesome day to me, because the field hands were away that day; the boys would be away frolicking at some place they had chosen. I resolved that I would break up, or put an end to my Sunday employment; so I studied a plan, while I sat down in the field one Sabbath, how I should accomplish it. First, I thought I would feign sickness; then I said to myself, that will not do, for they will give me something that will physic me to death. My next contrivance was that I would pretend that I had the stomach ache; then, I said again, that will not do either, for then my mistress will make me drunk with whisky, as she had done before by her repeated doses. I devised another scheme, I thought the best of all, and that was to pretend that I had broken my leg again. As this plan was satisfactory to my mind, I arose from where I was sitting and resumed my work. Monday morning I returned to the field, as usual.

All at once I intentionally struck my foot against a stone. I made out that I had broken my leg again. When I came to the house, Jinny, the cook, saw me; her first exclamation was: "Why, chile, what is de matter?" In reply, I only gave a deep, mournful sound, and made a dreadful time about my leg, how it pained me, and so on. The cook, after looking pitifully at me, took my hand and helped me into the kitchen; while there I gave a sad account about my leg; I complained of feeling faint, and desired something to drink that I might feel better. She took a blanket into the adjoining room, and invited me to lie down on the floor. [This adjoining room was a little bedroom attached to the kitchen]. Every effort I made towards lying down I would groan piteously, and whimper as though it hurt me dreadfully. While I was on the floor Mr. Mitchell and the family were at breakfast in the "great house."

Alfred, the servant boy, carried the news to the family that I had broken my leg. As soon as Mr. Mitchell heard of this, he said, with an oath, that he would tend to it when he had eaten his breakfast. It was not long before I heard his speedy steps, as he was coming towards me; just this moment, I said to myself; this day it is either victory or death.

As he stepped into the kitchen he called out to Jinny, the cook, "Where is that one-legged son of a b— ?" She replied that I was in the adjoining room, very badly hurt. He, with an awful oath, said that he would break my other leg. When he came into the bedroom where I was he sang out with a loud voice, and, with a dreadful oath, commanding me to rise, or else he would take every inch of skin off from my back. I told him that I was so much hurt that I could not get up. My complaints only vexed him the more, so much so that he told Alfred to go into the house and bring him the rawhide, and said that he would raise me.

By the time the boy had returned, I was up on one leg choking down the sobs now and then. Mr. Mitchell told me to take some corn and replant those hills I had allowed the crows to pull up. I took the corn and started to do my work, groaning and crying at every step; I did not get far before he called me back and asked me if I had eaten my breakfast; I told him I had not. As his passions had subsided, he told me to get my breakfast and then go out and plant the corn. I first went into the kitchen, and then to my room to lie down on the floor. Jinny came to me and asked me if I would have something to eat; I told her I was in too much pain to eat. (Just that moment I was so hungry that I could have eaten the flesh of a dead horse.) After Mrs. Mitchell had removed the breakfast things she came into the kitchen to see how I was, and found me groaning at a great rate, as if in great distress. She put her arm under my head to raise me, for I pretended that I was in so much pain that I could not raise myself.

Mrs. Mitchell was a very tyrannical woman, but notwithstanding her many failings she occasionally manifested a little kindness. She rolled up my pantaloons and commenced bathing my knee with opodeldoc (a saponaceous camphorated liniment) that she used for such purposes; after which she bound it up nicely and then laid me down again. Mr. Mitchell never came after me any more. Mrs. Mitchell rebuked her husband by telling him that he had no business to send me out in the field among the stumps to attend to the crows, for I was not able to be there.

I lay on the floor in my room about two weeks. In the course of the afternoon Jinny came into my room and asked me if I would have something to eat; I told her I would try and eat a little something, (just then I was hungry enough to eat a peck). When she returned with some bacon and corn-cake, (meal cake) I did not dare to eat much for fear that the rest of the family would mistrust that I was not sick. At the end of two weeks I asked one of the field hands if the crows had stopped coming to trouble the corn, his reply was, "yes, it was so, for the cherries were getting ripe and they were eating them instead." After hearing this joyful news I began to grow better very fast. The first day I sat up nearly all day; the next day I was able to go out some. When Saturday came I could walk quite a distance to see my mother, who lived some ten miles off.

Being lame, I was not very profitable on the plantation, so I went back to live with my mother till she died. At this time my eldest sister kept house for my father till the younger children were old enough to be hired out. My young master had become of age, and had his slaves divided between himself and his brother, each taking his half. It was at this time that my young master took me and put me in charge, or intrusted me to the care of his uncle, in Fairfield, to learn the shoe-maker's trade. I served four years, during which time my father died. After I had learned my trade, my master took me home and opened a shop in Heathsville, Va., placing me in it.

CHAPTER III.

LIFE IN HEATHSVILLE.

Hired out—Religious experience, conversion—Work as an exhorter—A slave prayer meeting—Over worked—A ludicrous accident—Love of dress—Love of freedom—Death of my master—Religious exercises forbidden—A stealthy meeting—The surprise—Fairfield Church—Quarterly meeting—Nancy Merrill—A religious meeting and a deliverance—Sleeping at my post.

I RAN the shop for one year, during which time my young master became jealous of me. He thought I was making more money for myself than for him; it was not so, he was mistaken about it. What little I did earn for myself was justly my own. While I was away enjoying myself one Christmas day, he took an ox-cart with my brother, for Heathsville. The driving devolved on my brother. My master carried off my tools and every thing that was in the shop; he hired me out to a man who was considered by every one to be the worst one in Heathsville, whose name was Mr. Lacky, advising him "to keep me very strict, for I was knowing most too much." I lived with him three years, and managed so as to escape the cowhide all the time I was there, saving once. I strove by my prudence and correctness of demeanor to avoid exciting his evil passions. While learning the shoe-maker's trade, I was about eighteen years old. At this time I became deeply interested in my soul's salvation; the white people held a prayer meeting in Fairfield one evening in a private house; I attended the meeting that evening, but was not permitted to go in the same room, but only allowed to go in an adjoining room. While there I found peace in believing, and in this happy state of mind I went home rejoicing and praising the Lord for what he had done for me. A few Sabbath's following, I united with the Church in Fairfield. Soon after I was converted I commenced holding meetings among the people, and it was not long before my fame began to spread as an exhorter. I was very zealous, so much so that I used to hold meetings all night, especially if there were any concerned about their immortal soul.

I remember in one instance that having quit work about sundown on a Saturday evening, I prepared to go ten miles to hold a prayer meeting at

Sister Gould's. Quite a number assembled in the little cabin, and we continued to sing and pray till daybreak, when it broke. All went to their homes, and I got about an hour's rest while Sister Gould was preparing breakfast. Having partaken of the meal, she, her daughter and myself set out to hold another meeting two miles further; this lasted till about five o'clock, when we returned. Then I had to walk back ten miles to my home, making in all twenty-four miles that day. How I ever did it, lame as I was, I cannot tell, but I was so zealous in the work that I did not mind going any distance to attend a prayer meeting. I actually walked a greater part of the distance fast asleep; I knew the road pretty well. There used to be a great many run-aways in that section, and they would hide away in the woods and swamps, and if they found a person alone as I was, they would spring out at them and rob them. As this thought came into my head during my lonely walk, thinks I, it won't do for me to go to sleep, and I began to look about me for some weapon of defence; I took my jackknife from my pocket and opened it; now I am ready to stab the first one that tackles me, I said; but try as I would, I commenced to nod, nod, till I was fast asleep again. The long walk and the exertion of carrying on the meeting had nearly used me up.

The way in which we worshiped is almost indescribable. The singing was accompanied by a certain ecstasy of motion, clapping of hands, tossing of heads, which would continue without cessation about half an hour; one would lead off in a kind of recitative style, others joining in the chorus. The old house partook of the ecstasy; it rang with their jubilant shouts, and shook in all its joints. It is not to be wondered at that I fell asleep, for when I awoke I found I had lost my knife, and the fact that I would now have to depend on my own muscle, kept me awake till I had reached the neighborhood of my home. There was a lane about half a mile from the house, on each side of which was a ditch to drain the road, and was nearly half full of water; as I neared this lane I fell asleep again, as the first thing I knew I was in the ditch; I had walked right off into it, best clothes and all. Such a paddling to get out you never saw. I was wide awake enough now you may rest assured, and went into the house sick enough; my feet were all swollen, and I was laid up for two or three days. My mistress came in to see me, and said I must have medicine. I had to bear it, and she dosed me well.

As soon as I was able, I went to work. I had a shop all to myself. My master lived five miles away, but would come once a week and take all the earnings; some weeks I would make a great deal, then I would keep some back for myself, as I had worked for it. In this way I saved at one time fifteen dollars; I went to the store, bought a piece of cloth, carried it to the tailor and had a suit made—I had already bought a watch, and had a chain and seal. You can imagine how I looked the following Sunday; I was very proud and loved to dress well, and all the young people used to make a great time over me; it was Brother Payne here, and Brother Payne there; in fact, I was nearly everywhere.

The other slaves were obliged to be on the plantation when the horn blew, at daybreak, but sometimes I did not get home till twelve o'clock; sometimes it would be night, and I always escaped a whipping. The first Sunday that I was arrayed in my new suit, I was passing the court house bounds, when I saw my master and a man named Betts standing near by. Betts caught sight of me; says he: "Lindsey, come here." Not knowing what he wanted, I went to him; whereupon he commenced looking first at me, then at my master; then at my master, then at me; finally he said: "Who is master; Lindsey or you, for he dresses better than you do? Does he own you, or do you own him?"

From a child I had always felt that I wanted to be free. I could not bear the thought of belonging to any one, and so when I ran away, my mind was made up all in a sudden. My master came as far as Philadelphia to look for me; and, my brother says, when he came back without me, he became a very demon on the plantation, cutting and slashing, cursing and swearing at the slaves till there was no living with him. He seemed to be out of his head; and for hours would set looking straight into the fire; when spoken to, he would say: "I can't think what made Lindsey leave me."

One day he ordered my brother and a man named Daniel to move the barn from where it set further out to one side. So my brother went to work, with two or three others, and had raised it about three or four feet, when something gave way; and, as they were under the barn, they all ran out. My master seeing this became furious. "How dare you to run? You shall stay under there, if you get crushed to pieces!" So saying, he went into the house and got the rawhide. "Now," says he, "the first one who runs, I'll cut to pieces." He then took his place inside the barn, and commanded them to go on with their work, while he looked on.

They began to turn the screw, when some timber from above fell right across the door, completely blockading it. Master was shut up in the barn, and it was impossible for him to get out. Why he did not jump out, when the creaking sound gave him warning, no one can tell; he seemed to sit back there, in a dazed sort of a way. There was a rush to rescue him, and he was found all mangled and bruised, with the rawhide grasped tightly in his hand. My brother says he only gasped once or twice after he was brought out.

When Nat. Turner's insurrection broke out, the colored people were forbidden to hold meetings among themselves. Nat. Turner was one of the slaves who had quite a large army; he was the captain to free his race. Notwithstanding our difficulties, we used to steal away to some of the quarters to have our meetings. One Sabbath I went on a plantation about five miles off, where a slave woman had lost a child the day before, and as it was to be buried that day, we went to the "great house" to get permission from the master if we could have the funeral then. He sent back word for us to bury the child without any funeral services. The child was deposited in the ground, and that night we went off nearly a mile to a lonely cabin on Griffin Furshee's plantation, where we assembled about fifty or seventy of us in number; we were so happy that we had to give vent to the feelings of our hearts, and were making more noise than we realized. The master, whose name was Griffin Furshee, had gone to bed, and being awakened by the noise, took his cane and his servant boy and came where the sound directed him. While I was exhorting, all at once the door opened and behold there he stood, with his white face looking in upon us. As soon as I saw the face I stopped suddenly, without even waiting to say amen.

The people were very much frightened; with throbbing hearts some of them went up the log chimney, others broke out through the back door, while a few, who were more self-composed, stood their ground.

When the master came in, he wanted to know what we were doing there, and asked me if I knew that it was against the law for niggers to hold meetings. I expected every moment that he would fly at me with his cane; he did not, but only threatened to report me to my master. He soon left us to ourselves, and this was the last time he disturbed us in our meetings. His object in interrupting us was to find out whether we were plotting some scheme to raise an insurrection among the people. Before this, the white people held a quarterly meeting in the Fairfield Church, commencing Saturday, and continuing eight days and nights without cessation.

The religious excitement that existed at that time was so great that the people did not leave the church for their meals, but had them brought to them. There were many souls converted. The colored people attended every night. The white people occupied the part next to the altar, while the colored people took the part assigned them next to the door, where they held a protracted meeting among themselves. Sometimes, while we were praying, the white people would be singing, and when we were singing they would be praying; each gave full vent to their feelings, yet there was no discord or interruption with the two services. On Wednesday night, the fourth day from the commencement of the meeting, a colored woman by the name of Nancy Merrill, was converted, and when she experienced a change of heart she shouted aloud, rejoicing in the richness of her new found hope. Thursday night, the next evening, the meeting still continued.

By this time the excitement was on the increase among both parties, and it bid fair to hold eight days longer; but right in the midst of the excitement some one came to the door of the church and nodded to the sexton to come to the door; as soon as he did go to the door some one there told him to speak to Nancy Merrill, the new convert, and tell her to come to the door, for he wanted to speak to her. She went, and, behold it was a slave trader, who had bought her during the day from her mistress! As soon as she went to the door, he seized and bound her, and then took her off to her cabin home to get her two boys he had bought also. The sexton came back and reported to us what had taken place.

This thrilling and shocking news sent a sharp shiver through every heart; it went through the church like wild-fire; it broke up the meeting entirely among both parties; in less than half an hour every one left the church for home. This woman had a daughter in Fairfield, where I learned my trade, and I hastened home, as soon as possible, to tell the girl what had happened to her mother. She was standing by the fire in the kitchen as I entered—she was the servant girl of John Langsdon, the man who taught me the shoe-maker's trade. As soon as I related to her this sad news she fell to the floor as though she had been shot by a pistol; and, as soon as she had recovered a little from the shock we started for her mother's cabin home, reaching there just in time to see her mother and her two brothers take the vessel for Norfolk, to be sold. This was the last time we ever saw her; we heard, sometime afterwards, that a kind master had bought her, and that she was doing well.

Many thrilling scenes I could relate, if necessary, that makes my blood curdle in my veins while I write. We were treated like cattle, subject to the slave-holders' brutal treatment and law.

The wretched condition of the male slave is bad enough; but that of the woman, driven to unremitting, unrequited toil, suffering, sick, and bearing the peculiar burdens of her own sex, unpitied, not assisted, as well as the toils which belong to another, must arouse the spirit of sympathy in every heart not dead to all feeling. Oh! how many heart-rending prayers I have heard ascend up to the throne of grace for deliverance from such exhibitions of barbarity. How many family ties have been broken by the cruel hand of slavery. The priceless store of pleasures, and the associations connected with home were unknown to the doomed slaves, for in an unlooked for hour they were sold to be separated from father and mother, brothers and sisters. Oh! how many such partings have rent many a heart, causing it to bleed as it were, and crushing out all hope of ever seeing slavery abolished.

Sometime before I left for the north, the land of freedom, I appointed another meeting in an off house on a plantation not far from Heathsville, where a number of us collected together to sing and pray. After I had given out the hymn, and prayed, I commenced to exhort the people. While I did so I became very warm and zealous in the work, and perhaps made more noise than we were aware of. The patrolers* going along the road, about half a mile off, heard the sound and followed it where we were holding our meeting. They came, armed to the teeth, and surrounded the house. The captain of the company came in, and as soon as we saw him we fell on our knees and prayed that God might deliver us. While we prayed he stood there in the middle of the floor, without saying a word. Pretty soon we saw that his knees began to tremble, for it was too hot for him, so he turned and went out. His comrades asked him if "he was going to make an arrest;" he said "no, it was too hot there for him." They soon left, and that was the last we saw of them.

As God had delivered us in such a powerful manner, we took courage and held our meeting until day-break. Another time I had a meeting appointed at a freed-woman's house, whose name was Sister Gouldman, about five miles in the country. I left home about seven o'clock on Saturday evening, and arrived there about ten; we immediately commenced the meeting and continued it till about daylight. After closing the meeting we slept while Sister Gouldman was preparing the breakfast. After breakfast we went two miles further, and held another meeting till late in the afternoon, then closed and started for home, reaching there some time during the night. I was very much fatigued, and my energies were entirely exhausted, so much so that I was not able to work the next day.

---

* The patrolers were southern spies, sent out, or were wont to roam at night to hunt up run-away slaves, and to investigate other matters.

The time when I was eighteen years old, when such a miraculous change had been wrought in my heart, I had had two holidays, and was up all night holding meetings, praying and singing most of the time. Not having any sleep, I could scarcely keep my eyes open when I went to work. While endeavoring to finish a piece of work, Mr. Lacky came and found me asleep while I was on my bench shoe-making. He told me that I had "been away enjoying myself for two days, and if he should come again and find me asleep, he would wake me up." Sure enough, he had no sooner left the shop when I was fast asleep again. As his shop was beneath mine, he could easily hear me when I was at work. He came up again in his stocking-feet, unawares, and the first thing I knew he had the rawhide applying it vigorously to my flesh in such a manner that did not feel very pleasant to me. After punishing me, he asked me "if I thought I could keep awake after this." I told him "I thought possibly I could," and did, through a great deal of effort till night. I never was satisfied about that whipping.

CHAPTER IV.

ESCAPE FROM SLAVERY.

Change of master–Plans of escape–Fortune telling–Zip–A lucky man–Farewell–
Beginning of the escape–A prosperous sail–Arrival at Frenchtown–Continuing on
foot–Exhausted–Deserted by companions–Hesitating–Terrible fright–A bold
resolve and a hearty breakfast–Re-union at New Castle–Passage to Philadelphia–A
final farewell–Trouble and anxiety–A friend–Passage to New York, Hartford and
Springfield–A warm welcome–Dr. Osgood.

NEAR the end of the third year I went to my young master and told him I
did not care about living with Mr. Lacky any longer. He told me that I
could choose for myself another man whom I could live with. I concluded
to live with one by the name of Bailey, who did not strike me during the
year, but threatened to, which made me mad. About the end of this time I
thought very strongly in reference to freedom, liberty; the precious goal
which I almost grasped. I pursued daily my humble duties, waiting with
patience till I could perceive some opening in the dense dark cloud that
enveloped my fate in the hidden future. Before I lived with Bailey, I had
some thoughts of this. I became acquainted with a man by the name of
Zip, who was a sailor; I told him my object in reference to freedom. He
told me that he also was intending to make his escape and to have his
freedom. This was in the year 1836. We agreed that whenever there was a
chance we would come off together. About Christmas, 1837, we made an
arrangement to run away. Zip was calculating to take the vessel that the
white people had left during their absence. He was left to take care of this
vessel till they returned; nevertheless he intended to use it to a good
purpose, for he took this opportunity to make his escape. We intended to
carry off seventy, but we were disappointed because we could not carry
out our arrangements. It was a very cold Christmas Eve, so much so that
the river was badly frozen, not making it favorable for us to capture her:
hence we gave that project up until the spring of 1838.

On the 6th day of May, 1838, Zip, with another one by the name of
Lorenzo and myself, each hired a horse to take a short journey up the
country to Lancaster, to see a sick friend of ours, who was very ill, for we

did not expect to see him again. His name was Lewis Vollin. We had calculated to make our escape in about two weeks; so we started one Sabbath morning and found our friend quite sick, and was only able to sit up a little while and talk with us. Lewis' doctor was an aged colored man, who was a fortune-teller also, and could unfold the past, present, and future destiny of any one. Our sick friend was at this doctor's home, for the purpose of being cured by him. While there, the doctor asked us to walk out and look at his place; we did so, and after a while we sat down under a large tree. The doctor then asked us if we would like to have our fortune's told; we told him "yes." He sent to the house for his cards, and after receiving them, told each of us to cut them; we did so, then he took my cut and looked it over, saying, "you are going to run away; I see that you will have good luck; you will go clear; you will reach the free country in safety; you will gather many friends around you, both white and colored; you will be worth property, and in the course of time will return back home, and walk over your native land." I asked him "how that could be; was I to be captured and brought back?" He said "no, you will come back because you wish to, and go away again." I told him "that was something that I did not understand." He said, "nevertheless, it is so."

He then told the fortunes of my two companions, Zip and Lorenzo. He examined their cuts, and said they would all go clear; but never said they would return, neither did they, for they died before freedom was proclaimed. Zip died at the West Indies, Lorenzo died on the ship in some port at the time the cholera broke out.

In the afternoon we started for home, reaching there about four o'clock. When we reached Heathsville, the place where we lived, we noticed as we rode up to the stable to put the horses away, (for we were on horse-back) that there were half a dozen or more young men, who appeared to be talking and whittling behind the stable. The stable where I put my horse was on one side of the street, and the stable where Zip was to put his was on the opposite side. Zip went up to the door to put his horse in, but found that it would not open readily, and while he was trying to open it those white young men whom we saw whittling, supposing that he had got in, began to assemble around the door. Now among these young men was a negro-trader who spoke to Zip, asking him "why he did not go in and put the horse away." Zip told him that "he could not get the door open." The trader then took hold of the door and it came open immediately. Zip was so astonished to think that the door opened so readily to the negro-trader, and did not yield to him, that he thought there must be something wrong about it. He refused to go in himself, and only fastened the horse's bridle to a fence, then went over to the tavern to tell the hostler that he might put the horse away. From there he went to his house, for he lived there in town, and as soon as he entered the house his wife warned him to flee for his life, for a trader had bought him, and had been to the house with several young men whom we saw behind the stable as we rode up, placed themselves there for the purpose of waiting till we came. Their motive was, when Zip went into the stable to close the door on him and capture him.

I knew nothing about this at the time. I put my horse away, went to the house, got something to eat, then started to go off some five miles to see some friends; but before I started I thought I would go into my shop and brush my coat; while there I sat down on my bench just for a few moments, and all at once I fell asleep. When I awoke the sun was just going down. I think I had been asleep about an hour. I did not have any idea of falling asleep when I entered the shop, for I intended to have gone out of town. As quick as thought I jumped up, took my hat and started for the door; just as I opened it there was a man passing by whose name was Griffin Muse, who belonged on James Smith's plantation about two miles off. He saw me as I opened the door, and said to me, "Lindsey, where have you been? I have been looking for you this two hours. I just started to go down home and give up the search, and to tell Zip that I could not find you." Said I, "what is the matter?" Said he to me, "did you not know that Zip was sold to a Georgian trader, who is trying to catch him." Said I, "where is Zip?" I am sure I did not know anything about this, I did not dream of such a thing; I saw this trader, with some young men behind the stable, but did not dream that he was after Zip. Griffin Muse said to me, "Zip is down on our plantation, and has sent me after you, and that his intention is to try to make his escape to-night to a free country, and if you are going with him to go to him as soon as possible." I was so astonished that I did not know what to do. I told him to "wait for me, and I would get ready as soon as possible." I went a few blocks where I kept my box, and in it I had three dollars, all the money I possessed in the world. On my way back I met a man who owed me fifty cents; I dunned him, and as good luck would have it he had the money and paid me.

I then went back to my shop and picked up all the things that I thought I would want to take with me. While I was making my arrangements my boss came into the shop. As soon as I saw him coming I pushed my bundle under the bench and sat down on the bench, pretending to be sick. He asked me if I "was going to church;" I told him I thought "I should not, for I was not feeling very well." After a while he went out and closed the door after him. Soon as he was gone I finished gathering up my things, then locked up the shop and went into the "great house" to put the key over the mantle-piece. Then Griffin Muse, Zip's wife and myself started for Smith's plantation, about two miles from Heathsville, where Zip was secreted.

When we arrived there Zip and Lorenzo were just starting; it was nearly eleven o'clock; they had waited for me till they thought I was not coming. They were just bidding the folks farewell as I arrived at the house where Zip stopped.* Two minutes more and I would have been left behind. If I had not fallen asleep in the shop I would have been out of town, and I should have been left, for Griffin would not have found me; and if I had slept one minute longer he would have passed by the shop and I would not have seen him; one minute more, either way, would have turned the scales.

All three of us, Zip, Lorenzo and myself, assembled together and started for the Cone River, about a quarter of a mile from where we were. There were a number of our plantation friends who went with us; Zip's wife and her mother, and a number of others. When we came to the river, we stood on the beach and embraced, kissed, and bade each other farewell. The scene between Zip and his wife at parting was distressing to behold. Oh! how the sobbing of his wife resounded in the depths of his heart; we could not take her with us for the boat was too small.

In the first place we took a small canoe and crossed the river till we came to a plantation owned by a man named Travis. He had a large sail boat that we desired to capture, but we did not know how we should accomplish it, as they took a great deal of pains generally to haul her up, lock her up and put the sails and oars in the barn. As it was the Sabbath day, the young folks had been sailing about the river, and instead of securing her as they usually did, they left her anchored in the stream with the sails and oars all in the boat. This was very fortunate for us, for the house was very near to the shore, besides they had very savage dogs there. So it would have been a very difficult matter for us to attempt to capture the boat, sails and oars if they had been where they were generally kept. So all we had to do was to run our canoe along side the boat and get on board.

It was quite calm before we started, but as soon as we got ready, and the sails set, the wind began to rise, and all that night we had all the wind we could carry sail to. Lorenzo and myself, by keeping our oars in motion, outran everything that stayed on the water. By the next morning we were

* These were Zip's plantation friends that were at this cabin home.

a great distance from home. We sailed all day and night Monday, and until Tuesday night about nine o'clock, when we landed just below French-town, Maryland. We there hauled the boat up the best we could, and fastened her, then took our bundles and started on foot. Zip, who had been a sailor from a boy, knew the country and understood where to go. He was afraid to go through Frenchtown, so we took a circuitous route, until we came to the road that leads from Frenchtown to New Castle. Here I became so exhausted that I was obliged to rest; we went into the woods, which were near by, and laid down on the ground and slept for an hour or so, then we started for New Castle.

I found I could not keep up with my companions, for they could walk much faster than myself, and hence got far ahead, and then would have to wait for me; I being lame was not able to keep up with them. At last Zip said to me, "Lindsey, we shall have to leave you for our enemies are after us, and if we wait for you we shall all be taken; so it would be better for one to be taken than all three." So after he had advised me what course to take, they started, and in a few minutes left me out of sight. When I had lost sight of them I sat down by the road-side and wept, prayed, and wished myself back where I first started. I thought it was all over with me forever; I thought one while I would turn back as far as Frenchtown, and give myself up to be captured; then I thought that would not do; a voice spoke to me, "not to make a fool of myself, you have got so far from home, (about two hundred and fifty miles), keep on towards freedom, and if you are taken, let it be heading towards freedom." I then took fresh courage and pressed my way onward towards the north with anxious heart.

It was then two or three o'clock Wednesday morning, the 8th of May. I came to the portion of the road that had been cut through a very high hill, called the "deep cut," which was in a curve, or which formed a curve; when I had got about mid-way of this curve I heard a rumbling sound that seemed to me like thunder; it was very dark, and I was afraid that we were to have a storm; but this rumbling kept on and did not cease as thunder does, until at last my hair on my head began to rise; I thought the world was coming to the end. I flew around and asked myself, "what is it?" At last it came so near to me it seemed as if I could feel the earth shake from under me, till at last the engine came around the curve. I got sight of the fire and the smoke; said I, "it's the devil, it's the devil!" It was the first engine I had ever seen or heard of; I did not know there was anything of the kind in the world, and being in the night, made it seem a great deal worse than it was; I thought my last days had come; I shook from head to foot as the monster came rushing on towards me. The bank was very steep near where I was standing; a voice says to me, "fly up the bank;" I made a desperate effort, and by the aid of the bushes and trees which I grasped, I reached the top of the bank, where there was a fence; I rolled over the fence and fell to the ground, and the last words I remember saying were, that "the devil is about to burn me up, farewell! farewell!" After uttering these words I fainted, or as I expressed it, I lost myself.

I do not know how long I lay there, but when I had recovered (or came to myself), the devil had gone. Oh! how my heart did throb; I thought the patrollers were after me on horseback. After I had gathered strength enough I got up and sat there thinking what to do; I first thought I would go off to the woods somewhere and hide myself till the next night, and then pursue my journey onward; but then I thought that would not do, for my enemies, who were pursuing me, would overtake and capture me. So I made up my mind that I would not loose any more time than was necessary; hence I crawled down the bank and started on with trembling steps, expecting every moment that that monster would be coming back to look for me.

Thus between hope, and fear, and doubt, I continued on foot till at last the day dawned and the sun had just began to rise. When the sun had risen as high as the tops of the trees, the monster all at once was coming back to meet me; I said to myself, "it is no use to run, I had just as well stand and make the best of it," thinking I would make the best bargain that I could with his majesty. Onward he came, with smoke and fire flying, and as he drew near to me, I exclaimed to myself, "why! what a monster's head he has on to him." Oh! said I, "look at his tushes,* I am a goner;" I looked again, saying to myself, "look at the wagons he has tied to him." Thinks I, "they are the wagons that he carries the souls to hell with." I looked through the windows to see if I could see any black people that he was carrying, but I did not see one, nothing but white people. Then I thought it was not black people that he was after, but only the whites, and I did not care how many of them he took. He went by me like a flash; I expected every moment that he would stop and bid me come aboard, (for I had been a great hand to abuse the old gentleman; when at home I use to preach against him), but he did not, so I thought that he was going so fast he could not stop. He was soon out of sight, and I for the first time took a long breath.

* The cow-catcher in front of the engine.

I was very hungry, for I had not eaten anything much for two days. We came away in such a hurry that we did not have time to prepare much food; we took only some corn-cake and a little bacon; I was almost starved to death; I became quite weak, and looked around on the ground to see if I could find anything green that I could eat. I began to fail very fast, I thought I should die there on the road. All at once I came to a house, and a voice seemed to say to me, "go to that house and see if you can get something to eat." I said to myself, "there are white people that live there and I shall be captured. They can but capture me, and if I stay away I shall die." I went up to the door and rapped; a lady came to the door and looked at me with a smile upon her countenance as I spoke to her. I said to myself, "I do not mind you white people's smiles, I expect you think to make money off of me this morning." I asked her if "she would give me something to eat." She said "she had nothing cooked, but if I would come in she would get me something." I thought to myself, "I know what that means, you want me to come in in order to capture me;" but nevertheless I went in, and she set a chair up to the fire-place and bade me sit down. Her husband sat there in one corner, and looking up said to me: "My man, you are traveling early this morning," I said "yes, I made an early start." (I did not tell him I had been traveling all day and all night for three nights.) He asked me "how far I was going," I told him "I was going to Philadelphia; that I had some friends there whom I had not seen for some time, and I was going to visit them, and then return in a few weeks." Very soon his wife had my breakfast all ready of ham, eggs, and a meal-cake, and put them on the table, and then asked me to sit down. I did so, without waiting for a second invitation, and the first mouthfull I took seemed to me as if it would go straight through me; I ate till I became alarmed, for I thought I would betray myself by my eating. I ate up most everything she put on the table, then I got up and asked "what I should pay for my breakfast," she said "twenty-five cents." I put my hand in my pocket and picked out a quarter, giving it to her, I started on my journey, feeling like a new man. I walked on till about noon, at which time I reached New Castle. The first one I saw was Lorenzo, who was one of the men who left me on the road. He came a little way out of the city to look for me, to see if I was any where in sight; we met and went into the city, found Zip, and once more we were together. The boat left there for Philadelphia twice a day. She had left in the morning before they had arrived, but she returned in the afternoon, only to start right off again the same afternoon.

By the time the boat had returned, I was there, so we three all went on board. How we ever passed through New Castle as we did, without being detected, is more than I can tell, for it was one of the worst slave towns in the country, and the law was such that no steamboat, or anything else, could take a colored person to Philadelphia without first proving his or her freedom. What makes it so astonishing to me is that we walked aboard right in sight of every body, and no one spoke a word to us. We went to the captain's office and bought our tickets, without a word being said to us.

We arrived safely in Philadelphia that afternoon; there upon the wharf we separated, after bidding each other farewell. Lorenzo and Zip went on board a ship for Europe, and went to sea. I started up the street, not knowing where I was going, or what would become of me; I walked on till I came to a shoe store, went in and asked a white gentleman, "do you want to hire a shoe-maker?" He said "I do not, but think you can find a place by going a little further." I proceeded a little further, and came to a shop kept by a colored man, whose name was Simpson. I went in and introduced myself to him the best I could. (I did not let him know that I was a fugitive.) We sat there a talked till most night; I then asked him if he "could keep me all night?" He replied "no, for it was not convenient for him to do so."

Here I was, hedged in, not knowing what course to take; I was down cast, and the thought of having no friend or shelter only sank me into deeper perplexity. He told me "he had a brother who lived on a certain street, who he thought would take me." Hearing this I felt somewhat encouraged, but not understanding the number he gave me, in order to find his brother, I was as badly off as before. As it was getting late he began to make preparation for shutting up his shop. My heart began to ache within me, for I was puzzled what to do; but just before he shut up, a colored minister came in; I thought perhaps I could find a friend in him, and when he was through talking with Simpson he started to go out, I followed him to the side-walk and asked him "if he would be kind enough to give me lodging that night." He told me "he could not, for he was going to church; that it would be late before the service closed, and besides it would not be convenient for him."

Here the same heavy cloud closed in upon me again, for it was getting dark, and I had no where to sleep that night. Circumstances were against me; he told me "I could get a lodging place if I would go to the tavern." I made no reply to this advice, but felt somewhat sad, for my last hope had fled. He then asked me if "I was free." I told him that "I was a free man."

(I did not intend to let him know that I was a fugitive.) Here I was in a great dilemma, not knowing what to do or say. He told me if "I was a fugitive I would find friends." "If any one needs a friend I do," thought I to myself, for just at this time I needed the consolation and assistance of a friend, one on whom I could rely. So thought I, "it will be best for me to make known that I am a fugitive, and not to keep it a secret any longer." I told him frankly that "I was from the South, and that I was a runaway." He said, "you are;" I said "yes." He asked me if I "had told Simpson;" I said "no." He then called Simpson and asked him "if he knew that this brother was a fugitive," He said "no." After finding this to be a fact, Simpson asked me if "that was so?" I said "it was." He then told me to "come with him, that he had room enough for me." I went home with him and he introduced me to his family, and they all had a great time rejoicing over me. After giving me a good supper, they secreted me in a little room called the fugitive's room, to sleep; I soon forgot all that occurred around me. I was resting quietly in the arms of sleep, for I was very tired.

The next morning Simpson went in pursuit of the two men who had been with me, but he could not find them. I have never seen them since. My parting with them at the Philadelphia wharf was the last I saw of them. Simpson then went among the Abolitionists, and informed them of my case; many of them came to see me. They talked of sending me to England; one Quaker asked me if I would like "to see the Queen." I told him that "I did not care where I went so long as I was safe." They held a meeting that day, and decided to send me to Springfield, Mass.; this was the fifth day after I left home. The next day, Friday morning, Brother Simpson took me down to the steamboat and started me for New York, giving me a letter directed to David Ruggles, of New York.

The nearer I came to New York the worse I felt, for I did not know how I should find Mr. Ruggles. Just as I reached the dock there was a lady whom I had never seen before; I went to her and asked her "if she knew of such a man, by the name of David Ruggles?" She told me that she "did know of such a person, and that he lived on her way home." She kindly consented to show me where he lived. I went along with her without any more trouble in mind about it. I gave Ruggles the letter, and we had a great time rejoicing together. I staid with him till Monday. On Monday, the ninth day of my travels, he gave me two letters, one to a Mr. Foster, in Hartford; and the other to Doctor Osgood, in Springfield. Mr. Ruggles sent a boy with me down to the steamboat, and I started for Hartford on a boat which sailed in the afternoon.

Towards night I went up to the clerk's office to pay my fare. I asked him "how much it would be?" He told me it was "three dollars." I told him it was a large sum of money, more than I possessed." He then asked me "how much I had?" I told him "two dollars and fifty-eight cents." He told me that "that would not do, and that I must get the rest of it." I told him "that I was a stranger there, and that I knew no one." He said: "You should have asked and found out." I told him "I did, and was told that the fare would be two dollars, and that was nearly all I possessed at that time." He requested me to hand it to him which I did, and it robbed me of every cent I had. I then took my ticket and went forward and laid down among some bales of cotton. It was very chilly and cold, and I felt very much depressed in spirits and cast down.

The climate had changed much since I left home, I was out of money and among strangers; my heart sank within me, for I was faint and hungry, and had no means to pay for my supper. I fell asleep while lying among the bales of cotton. After tea was over with the passengers, one of the waiters came and awoke me, and asked if "I wanted any supper?" I replied "no," knowing that I had no means to pay for it. Soon another one came and cordially invited me to partake of some, that it would cost me nothing. I went to the cabin, and had an excellent supper. The old saying proved true in my case, that "a friend in need is a friend indeed." Before I retired for the night, some one came through the cabin and told the way-passengers that they must come to the captain's office and leave the number of their berth before they retired for the night. I did not know what he meant by that saying; I thought it meant all the passengers to pay extra for their berths. Now, thought I, if that is the case, and I sleep in the berth all night, and in the morning have no money to pay with, I shall be in trouble sure enough. As I was very tired, I desired very much to lie down and rest; so I thought I would risk it and lie down and sleep till daylight. I reached Hartford quite early the next morning, so I lay till I thought the boat was along-side the wharf; I then got up and dressed myself and looked at the number of my berth, as I was told to see what it was, so if I should meet the captain I could tell him. I then started for the deck, and on reaching there I looked around, and wondered how I should find Mr. Foster. While I was looking, I saw a colored man standing, and seemed to be looking at me; I went up to him and asked him if "he knew a man by the name of Foster?" He replied: "Yes." I asked him if he would show me where he lived? He said: "Yes." So he went along with me, and I found Mr. Foster's residence, by directions given; and, finding him at home, I presented the letter. After he had read it, he began to congratulate me on my escape. When he had conversed with me awhile, he went out among the friends, (Abolitionists), and informed them of my circumstances, in order to solicit aid to forward me on to Springfield.

Many of them came in to see me, and receive me cordially; I began to realize that I had some friends. I stayed with Mr. Foster till afternoon. He raised three dollars for my benefit and gave it to me, and then took me to the steamboat and started me for Springfield. I reached there a little before night.

When I had reached the wharf I stepped ashore, and saw a man standing on the dock; and, after inquiries concerning Doctor Osgood's residence, he kindly showed it to me. The Doctor, being at home, I gave him the letter, and as soon as he had read it, he and his family congratulated me on my escape from the hand of the oppressor. He informed me that the letter stated "that he could either send me to Canada, or he could keep me in Springfield, just as he thought best." He said: "I think we will keep you here, so you can make yourself at home." The family gathered around me to listen to my thrilling narrative of escape. We talked till the bell notified them that supper was ready. An excellent meal was prepared for me, which I accepted gladly, for the Doctor was a very liberal man, saying: "Friend, come in and have some supper."

Wheat bread was the same as cake to me in those days, for my food at the South was principally corncake and bacon. While I was eating, his daughter said: "Don't be afraid, but help yourself." Not being accustomed to eating at the "great house" at home, you must imagine that it produced some embarrassment in my mind. When the supper was over, the family gathered in the sitting-room for prayers, as it was their custom to read a portion of the Scriptures before retiring for the night; and I was asked to read with them. Before conducting prayers the Doctor sang one of his favorite hymns, in which all the family united. I listened with pleasure, and my whole soul entered into the holy service.

The next morning the Doctor asked me "how I rested?" I replied, "very well sir." He informed me that breakfast would soon be ready. It was customary for them to have prayers before the morning meal, which was something new to me; it seemed more like a meeting to me, to attend prayers with such a pious family. Dr. Osgood was very benevolent, and his charitable deeds were many; none were turned away hungry from his door. I was much impressed with his genial spirit, consistent and zealous piety, and activity in the cause of Christ. His life was upright, pure, and good, and his Christian faith unfaltering. None in want every appealed to him in vain. Truly that passage of Scripture can be applied to him, "For I was an hungered and ye gave me meat: I was thirsty and ye gave me drink: I was a stranger and ye took me in: Naked and ye clothed me: I was sick and ye visited me: I was in prison and ye came unto me." "Verily I say unto you inasmuch as ye have done it unto one of the least of these my brethren, ye have done it unto me."

Rev. Dr. Osgood who "always abounded in the works of the Lord," was in the habit of rising very early, and held prayer meetings twice a week, from five to six o'clock in the morning. The young and the aged gathered at the chapel, which was half-a-mile from the Doctor's residence. The day laborers who "earned their bread by the sweat of their brow," attended before going to work; also, the wealthy were there, and it was an hour of refreshing to many souls. The invigorating air of the early morning seemed to make the conference room a fitting place for the holy spirit.

The opening hymn was most generally sung, beginning thus:

"Lord, in the morning thou shalt hear
My voice ascending high:
To Thee will I direct my prayer,
To Thee lift up mine eye.

"Up to the hills where Christ is gone,
To plead for all His saints,
Presenting at His Father's throne
Our songs and our complaints."
* * * * * * *

Which echoed beautifully as the birds sang in the spring their sweetest carols, as they flew among the branches of the large elm tree which stood before the door of the chapel. All were very devotional, unlike as it is with us, for every one bowed the head in silent prayer as they entered the house of God, and really it did seem like a heaven below.

Dr. Osgood was pastor over a large congregation. His church was a large, white Presbyterian church, on a beautiful green lawn not far from the chapel. The early morning services resulted in a large revival, in which one hundred came out on the Lord's side, rejoicing in their new-found hopes. All were made welcome, and Christian fellowship was truly exhibited towards all.

CHAPTER V.

LIFE IN FREEDOM.

Employment in a shoe shop—Education at Wilbraham—Licensed to preach—John M. Brown—Mrs. Cecelia Platt—Elizabeth Osgood—Sabbath and Mission Schools—Return to Springfield—Engagement with Dr. Hudson—Experience at Saybrook—Persecutions of Abolitionists—Lecturing—Courtship and marriage.

DR. OSGOOD felt an interest in my safety, for my master was on my track, and had advertised me through the press, trying every means to get me, if possible. The Doctor secreted me in a little room, called the fugitive's room. As I was secreted, all schemes to capture were baffled.

After keeping me for a while, the Doctor endeavored to find employment for me as a shoe-maker. He went to several persons, but found none that would take me. Finally, for safety—and the last resort—he went to see Mr. Elmore, an Abolitionist, who was a wholesale shoe dealer on Main Street. He readily took me, saying: "Bring him to me, I want to see him." I went to him one night with the Doctor, and he made a bargain with me, and also gave me some work to do in his work-shop, secreted from public gaze. It was the first work I had ever done in the like of a freedman, which gave me strength to think I was a man with others.

I stayed with him one year, and during that year, besides clothing myself and paying my board, I saved one hundred and thirty dollars. I soon became a great favorite with all the hands in the shop. I well knew a man in Springfield who commenced with only six cents in his pocket—for he was once a poor apprentice boy—who, in the course of time became a wealthy man, which gave me great encouragement to save my earnings.

As I never had had any advantages for obtaining an education, I felt the importance of it at this time. I made known my desire to Mr. Elmore, who said it was a good project, and advised me to attend school by all means. The old saying is, "it is money that makes the wheels turn, but after all, education moves the locomotive." I then made preparation to attend school at Wilbraham, Mass. After I had been there a while I became quite proficient in my studies, especially in mathematics, it being my favorite study. At first I found it difficult to keep up with the course of study; I

overcame it, however, and progressed so rapidly that the students and the
faculty of the academy gave me great praise. I remained two or three
years. As I was a poor student, I worked at my trade to pay my board and
tuition. So many hours were given me for work, and so many for study;
and thus I kept myself busily employed while at Wilbraham.

The reason I attended school there was because it was a more retired
place for me. I was very ambitious to learn, for I knew I would be better
qualified to enter into business for myself, which I had some thoughts of
doing then. While I was at Wilbraham I was licensed to preach the Gospel;
I held meetings in Springfield and Ludlow, and the Lord blessed me in my
endeavors. I had a fellow-student who occupied the same room with me;
this chum of mine was a young man from Philadelphia, by the name of
John M. Brown, who was then preparing for college. After completing the
academical course, he attended Oberlin College, and graduated with
honors, and then became professor of Wilberforce College for young men.
He expressed a strong desire for me to finish my education at Oberlin, but
not having sufficient means to pay my expenses, I did not go.

As we were firm friends, it was sorrowful for us to part, as I found much
pleasure in his company. We walked together, spent our hours of
recreation together, conversed on themes that interested us the most while
we were students at Wilbraham.

In the course of some years he was chosen presiding Bishop of the
Methodist Episcopal Churches of color. While at Wilbraham, Mr. Brown
and myself held a series of meetings in Springfield, at the house of a Mrs.
Cecelia Platt, for the colored people had no church of their own at this
time to worship in. Mrs. Platt was a devoted Christian, of many remarkable
characteristics, and zealous in the works of the Lord. She long since has
been summoned to reap her reward; she died in the triumph of faith. Her
house was the welcome home of strangers and friends, whom she always
made happy and comfortable. Her home was called the "pastors' home,"
for they were always made welcome whenever they came. Some of the
students, those studying for the ministry, would come in from Wilbraham
on Saturdays, and stop at the home of Mrs. Platt, in case of a storm, or
being fatigued by the journey, and return on Monday morning. She was
very charitable to the needy; as a Christian, very few were her equal. It was
there where the first preaching service was held, and the first Sabbath
School began. In referring to the Sabbath School, I must acknowledge that
those who were engaged in this great work were ardent and active workers,
for there were no timid drones.

Mrs. Stebbins—better known as the teacher among the freedmen in the barracks in Washington has since gone to rest from her labors; peacefully fell asleep in Jesus—was one of the most faithful co-workers of this institution.

Miss Elizabeth Osgood, the daughter of Dr. Osgood, was very enthusiastic in this mission; her deeds attracted more than a passing notice, and through her instrumentality many poor children were clothed so as to be presentable for the Sabbath School. She went out into the highways and hedges and gathered them in with their tattered garments, with the promise of a new suit of clothes; and thus many a little heart was made glad.

Miss Osgood was then a member of the Washingtonian Society. The object of this society was for the benefit of the poor. Useful articles of all kinds of wearing apparel were made for the needy.

We now turn our thoughts to the Sabbath School. In establishing the school the co-workers took pains, in the course of the week, to notify all the children of the neighborhood, and went out into the lanes and hedges, urging them to come into the proposed school. They were taught Bible truths, thus preparing them for future usefulness. Many of the scholars were newly impressed with something that would go with them through the week, and restrain them from sin; also, keeping them in the fear of God. The influence of the Sunday School was felt in the community. The scholars became interested in the lessons, and loved and respected their instructors. Through the aid of the Presbyterians this school was organized; and, opening with five scholars, the number increased to twenty, and then to one hundred. A small library was procured. A lady aged ninety years, who attended the school, learned to read the Bible, and the perusal of its sacred pages was a great comfort to her.

After awhile, when the school was fully established, we opened a class-meeting, and the parents of the children, and other adults, began to flock to the house of prayer. They came from all quarters to enjoy one another's experiences, feeling it was good for them to be there. As the people came in such numbers, there was not sufficient room in Mrs. Platt's home for the convenience of the people. We found it necessary to build a Chapel near by, and accomplished it within a year's time. It was plainly built, only for temporary use, till we could do better. Before entering it, however, a large revival broke out, which resulted in the conversion of souls.

During the revival I generally made it a point to come in from

Wilbraham—a distance of nine miles—Saturday afternoons for the purpose
of assisting in the meetings on the Sabbath. Occasionally the white
students of Wilbraham Academy would favor me with a pleasant drive in a
buggy. Those who had relatives in Springfield often visited them on
Saturday. They came to our quarterly and revival meetings, and seemed to
take quite an interest in them. They were very enthusiastic, and helped us,
by their remarks and testimonies, making the meetings a power for good.
Many of the faithful, who sustained these meetings, have long ago been
called to the great "Harvest Home," where, I doubt not, there will be
gathered many rich and precious sheaves.

At this time the colored ladies of the Chapel resolved to organize a
Sewing Society, which consisted of a President, Vice President, Secretary
and Treasurer. There was also a committee of ladies who went around to
solicit funds to carry out their plans. They had no regular sewing room,
but went around from house to house.

After accumulating thirty or forty dollars' worth of sewing, they opened
a fair in Masonic Hall; the proceeds were used towards building a more
commodious Church for worship. A fair audience attended; the hall was
profusely trimmed with evergreens, and the galleries with floral wreaths,
intermingled with evergreens, and flags placed at different points. Certain
parts of the hall were devoted to the sale of useful articles, which had been
generously donated to the ladies by the merchants. There were fancy
articles of all descriptions, and the needle-work was finely executed. The
ice-cream, lemonade, and pastry were served by competent ladies, who
received a liberal patronage. The ladies labored arduously to make the fair
a success, and their untiring efforts were well rewarded. The committee
received from time to time, sums of money from benevolent persons to
encourage them in the great work they had undertaken. God prospered
them, and in the course of a few years, a Methodist Church was built on
Main Street. Now they have two churches; the second church is on Elm
Street.

Many changes have taken place in Springfield; the house where we held
our first meeting has long since been completely demolished, and given
place to rail-road tracks, on which street cars and omnibusses run. In going
to Chicopee it looks like a level plain as far as the eye can reach. This
village is now a part of Springfield, making it a city of many manufacturing resources, and in consequence is a thrifty and enterprising
city. So time changes all things.

Finally I left school and returned to Springfield. I became acquainted with Dr. Hudson, an Abolitionist of great note in those days, who was an anti-slavery lecturer. It was no small thing to be a worker in such a cause. The Doctor engaged me to travel with him for one year; I, according to agreement, accompanied him, for I desired to do all the good I could. We had great success in our mission; we traveled all through the eastern and western part of Connecticut, and a part of Massachusetts. We had some opposition to contend with; it made it much better for the Doctor in having me with him. Brickbats and rotten eggs were very common in those days; an anti-slavery lecturer was often showered by them. Slavery at this time had a great many friends.

When we were in Saybrook there was but one Abolitionist in the place, and whose wife was sick. As we could not be accommodated at his house, we stopped at a tavern; the inmates were very bitter toward us, and more especially to the Doctor. I became much alarmed about my own situation; there was an old sea captain who was there that night, and while in conversation with the Doctor, had some very hard talk, which resulted in a dispute, or contest in words; I thought it would terminate in a fight. The captain asked the Doctor, "what do you know about slavery? All you know about it I suppose, is what this fellow (meaning me) has told you, and if I knew who his master was, and where he was, I would write to him to come on and take him." This frightened me very much; I whispered to the Doctor that we had better retire for the night. We went to our rooms. I feared I should be taken out of my room before morning, so I barred my door with chairs and other furniture that was in the room, before I went to bed. Notwithstanding, I did not sleep much that night. When we had arisen the next morning and dressed ourselves, we went down stairs, but did not stay to breakfast; we took our breakfast at the house of the man whose wife was sick. We gave out notice, by hand-bills, that we would lecture in the afternoon; so we made preparation, and went at the time appointed. The hall was filled to its utmost capacity, but we could not do much, owing to the pressure that was so strong against us: hence we had no success in this place. We went to the tavern and stayed that night. The next morning we went about two miles from this place to the township, and stopped at the house of a friend; one of the same persuasion. He went to the school committee, and got the use of the school-house. We gave out notice that there would be an anti-slavery lecture in the school-house that night. When it was most time for us, word came that we could not have the school-house for the purpose of such a lecture.

We thought that we would not be out-done by obstacles. The man at whose house we were stopping cordially told us that we might have the use of his house; so we changed the place of the lecture from the school-house to his house. The house was full; and we had, as we thought, a good meeting. At the close of the lecture the people retired for home. After awhile we retired for the evening, feeling that we had the victory.

The next morning the Doctor went to the barn to feed his horse, and found that some one had entered the barn and shaved his horse's mane and tail close to the skin; and, besides, had cut our buffalo robe all in pieces; besides shaving the horse, the villians had cut his ears off. It was the most distressed looking animal you ever saw, and was indeed to be pitied. The Dr. gathered up the fragments of the buffalo robe and brought them to the house; it was a sight to behold!

We intended to have left that day, but we changed our minds and stayed over another night, and held another meeting. The house was crowded to excess that evening; at the close of the service the Doctor told how some one had shaved and cut his horse, and brought out the cut robe and held it up before the people, saying: "This is the way the friends of slavery have treated me. Those who have done it are known, but I shall not hurt a hair of their heads. I hope the Lord may forgive them." The people seemed to feel very badly about it.

We left the next day for another place; the name I cannot recall now. We had better success when we went to Torringford, for here the people had just passed through a terrible mob, on account of an anti-slavery lecturer. The mob broke the windows of the church, and the lecturer had to escape for his life. We arrived here on Saturday, and put up with one of the deacons of the church. The next morning, after breakfast, he harnessed up his horse and sleigh, (for it was winter), and he and his family and I drove off to the church. Every eye was upon me. The deacon said to me: "Follow me, and sit with me in my pew." I did so, and every eye was fixed upon me, I being a colored man; and, being seated in a deacon's pew, caused quite a stir or bustle among the worshipers. There was such a commotion that the minister could hardly preach.

At the close of the service one of the other deacons came to the one that I was with, and seemed to be much excited. My friend asked him: "What is the matter, you appear to be mad?" "No," says he, "I am not mad; but grieved to think that you have taken that nigger into the pew with you; I think you had better promote your own niggers instead of strangers." My friend told him that "the pew was his; that he had paid for it, and that he had the right to have any one sit with him whom he chose; and that he did not think that it was anybody's business." When the controversy was over we went home and ate dinner.

In the afternoon we started for the church again, and after arriving there I took my seat with the deacon; it did not affect the worshipers so much this time as it did in the morning. After the meeting closed we started for home, and ate our supper; and in the evening the Doctor and I intended to have the church for our lecture.

On arriving there, Oh! such a crowd met us at the door that we could hardly get in. Through perseverance we made our way to the pulpit and took our seats. Some of the men who were engaged in the mob a few months before came and took the front seats, and looked as though they could devour us. I did not know what would become of us that night.

We began our meeting. The Doctor spoke first. They did not intend to have him speak, (being a white man), for the men were desirous to hear me; they kept quiet, however, for the sake of hearing me. When the Doctor was through I took the stand, and before I had finished my talk took all the fight out of them; some of them wept like children; so you see that it changed those men's hearts towards us, for a sympathetic feeling seemed to pervade through their hearts. I made many friends for myself that night. I heard one of them say that "if my master came there after me he would fight for me as long as he had a drop of blood in him." There were no more mobs in Torringford after that.

We then started for other parts of the State, and the work of the Lord prospered in our hands. I went back to Wilbraham and lectured in the hall to a large audience; and from there I went to South Wilbraham, and spoke in the M. E. Church to a full house. Many that heard of the sufferings of the poor slave, wept like children; many turned from slavery to anti-slavery. I went from South Wilbraham to Boston, and spoke in the Spring Street Church before a large assembly. I spoke in Worcester, and many left the slavery ranks and joined the anti-slavery. I have spoken in some places in Connecticut where the people have acted as though they had never seen a colored man before; they would shake hands with me and then look at their hands to see if I had left any black on them. I met with success every where I went; I traveled all the winter of 1842 with the Doctor, and in the spring following I left him and returned to Springfield, to resume my trade again, (boot and shoe-making), and worked a few months.

During my first year with Mr. Elmore I formed an acquaintance with a young lady, Miss Emeline Minerva Platt, who was visiting one fourth of

July a friend of mine, at whose home I boarded for a time. At this time I had made up my mind to settle North, and had given up all idea of ever visiting my Southern friends. As I had often seen this lady, in company with other friends, I thought it would be a good opportunity, on this occasion, to offer my hand in marriage.

Four years from my first acquaintance, in the spring of 1842, we were married. I have three daughters and one son.

CHAPTER VI.

LIFE IN NORWICH, CONN.

Came to Norwich—Started business—Purchase a house—Persecutions and difficulties—Ministerial labors—Church troubles—Formation of a new Methodist Church—Retiring from ministerial work—Amos B. Herring—Mary Humphreys—Sketches of life and customs in Africa.

IN coming to Norwich, Conn., in 1842, I took a shop on Main Street, near where Perkins Block, now stands; here I remained one year. The next year, 1843, I moved across Franklin Square, in the rear of Chapman's Block, the place now occupied by R. R. Armstrong as a fish-market; here I remained till I was burned out. This shop contained a side-room, which was occupied by John Wells, who hired it of me, and was employed as a boot black. On the night of the fire he was asleep in his room, and came very near loosing his life; by breaking his door open he was rescued from the burning flames. This shop was burned to the ground. I then moved to a shop on Shetucket Street, and from here to a shop in Chapman's Block, where I remained for a number of years. I then secured a shop on Bath Street, where I am located at the present time.

In first coming to Norwich, I established myself in business with a full line of customers. I then looked about for a tenement to live in and succeeded in finding one, through a friend, on Franklin Street, and then I returned to Massachusetts for my wife, who came in June. After living two years and-a-half on this street, I moved to a tenement on School Street, where I remained one year. The next year I had accumulated money enough to pay one-half for a frame house—only a few steps from where I then lived—before taking possession of it. Three years from this time I paid off all the mortgage on the house; then I truly felt that it was my own, since through my energy and toil, I had gained it.

In establishing myself in business, Mr. Gurdon A. Jones, a wholesale shoe dealer, patronized me by giving me his custom work. He was the first shoe dealer who gave me work, and thus greatly assisted me towards my accumulations.

As the years rolled on my family began to increase so that I deemed it necessary to procure a larger house. Having made several attempts, I bought a desirable one on Oak Street. After a struggle of a few years we moved into our new home. Reader, you must not think that I obtained it without any trouble. Ah! no; it was under difficulties; I had many a heart ache: I was persecuted on every hand for getting a home. While many would be encouraged for their industry and toil, my people are subject to all sorts of abuse for buying desirable homes for their families. We were in Norwich when colored young men were not allowed to attend the High School that was kept for young men on School Street. A promising young man of color applied for admission, and was promptly rejected. It is owing to being deprived of the chance to acquire an education that many of the old inhabitants, and the young, are ignorant to-day.

We were waiting with anxious expectation for the day to dawn, to enjoy all our privileges and equal rights as citizens. We have waded through many trials, and suffered every thing but death itself, in endeavoring to educate our children; many a time they have been to school with a heavy heart while trying to solve some problem or translation. Oh! how my heart went out for them; they were not easily daunted, for they were filled with enthusiastic ardor; they strank from no obstacles. The old saying is, "the darkest hour is just before dawn."

My two daughters, Louie Amelia Smith, and Emma J. I. Smith, after completing, the former a classical and the latter an English course at the Norwich Free Academy, in Norwich, graduated from that institution, and thus qualified themselves for future usefulness. They have proved very successful as teachers in Washington, D. C. My eldest daughter, Sarah Ann Smith, a graduate from the Normal Grammar School, is living at home and making herself useful. My son, James H. Smith, follows the trade of his father.

The first commencement of my ministerial labors, after I came to Norwich, was in a Union Church on Allen Street. There were two colored denominations which worshiped in this church—the Methodists and Presbyterians; both societies had a share in this church. The agreement was that each denomination were to take their turns in leading the meetings. The Methodists were very anxious to have me preach for them, and the Presbyterians desired a pastor of their own persuasion. The upper part of the church was used for the Sabbath school, and the basement for the preaching services. The reason for this was, because the regular audience room was not finished. The stove was moved to either part of the house, to suit their convenience. Prayer and class meetings were often held during the week at private houses. The Methodists were very zealous, and generally conducted the services on the Sabbath that the Presbyterians rightfully claimed. This caused a strife among them, and then a controversy arose with reference to the two ministers.

One evening while I was preaching, a red hot stove was carried out from the upper part of the church into the street by the opposite party; when the heat had abated somewhat, they carried it into the basement. The lights were put out, leaving me in total darkness; the meeting got fairly beyond control; the seats and floor were well besmeared with oil. More lamps were procured from the neighboring houses, and I continued the services till we were completely frozen out, and were obliged to close before the usual time. The other party continued till after nine o'clock.

The two societies never became reconciled to each other, and consequently there was a split in the church. The Presbyterians stayed at their post, while the Methodists went off by themselves, and gave up all they had put in the church to the Presbyterians. To keep themselves together, they held meetings at private houses, of great spiritual power. This separation weakened the Presbyterians somewhat, and they disbanded soon after, as the Methodists formed the larger part of the congregation. Prior to this a singing school was opened, and they made a vast improvement in the singing. Thus was the beginning of my first trials in the ministry.

The Methodists, after awhile, bought a building lot in the rear of Franklin Street, of William Prentice, for which they paid him two hundred dollars. Rev. Leaven Tilman came to Norwich to aid us in organizing a Methodist Church, as it was his business to organize churches wherever they were needed. He went around to solicit funds for that purpose, and was very zealous in the work. Myself and others, with his aid, solicited funds for purchasing the ground, and for the building. After the house was completed it was dedicated to the Lord. At the dedication, Bishop Quinn, Bishop Clark, Rev. H. J. Johnson, and others, were present and conducted the services.

We opened a Sabbath school and were prospered in our good work; we formed a bible-class, and opened a singing school. The bible-class consisted of young men who had formed themselves into a club called the "Young Men's Christian Association." Every Sabbath they were found in their places, and the class was in a flourishing condition.

The church was under the supervision of our New England Conference, which supplied us with ministers. I preached for the people of this parish for twenty years. We experienced many refreshing seasons; death invaded our ranks, calling out some very faithful and efficient helpers. The Sabbath school was broken up on account of the death of its prominent leaders.

At the time of the great rebellion the young men of the church disbanded and responded readily to their country's call. Although there were many obstacles to retard the progress of the church, yet there were a few who held on and hoped for better days. I was ordained Deacon, at the New England Conference, and after being with them four years, they appointed me Local Deacon. During my whole ministry in the church, I had no regular salary; I worked at my trade to support myself and family. I was compelled, by growing infirmities to retire from my pastoral labors, feeling that the days of my active usefulness were almost over. The house of worship became so dilapidated as the years rolled on that we sold it, and it passed into other hands.

After Mr. Gurdon A. Jones' decease, the well-known firms of E. G. Bidwell, J. H. Kelley, and J. F. Cosgrove employed me for years to do their custom work, which was quite a pecuniary assistance and help to me.

During my stay in Springfield, Mass., I became acquainted with a man by the name of Amos B. Herring, a native of Africa. It seems he had been on to Springfield once before, but, not having finished his education, he had returned to complete his course at Wilbraham Academy. He was a widower with six boys, the two eldest of whom he had left in Paris, to be educated, while he had come here. His wife had been dead four years; so he left his beautifully furnished house in Monrovia in charge of a housekeeper, paying her a dollar a month—just here you will see how low wages were in Africa. He told me every thing was nearly as cheap as could be. He had not been in Springfield long before he became acquainted with a Mrs. Lucy Terret, of Washington, D. C. They married; but upon his returning to Africa his wife did not long survive. She had made a great many friends during her stay in Springfield, and when he wrote back that his wife was dead we could not but regret that she had ever left us. Soon after her arrival in Monrovia she was attacked with a fever, from which she died. She was very fond of the tropical fruit which abounded, such as bananas, bread-fruit and dates, and had been cautioned about eating it before she was fully acclimated. At one time it was thought she would live through the attack, but she insisted on tasting the fruit, which she appeared to enjoy better than any thing else. A daughter by a former marriage—a sweet and attractive child—also found a grave in a foreign land.

Another friend of mine, Miss Mary Humphreys, also went to Africa as a missionary, and established a school in Monrovia. Her sole object in going was to do all the good she could in the way of enlightening her people. Soon she was smitten down with the African fever. So we see it is almost impossible for persons from this country to live in that climate. Very few survive the fever, and the fever they must have. I remember when there was so much talk about emigrating to Liberia that quite a number of my people embarked for the foreign land. Accounts afterwards showed that most of them died, if not on shipboard, soon after they reached shore.

Mr. Herring and myself often enjoyed many pleasant conversations. I used to love to hear him tell of Africa I had read so much about. He said that Monrovia was quite a thriving town then, and a great speculative mart for merchants of all nations. Many of the merchants who live there can not own lands, but can hire them. In passing the king, the white man is obliged to take off his hat. It is necessary, in presenting yourself before a chief or king, to carry a lot of presents to insure a welcome, notwithstanding they may not be of very great value; but they must be showy, such as bright colored shirts, and red cloth which is worn to adorn the breast pocket. Only a few of the Africans are able to wear stripes of red cloth. Some are clad entirely in shirts made of leather, which they skillfully prepare. I was quite amused at his account of a chief who consumed daily a sheep and the milk of seven cows.

The king partook of a kind of macaroni, prepared from wheat, with a rich seasoning of butter; while the natives ate apples pounded up and simmered down, in the place of real butter, which they considered very good. The natives burnt a kind of brush to keep the panthers and hyenas away, which abounded in large numbers.

In speaking of Africa, I would say that slavery still exists there. Slave ships are traveling to and fro from Africa to many of our foreign ports laden with slaves. We look forward to the day when Africa shall be free, and my people shall have that liberty that rightfully belongs to them. Many missionaries have gone out there to enlighten and teach the natives the "Good Way;" but after awhile we find most of them more interested in the gold and silver than in the civilization of the people.

In referring to the chief who consumed a sheep every day, you must not think this species were as large as the American sheep. These animals were not fattened like the sheep among us. They were very lean, and scarcely any fat on their ribs. They resided in the dense forests, and sought their own food, and subsisted on all kinds of nuts, tropical fruits, or anything they could find to eat. They inhabited the interior of Western Africa, and other parts of the country. The cows, also, for the want of care and green pasture fields to feed in, were not as large in size as those in America; and, for this reason, they gave a small supply of milk daily. It required a supply of milk from seven cows in order to obtain milk enough for the chief.

CHAPTER VII.

THE WAR OF THE REBELLION.

FOR many years, while slavery existed, I have never ceased to pray that God, in his all wise providence would bring it to pass that I might return to the land that gave me birth, and see my former friends. As the signs of the times looked dark and doubtful, I began to think I should never realize such a blessing; but time passed on, and with it the rebellion increased in strength, war rumors were afloat, and the very air seemed to bespeak war. God gave us war signs which spoke of the dissolution of the Union. Some said in case of war between the North and South, that it would result in the liberation of the slave. I said it would be too good a blessing to be true, not dreaming that such a course would lead to it; not knowing which way the scales would turn. We all know the immediate cause of the rebellion. The North and South were at length arrayed against each other in two great political parties on the question of slavery. The Northern party triumphed, and though no unlawful act was charged against it, and no simulated claim or assumption offered that it had not succeeded in a lawful and constitutional way, the defeated Southern party refused to accept the decision of the ballot box, and rushing into open revolt proceeded to organize a government of its own. Not being satisfied in what they already possessed they craved for more territory, and fired on Fort Sumpter for that purpose in the spring of 1861, little dreaming that they themselves were destroying their beloved institution.

The first sound of the cannon that saluted the ears of Major Anderson, and his starving garrison, was the death knell of slavery. The heart of the nation beat in unison; every telegraph wire vibrated with the news, "Sumpter has fallen." The news spread like the flash of lightning through the country; it united the people and aroused the nation to a sense of its duty; the proud sons of America responded as one to the call of their country. It was then this war began in which we have all had to take our part. When President Lincoln called for men to defend the country, the call was for white men. Our martyred President, proud in the strength of his high position said, "the Union must be saved with slavery, if it can, without it, if it must." Did he forget that at the great wheel of state there was a guiding hand, stronger and mightier, and more just than his. Truly, "God moves in a mysterious way, His wonders to perform."

At the beginning of the war, few anticipated the great and important changes so soon to be wrought by it. To the observing eye, the hand of God has been seen in the war; seen in the overthrow of the proud, and uplifting of the lowly; seen in the fall of the taskmaster and the emancipation of the slave. Many fought for the liberation of the colored man, although they hated him. How well do I remember the time when our Northern army undertook to go into battle at Bull Run. The Northerners, corrupted by unexampled prosperity, and forgetful of the traditions of their forefathers, the vital and animating principles underlying the very foundation of this government, severed their course from the cause of liberty and every hope by which the black man might take courage, proclaiming it to be the white man's war exclusively. The Northerners, eager for glory and greedy for honor in that eventful hour disdained the proffered service of the colored man, and would not even permit him to drive a wagon in train of their army; and even more, would not allow him to wear the cast-off clothing of their soldiers for fear the imperial blue of this great republic would be dishonored by them, and perverted from a sacred purpose.

Under such circumstances, the Northern troops, filled with pride and hautiness, promptly responding to the call, "On to Richmond," moved in military order to plant their standard on the walls of Richmond. Not a military instrument of music, or drum cheered the march; the deep silence broken only by the muffled tread of the advancing host, or the heavy rumbling of the artillery carriages. On their march they were confronted at Bull Run by an army animated by a sterner and more determined will. The rising sun of the ever memorable 21st of July, 1861, beheld the Union troops in "war's bright and stern array;" their polished arms shone in the morning's light, and their silken banners glittering in the sun. The long line of bayonets flashing in the sunbeams, extended rows of army wagons with their white tops, winding columns of cavalry, the dark looking ambulances, all combined to form a scene of thrilling interest, and presented a magnificent spectacle.

But the parting rays of that same sun looked down on defeated, routed and disgraced men; their bright arms thrown away, and their silken banners were taken by the exulting Rebels as trophies of war, or trailed in the dust. Then, forgetful of all their proud boastings, our Northern troops made a hastry retreat towards Washington. The panic was disgraceful in the extreme; for miles the road was black with men running in all directions. Hosts of Federal troops, some separated from their regiments, were fleeing along the road and through the fields, all mingled in one disorderly route. Horses galloped at random, riderless from the battle-field, many of them in the agonies of death swelling the wild commotion. Then the heavy artillery, such as was not destroyed, came thundering along, overturning and smashing every thing in its passage. Hacks conveying spectators from the battle-field were completely smashed, leaving the occupants to the mercy of the way. Sutler's teams, carriages and army wagons blockaded the passage way, and fell against each other amidst the dense cloud of dust. Men lying seriously wounded along the banks entreated, with raised hands, those on horse-back to lift them further back, so they might not be trod on.

The Northern troops, in this celebrated race of twenty-five miles, with forty thousand entries, was made without stopping; for the goal was Washington, and the prize safety. Though taxed to their utmost, it is sorrowful to reflect that all this haste and endurance were needlessly expended. We have the facts in history that the Southerners did not pursue the Union army, and they did not find out the mistake till after the flight. This lesson was terrible to the North, but it was not sufficient to teach them to do justice to the down-trodden of my people; and, still relying on their superior numbers and almost boundless resources, the government called for three hundred thousand more men.

It was at this time that the whole North, humbled by defeat, and eager to revenge the Rebels, sprang to arms. Soon there was a gathering of the clans from the rivers to the lakes, and from ocean to ocean. Geo. B. McClellan, of the West, led a mighty host towards Richmond, and by a new route. The earth shook beneath the tread of his army, and the ocean was filled with his iron-clad war ships. Being chained down by fate in the pestilential swamps of the Chickahominy, daring not to strike, and unwilling to retreat, he permitted the golden moments to pass until his army was decimated by disease. The South then took fresh courage, and gathered from her broad dominions her best and bravest sons and threw them, with irresistible force, upon his defeated army. Indignant and morose, our army sought safety beneath the guns of the fleet, otherwise every one of them would have been annihilated.

It was under these circumstances of gloom and despondency that our beloved martyr President lifted himself to the height of his great duties; issued the immortal proclamation of emancipation, proclaiming liberty to the oppressed millions made in the image of God; severing the chains from the limbs of hundreds of thousands. Their shouts of joy for new-born liberty had rung over distant hills, and through wooded dales.

I was then keeping shop in Chapman's Block, on Franklin Square, when the proclamation of freedom was proclaimed; it sent a thrill of joy through every avenue of my soul. I exclaimed, "Glory to God, peace on earth, and good will to men," for the year of jubilee has come! His glorious Proclamation of Emancipation will stamp the first of January, 1863, as the day of days; the great day of jubilee to millions. When that battle cry resounded throughout the land, o'er river and plains, o'er mountains and glens, even then the government could not entirely emancipate itself from the hateful spirit of caste. Still awed by the traditions of the past, it had not the courage to say to the freedmen: "We want you to fight in defence of the life of the nation;" but they said: "We want you as laborers, and for your better organization and control we will enroll you in companies, and form you into a regiment, and for your protection, we will arm you."

It was by this sneaking, back-door arrangement, that they were smuggled surreptitiously into the service of our country. It was plainly seen that the American people, at first, were unwilling that the colored man should go into the battle—it was "the white man's war, and negroes had nothing to do with it." When the Governor of the State of Ohio was asked if he would accept of a colored company, he replied that they "did'nt want negroes,"—and for the love to their country went to Massachusetts and enlisted, with the promise of the pitiful sum of seven dollars a month. And not until the Massachusetts Governor received the colored man as a soldier did the governors of the other Northern States think they could condescend to give the negro a musket and a suit of blue. These are facts that can not truthfully be denied. It was not the intention of the government at the beginning of the war to free the slaves, but they soon learned that men of color were made for a nobler purpose than to be "drawers of water and hewers of wood."

As a war necessity, the Americans bestirred themselves for their protection; they were driven to take measures that neither God, justice nor humanity could induce them to adopt, knowing that the Rebels armed the slaves to fight against them, for they saw that they were likely to be defeated. It has been said that colored men will not fight for liberty, but will run at the first fire. They questioned their loyalty, and distrusted their fighting qualities. When we think of the Bull Run race, we have nothing to say about running. Let me direct your attention to that brave fifty-fourth Massachusetts colored regiment, who marched in the line of battle when more than one-third of their number had fallen, their color-bearer lying in the cold embrace of death, when a Mr. Wall, of Oberlin, grasped the flag, mounted the parapet and waved over the conquered enemy the stars and stripes. If that is not bravery, I ask what is? Is it running? We find them running to replace the flag of our country in the very capital of the Rebels, and we as a nation need not be ashamed of this kind of running.

I commend the daring and noble deeds of our soldiers, and hand them down to posterity as worthy of imitation, and that they have won for themselves a proud position on the pages of American history. Thanks be to God the colored men, as soldiers, have shown to the world their true patriotism in their valor and courage, and displayed as dauntless bravery as ever illuminated a battle field. Thousands have fought and died. They met death calmly, bravely defending the cause that we revere. The world has looked on with admiration and wonder at the boldness and daring of their victorious host, for they have contributed largely towards some of its splendid victories. They have come forward by thousands, and rallied around the so called "banner of the free," hoping that by preserving it from the hands of the enemy to make our dear beloved country free—what she has so long been called in song and story: "The land of the free and the home of the brave,"—after two hundred years or more of oppression and injustice, and having not only their rights as citizens, but their manhood ignored; and, besides, a thousand other wrongs calculated to kill the patriotism in any other than a black man.

An incident of bravery of the colored troops at Port Hudson, I am about to relate, sends a thrill through every avenue of my soul. I wish it could be burned into our hearts with the words of fire, so that no tongue would henceforth dare to utter or repeat the old slander that "black men will not fight for freedom." Let the vaunted Anglo-Saxon stand back abashed before this sublime exhibition.

In 1863 the Fifty Second Regiment Massachusetts Colored Volunteers were ordered to charge the enemy's works, and did it magnificently. Just before they reached the forts they came to a ditch thirty feet wide and ten feet deep, full of water, which was absolutely impassable; they were ordered forward again; they could only do and die, yet on, right on they went to the hopeless charge; into the storm of grape and musket balls; on, with no chance of doing any thing but to die like brave men; on, where their white officers dare not to lead, till nearly half their number were dead or dying. Five times more they charged up to this bayou, when they were withdrawn.

When I think of these torn and bleeding veterans as they wended their way to the hospital, it seems too horrible to relate. Nevertheless it is so, for I have the facts. I can hardly speak of it but with many tears. Bless God that they have shown themselves worthy to be free, and entitled to all the inalienable rights, among which are "life, liberty, and the pursuit of happiness;" having won the rights for all their posterity, without having them infringed upon, for they are blood-bought rights. Can a people into whose hands arms have been placed, and who have been drilled in the art and science of war, become again slaves? And can this nation, that has advanced so rapidly in the cause of freedom, go backwards so much as to re-enslave a people that have assisted in fighting its battles? Forbid it, justice! forbid it, humanity! forbid it, ye spirits of our fathers, still hovering over us! forbid it, our Country! forbid it, Heaven!

In the spring of 1865 the war closed; then the lovers of the Union, and freedom, were giving thanks to God for recent victories they had gained, and rejoiced that right and justice had triumphed over wrong. City after city fell, until Richmond itself was surrendered to a band of colored warriors.

There are times when the human heart is so overwhelmed with joy and gratitude, with thanksgiving and praise, that words seem meaningless, and language fails to convey the deep emotion felt. Words were inadequate to convey the joy unspeakable, and almost full of glory, that the lovers of the Union felt at that hour of triumph. Great were the rejoicings over the fall of Richmond; beautiful were the displays made in all the places, far and near. Flags were thrown out to the breeze, bells resounded, bonfires, illuminations; the rocket's red glare, and the cannon boomed forth its peals of thunder. The innumerable lights which flashed forth their brilliancy threw into magnificent relief the gorgeous decorations of the buildings. Crowds of human beings of all sexes, nationalities and colors assembled in the streets; they were wild with excitement; they were crazy with joy; enthusiasm cannot describe it. Men hugged each other, struck one another, yelled and screamed like wild men.

Peace, with its snowy wings, seemed to be hovering in the air, ready to shed its blessings on the distracted and blood-drenched country. Richmond, for four long years of blood and tears, of fire and sword, was at last convulsed in its last death-throe. Events of magnitude crowded upon us in such rapidity that before we could duly digest the one, another of more startling importance rushed in and pushed it aside. Before we had half thought out the evacuation of Richmond, then came the sudden news of the surrender of Gen. Lee, and the Confederate army of Virginia.

But ah! our day of rejoicing had scarcely passed when the same wires that brought the tidings of the surrender of Lee, brought the sad intelligence that our beloved President was dead—fallen by the hand of an assassin! Oh, what a shock to the American people. Our rejoicing was turned into mourning: the whole country was draped in mourning; every eye was dimmed with tears. Pen can not begin to describe the sadness; deeply the people felt the loss of one whom they loved as a father. The American Nation has lost a pure patriot; humanity a tried friend; freedom a great champion. He was stricken down at the time when his great wisdom was so much needed in bringing his distracted and blood-drenched country into the harbor of returning peace and prosperity. His course, from the time of his inauguration, had been marked with wisdom and justice; his manner had been unfaltering; his feelings could be touched by all classes of the nation, from the highest to the lowest—an instrument in the hands of God in avenging and redressing the wrongs of years, and the emancipator of my heretofore enslaved brethren of the South. None were afraid to approach his Excellency, and justice was always meted out, as the circumstances of the case required. It was my desire that he might have witnessed the end of the beginning; but, as Moses, he viewed, but was not permitted by Divine Providence to reach the end of the beginning, which began to loom up with such splendor. The position he placed us in, as a people, causes us to feel as did the children of Israel when they passed through the Red Sea, and were freed from the hand of Pharaoh and his pursuing host. ABRAHAM LINCOLN has gone but a step before us, but ever memorable will be his name in the hearts of the loyal millions.

IN MEMORIAM.

We also pay tribute to the late Senator Sumner, that in his death, we, and the friends of freedom everywhere have lost a sincere and earnest friend, an able and untiring philanthropist and statesman; the principle of freedom he strove so earnestly to inculcate into the minds of all, irrespective of complexion. It was his last and most deeply cherished wish to lift up the colored race to the plane of perfect equality. "See to the Civil Rights Bill, don't let it fail," were among his last utterances to his colleague, who stood beside the dying Senator. Probably at no period of his life did he more forcibly illustrate his perseverance, his energy, his zeal and eloquence than in the many efforts he made to pass this bill. That bill was the great work which was to crown his labors. We never can express the sentiments of gratitude which his name awakens in the breast of every colored American. In defending the rights of my people by the most generous sentiments of his aspiring nature, by his sincere love of justice, he has acquired an immortal title to all their descendants. The Civil Rights Bill, passed April 9th, 1866.

OUR STANDARD BEARERS.

Thomas Garrett, James and Lucretia Mott, Francis Jackson, Wendell Phillips, William Lloyd Garrison, Henry C. Wright, Owen Lovejoy, Lydia Maria Childs, Abby Kelly Foster, the Phelpses, Samuel Budgett, and many others, by their pen and voice poured floods of light upon the minds and hearts of the public, through evil as well as through good report, until they have created unto God, and developed that moral and religious influence which has always accomplished that to which they consecrated themselves, and for which they strove with a devotion as constant as truth, and with an industry and zeal as unwavering as justice, and with a fidelity as pure as their cause was patriotic and sacred. Let them, and many others shine as stars, for they were as beacon lights for freedom. They spoke when speech cost something; their greeting was the violence of the mob, and their baptism fire and blood. They did not "count their lives dear unto themselves." The sufferings and death of Torrey Lovejoy and John Brown, has sent a thrill through the hearts of the nation, for they possessed a self-sacrificing spirit. Let their names be written as with a diamond; let the historian stamp them with letters of fire upon tablets of gold; let the poet sing them in sweet strains; let the scholar, with the graces of literature, embalm them; let the great of humanity enshrine them. Their deeds can never be effaced, but will exist as an imperishable memento, engraven on the hearts of the people.

CHAPTER VIII.

AFTER THE WAR.

AFTER the Fugitive Slave Law was passed, terror struck the hearts of
those who had escaped to the free States, as no earthly power could
prevent them from being returned to their masters. Very many were taken
back. For my part, I was very much frightened, and was continually
haunted by dreams which were so vivid as to appear really true. One night
I dreamt my master had come for me, and, as he proved property, I was
delivered up to him by the United States Marshal. In the morning I told
the dream to my wife. She said she "believed it would come true," and
was very much worried.

I went down to my shop, and, in the course of the morning, while
looking out of my window I noticed a number of persons who had just
come in on the train, and among them I was sure I saw my master. You
may rest assured I was pretty well frightened out of my wits. What to do I
did not know. This man did certainly walk like him, had whiskers like him;
in fact his whole general appearance resembled his so much that I was sure
that he had been put on my track. I peeped out at him as he passed my
door and saw him go up the steps leading to the office of the U. S.
Marshal, then I was sure he had come for me. I could do no more work
that day.

As my friends came in I told them of what I had seen, my fears, etc.; and
they assured me they would be on the look-out and see if such a man was
in town, find out his errand, etc. Accordingly one of them who was a town
crier, Dunton by name, went to the hotels and searched the registers to see
if a man by the name of Lackey was registered there. At night he reported
that no such name could be found. My friends declared that I should not
leave this town. One even went so far as to go to the U. S. Marshal and ask

if "any one should come, looking for me, what he would do; would he give me up?" He replied: "No, he'd resign his position first." Another bought a revolver, and told me that "if they had me up that, by some means, he would manage it so as to get it into my hands that I might in some way defend myself." I had determined never to be taken back alive. Death was preferable to slavery, now that I had tasted the sweets of liberty. As it was, dreams of this kind ceased to trouble me, and the effects and fear wore off.

It was not till after the Emancipation Proclamation that a man who is living in Norwich to-day, told me that after I left the South, and had settled here, he went to Heathsville, to the very place where I used to live, saw my master, who asked him whether, in his travels North, he had ever come across a man who was lame, shoemaker by trade; that he would give him two hundred dollars, cash, for any information which would lead to his discovery. He returned home, said nothing whatever to me, for fear I would be alarmed, sell out and leave the place; said nothing to any one about it till after January 1st, 1863, when freedom was proclaimed throughout the land.

During one of my visits to Heathsville, on which I always carried a large stock of clothing, shoes, etc., I formed a plan for some amusement among the young people. On Sunday it was announced that on a certain evening during the week there would be a Christmas tree. All were invited to come; accordingly when the time arrived, the church was packed; many came from miles away. I selected a young man who I intended should represent Father Christmas, as he is called there. I put on him a long swallow tail coat, the ends of which almost touched the floor, then he was filled out so as to be very large; he had on an extremely sharp pointed collar, which extended far out from his face, which was hidden behind a mask. I opened with an address, and at a given signal, Father Christmas made his first appearance. Many of the children, even some of the old people were frightened nearly out of their wits; one child ran forward, crying to his Uncle John to save him; some fell over each other to get out of the way. Well, I laughed till I could laugh no longer, and finally I was obliged to dispense with Father Christmas before anything like order could be obtained. Then the different articles were distributed, and if you could have heard the many prayers that went up from thankful hearts for the gifts received, no one would tire of this good work. General satisfaction reigned, and after a hymn of thanksgiving they dispersed to their homes.

January, 1867, I was called to visit Washington, to see about a school for my daughter. While there I was invited by the pastor of Israel Church to preach on the Sabbath. At the close of the service many of my former friends came forward to greet me, and informed me of the old plantation where my brother and two sisters still resided. I immediately wrote to my brother to let him know that I was still alive, and that I should visit Heathsville at such a time, and asked him if "he thought there would be any danger in coming." He informed me that "there was no danger, for Virginia was free." When he received the letter it seemed as from one risen from the dead. My sister took the letter and went round amongst her friends, wild with joy.

A few weeks after this I made preparations to start on my long-premeditated journey, in the middle of June, 1867. I went by way of Washington. As I was proceeding down the old Potomac River her red banks looked natural to me, so much so that I could hardly suppress the feeling of joy which arose in my heart. That night the boat stopped about forty miles from Heathsville. The next morning, about light, I went ashore, as I was very anxious to tread once more on the old Virginia soil. Very soon the bell rang for the boat to start; I hastened on board again. By this time she had got underway, and I reached Cone Wharf at six o'clock—the very spot from where I started thirty years before. It seemed to me more like a dream than a reality. No one can imagine how I felt; I could not believe that it was possible that I was going home to tread on free soil. I asked myself the question: "Can it be possible that Virginia is free?" I looked ashore before the boat reached the landing, and saw those old ex-slave-holders standing on the dock, which sent a thrill all over me. But soon the boat rounded up to the dock, and as soon as the gang-plank was put out there were some white young men who came aboard and stepped up to the bar and began drinking. A colored man, also, went up to get something to drink. There was a row that commenced with the white men and the colored man, and came very near ending in a fight. Here I saw the old spirit of slavery exhibited by the whites. This somewhat increased my fears; but quiet was soon restored, and I stepped ashore almost on the same spot where I was thirty years before.

Things looked changed somewhat since I left, but after awhile I came to myself and found that I was really home again, unmolested where I was once a slave, and my joy knew no bounds. I was soon discovered by some of my friends, and we congratulated one another like old friends, for I seemed to them like one risen from the grave. I felt as though I wanted to get down and kiss the free ground upon which I stood. I could hardly restrain my feelings, for it was a new day with me. This visit was fraught with many sad reminiscences of the past.

After looking about and seeing the many changes that had been wrought in thirty years, I was taken by my friends and conveyed to my brother's house. On my way, I came to the old mill, gray with age, where I used to work. In the mill was a little room partitioned off where I had in former days done shoe-making. We stopped, and I went into the little room and saw where my bench used to stand, and the old, quaint fireplace where I used to make my fire. While I was there I remembered the joys and sorrows that I had passed through during the time I occupied that room. I then went to look for the old spring where I used to get water; I found it and knelt down by the side of it and drank therefrom. No language could express my feelings while I knelt over that spring. I then arose and continued my journey till I came to a cross-path, which I traveled in my former days. I asked the driver if "he would halt and let me get out of the wagon," and told him that "he could drive around and I would go across." As I viewed the place, old scenes seemed so natural to me that I could not help praising God in the highest for bringing me back to the place of my birth. I waited a few minutes, and then proceeded on. We then came to the old Heathsville spring, here I got out also and stooped to drink. We then came to the village of Heathsville, and as soon as I entered it, I was recognized by old friends who knew me in former days. I alighted from the wagon and we clasped each other, and a full tide of joy rushed over our souls. Here I found my brother's wife, he having been sold years before. After looking around at the different places where I had lived, and the different shops where I had worked, I started for my brother's house, located about two miles out of the village of Heathsville. When I was within half-a-mile of his house, I met my brother coming out of the house of a friend, and as soon as I saw him I knew him, although I had not seen him for years.

Dear reader, you should have been there in order to have realized the scene of our meeting. We got hold of each other and put our arms around each other's neck without speaking for some minutes; the silence was broken, and I exclaimed: "Dear brother, is it possible that we are standing on Virginia's free soil, and we are free?" My brother replied, "yes, dear brother, and you too have been living in the 'land of the free and the home of the brave.'" We wept and rejoiced, and praised God for his goodness in bringing us together once more on free soil. For a short time all was excitement and confusion. When it had subsided we started for the house, where I met my eldest sister. She pressed eagerly forward to greet me, and we seemed to each other as one risen from the dead. We, too, fell on each other's neck and clasped each other and wept. News spread like wild-fire that Lindsey Payne (for that was my name before I escaped from slavery,) had returned home again. Many of my old friends who once knew me, came flocking in to see me. My listeners were never weary, as I related to them the history of my life at the North, and described the varied scenes through which I had passed. My joy and excitement rose to such a height, that I scarcely knew whether I was in the body or out.

In the afternoon I went down to the "great house," so-called in the days of slavery, where Mrs. Sarah Winsted lived, who was formerly my mistress. She was the second wife of my former master, Mr. Langsdon. She survived him, and afterwards married a Mr. Winsted, who died before her. When I got within two hundred yards of the house she saw me coming, and knew me. It being warm weather she threw on her sun bonnet and came to meet me, and was so glad that she wept and grasped my hand for a minute before either spoke. At last she broke the silence by saying: "Oh! Lindsey, is this you?" I replied: "This is me, what there is left of me." Says Mrs. Winsted: "Let us go to the house." Mrs. Winsted then introduced me to her daughter, who had been born since I left, and then set the table and would have me take dinner with her. Although I had ate dinner, I accepted her cordial invitation as an appreciation of her kindness.

After dinner she told me "to relate to her the narrative of my escape from slavery; how I got away, and how the Yankees had treated me since I had been up amongst them?" I set my chair back, and told her the whole story of my escape. When I told her how frightened I was by seeing the cars, and thought the engine was the devil coming after me, she really did shake with laughter. I also informed her of our sail up the Chesapeake Bay in a small boat, and how we were overtaken by the storm of wind and came very near being lost, but we reached the land of freedom in safety; that the Northern people had treated me comparatively well; and that I had bought me a comfortable home. She seemed to be very much pleased with my recital. I gave her a nice pair of shoes, for which she was very thankful.

While on this visit I saw a great many places of my childhood among them were Hog Point, where I spent many of my boyhood days; and, also, the very spot where I was made lame. I saw the old oak tree that stood near my mother's cabin home, which I have mentioned in the first part of this work, on a limb of which Mr. Haney hung one of his slaves, and whipped him till the ground beneath him was stained with his blood. I tried to find the same limb, but although the tree appeared to be in perfect health and strength, that limb seemed to have withered and dropped off. While I was meditating under this tree, many scenes of my boyhood came vividly to my recollection. I then searched for my mother's cabin home, but no humble cabin, like the one in my memory, met my eye; it had given place to a dense pine forest. The logs of the cabin had either been burned, or rotted with the dust of the earth. All was desolate in the extreme. I called, but there was no response; no voice of a kind mother greeted my ear; no welcome of the eleven brothers and sisters greeted my approach; all was speechless as the grave. Nothing occupied that sacred spot but the reptile and the owl. As I gazed and thought, I became faint and sorrowful. I turned from here in pursuit of the spring from which I had carried so many buckets of water. After much search and labor, crawling through the bushes and fallen trees, I found the old spring and drank therefrom. The old gum tree that was near this spring in my childhood days, I found there still, being bent with age; its branches hung over this spring. It was once noted for its healing properties, the berries of which were used for medicinal purposes.

These three springs that I have mentioned, have served to quench the thirst of many a weary soldier as he stooped to drink, at the time of the great rebellion. I knelt, and offered my heart in prayer and thanksgiving to "God, who doeth all things well." I thought how often my brothers and sisters with myself, came to and from that spring; but now we were separated, nearly all of us, never more to meet, till we meet in that heavenly land where father, mother and children shall never part, "where the wicked cease from troubling and the weary are at rest." From there, with a heavy heart, I went in search of our neighbors; they, too, like the cabin, were gone; they had been committed to the dust, and their spirits had returned to "God, who gave them." Their houses were occupied by others; with a sad heart I retraced my steps to the home of Mrs. Winsted, and then to my brother's.

I spent three or four weeks in Heathsville, and while I was on this visit I went a second time to see Mrs. Winsted, and found her in the garden, in the hot sun, hoeing. Said I, "is it possible that you can work out in the hot sun?" She replied, "Lindsey, we can do a great many things when we are obliged to, that we once thought we could not do." I saw the changes that freedom had wrought, and I thought, "how people can accommodate themselves to circumstances." When we were on the plantation together she would not allow herself even to walk out doors in the hottest part of the day, without a servant to hold an umbrella over her.

Many a man who was very rich, has been reduced to beggary. Many of those negro traders, who used to buy up a large number of slaves and carry them down to the lower States and sell them, have become so poor that they have not clothes to hide their nakedness. They go around among the freedmen and beg for something to eat. I know a man who was once very rich, worth about half-a-million, who has since been reduced to such poverty that he has been obliged to hire himself out under the United States service to work on a mud machine, as a common day laborer, and is not allowed to go and see his family but once in three months, he being in Norfolk and his family in Baltimore. Others, who were rich, are even worse off than he. This description does not include all the slaveholders, for those who were kind and humane towards their slaves are far better off in circumstances than the others. The slaves, as a general thing, did not leave them in the time of the war, but stayed with them to protect their property, while their masters were on the battle field. Those who brutalized their victims seem to be marked by the vengeance of the Almighty; they are wasting away like the early dew, for many have nowhere to lay their heads, except among those whom they have abused.

The colored people, unlike all other nations on the face of the earth, are ready to fulfill that passage of Scripture: "Therefore, if thine enemy hunger, feed him; if he thirst, give him drink; for in so doing thou shalt heap coals of fire on his head." Many of them, when bleeding from the effects of the knotted whips applied by their cruel task masters, could have risen and made the land knee deep with the blood of their oppressors, and thus avenged themselves of the host of cruel wrongs which they have suffered; but, instead of raising an insurrection, they calmly left the plantations without injuring a hair of the heads of their masters, and went on the Union side; and not till the United States put arms into their hands, and bade them go forward in the defence of their country, did they attempt to show any signs of revenge.

During my first visit I noticed that very many of the houses looked very ancient and dilapidated. The old slave pens, and the whipping posts, stood just as they were when I left. The fertile soil which once brought forth in abundance, and the cotton and corn, presented an unbroken scene of barrenness and desolation. The place was almost depopulated—plantations forsaken.

The South has been subjected to a fearful waste of population.

Thousands of the colored people during the war, and many thousands of whites also left, to say nothing of those who have been killed. I only found one brother and two sisters living. Since that time my eldest sister has died, leaving four or five children, three of whom had been torn from her, and sold into slavery, and she never heard from them again. She was a great sufferer, owing to the want of proper care, and sorrow reigned in her inmost soul. Finally the Angel of Death came and severed her from her sufferings. Her husband survives her, as I write, "The fountains of bitter sorrow are stirred by the healing branch that God can cast." As soon as I struck the Virginia wharf, the words of the aged colored doctor came vividly to my mind, who told me my future destiny: "that in the course of time I would return to my native land." Sure enough I had returned after thirty years' absence.

A day or two after I had made my escape from slavery, Thomas Langsdon, supposing that the old doctor was accessory to my running away, fell on the man and beat him in a brutal manner, most shocking to behold. The doctor never recovered from his injuries; being a free man he did not have any one to intercede for him. After I had been home a few days, I inquired after the doctor, and found, to my great sorrow, that he had gone to his long home, where no foe nor hostile bands will ever enter its peaceful inclosure. In my repeated visits to Heathsville, I observed but little improvement since the great rebellion; there have been but few houses built for the last thirty years. The condition of the colored people is improving very fast, for many of them are buying lands and building, and thus preparing homes for themselves. Their condition is much better than those who once owned them. The old ex-slave holders are dying off very fast. As they have no one to cultivate their large plantations, and can not do it themselves, they are obliged to divide them up and sell them to the freedmen, as they are growing over with dense forests.* I think that eventually, Virginia will be in as flourishing a condition as any section of the United States.

The Northern people are beginning to emigrate there. The steam whistle from the factory and sawmill, which serve for the employment of many, is beginning to be heard morning, noon, and night. Things begin to wear a Northern aspect considerably. The log-cabin begins to disappear in some

*These pine trees had grown up from the larger trees, (saplings as they are called,) and reminded me of past days, when we slaves had to fell them for fire-wood for our masters. The woodlands were owned by them, and nothing could induce them to buy fuel to burn as long as they had slaves to labor in felling trees.

places, giving way to houses of modern construction. The broad long handle Southern hoe is giving place to a more modern make. This improvement is more or less seen, except among the class that bought and sold human flesh, and obtained their living from the bones and sinews of others. But now have the ex-slave holders—that is including all of them in the South—treated the freed people since the great rebellion of 1861? The colored people of the South have suffered every thing, even death itself. Some were violently beaten, or rudely scourged; many were deliberately shot down in open day, on the public streets; others were way-laid and cruelly butchered, and some, God only knows the fate they have suffered. There has been an awful destruction of human life. The streets have been drenched with their blood, for it has flown freely. Many worthy and willing hands were left without employment, while others worked for a mere pittance to get their living, while still others toiled on as formerly, without any agreement or probability of due return. When the civil rights bill was passed, April 9th, 1866, the condition of the colored people was ameliorated in many instances.

During the rebellion some were driven from their cabins during the absence of their owners, who were on the battle field. The cabins, many of them, were stripped of all their contents, leaving the occupants nothing. Oh! how many have suffered malice and revenge, the bitter wrath and vengeance of those who justly shared the disappointments and misfortunes attending the overthrow of slavery and rebellion.

My brother is doing well, and has bought himself a nice farm, from which he raises crops every year. He is a Baptist preacher; and, besides presiding over his own church, he has the oversight of the Lancaster Baptist Church, in Lancaster County; thus supplying two churches, the Northumberland, and the Lancaster churches. My younger sister, who resides in Wycomco, in Northumberland County, Va., has four or five children; and, through her and her husband's industry have procured a small farm, from which they have obtained principally the support of their family.

During my repeated visits to Heathsville I have carried boxes of clothing and a large trunk closely packed, for the benefit of the freedmen and their families. The little sacks and other children's clothes were presented to mothers whose little children stood in great need of them, and were very thankfully received. "God bless the friends of the North," was the hearty exclamation of many. I found the colored people industriously employed in doing something, and thus they seemed contented and happy.

In December, 1879, during my visit, I went down to Fairfield, some five or six miles from Heathsville, where I had learned my trade, and found the old place much dilapidated. The fields from which were raised corn and wheat were all grown over with thick forests. The "great house" had been burned to the ground. Mrs. Winsted had passed from time into eternity to try the realities of the other world. The old shop that I used to work in had been torn down, and desolation seemed to mark the place. The foot of the war horse had been there. I tender my thanks to the kind friends of Norwich for their generous gifts.

CHAPTER IX.

CONCLUSION.

The Fifteenth Amendment Celebration–The parade–Address–Collation–Charles L. Remond–Closing words.

FROM 1867 to 1869, great changes were taking place in the government. Amendments to the Constitution were being made; among them was the fifteenth amendment. When that was passed, the colored Americans of Norwich called a meeting and passed a resolution proposing to celebrate that great event. In May, 1870, we appointed a committee to arrange for the same. I was appointed chairman of that committee. A motion was made to extend a call to the Hon. Charles L. Remond, of Boston, to deliver the oration. The motion was unanimously passed to that effect.

The Fifteenth Amendment Celebration took place on June 16th, 1870. At early dawn the booming of the cannon was heard from some distant hill, that aroused the participants to the more arduous duties of the day. The din and smoke reminded one of the war, where our veterans fought so creditably. The first part of the morning the weather did not look very favorable for us. There was a misty appearance in the air, but as it advanced towards ten o'clock that hazy look wore off, and the half-veiled sun shone in all its splendor. On that eventful morning the committee of arrangements labored faithfully to make the affair a success, for it was a scene of bustling activity. Flags that bore the national colors, and banners bearing mottoes appropriate for the occasion were waving in the breeze. Every effort was made by some to make it a failure, but their plans were frustrated by our eminent citizens. When undertaking a good project for our fellow-men, we are often defeated by our enemies. In this we almost lost our balance, which we soon regained in our full strength, and we came off victorious, to the astonishment of our opposers.

The generous contributions of the citizens, by way of provisions and money for the celebration, evinced their appreciation of our efforts; the arrangement reflected great credit upon those who had it in charge. The procession formed on Franklin Square, headed by the Norwich Brass and

String Bands, proceeded from the Square up Washington Street, down Broadway, up Franklin Street: thence to Rockwell's Grove, where a platform was erected, upon which sat the speaker of the day, and a few of our leading citizens. One feature of the procession that attracted much attention, was a tasefully decorated car, drawn by two horses, filled with young ladies dressed in white, bearing aloft the banner of beauty and glory. The selectmen, common council, clergy, and other citizens participated in the celebration, and helped to swell the number.

A goodly number stood beneath the trees in the shady grove, and fanned by the gentle breeze that came laden with the perfume of peaceful fields, under the canopy of the deep blue heavens, listened to the oration of the Hon. Charles L. Remond. The exercises opened with prayer by one of our citizens, invoking the blessings of Heaven upon all. After which Mr. Remond proceeded in a most able and eloquent manner to review, in fine style, the most important incidents connected with the event we had met to celebrate. His theme was: "The Advancement of the Colored People." He referred to the present condition and future prospects of my people. Every word was sparkling, brilliant, convincing and touching, and was received with great applause. His speech was full of thoughts that breathe, and words that burn, and was listened to with marked attention and interest.

After the address was a collation, to which the people did ample justice. The long tables were arranged with much taste, by competent ladies, and others, who had them in charge. It was an enjoyable occasion for every one present. The Norwich Brass Band played in fine style the pleasing national airs; among them were "Hail, Columbia," and the "Star Spangled Banner," which always stir up the patriotism of every true American, and were loudly encored. It was an event long to be remembered in the hearts of my people, and is one of the greatest and brightest events that has ever occurred in our history as a people, and should be handed down from generation to generation. We tender our thanks to the citizens of Norwich, for their generosity and kindness in aiding us in that great and good cause.

IN MEMORIAM.

The Hon. Charles L. Remond is no more, for his earthly career is ended. By his untiring energy he became one of our first men, and advanced, step by step, till he became a custom house officer at Boston. His well-known qualifications as a man were more than of ordinary mark, and well-fitted him for the position and duties which he was called to fill. He always wielded his pen for the benefit of his people. As an orator, he has had few the scourging lash must have a significance in the work of civilization, or God is not wise or just.

The filling up of their years with misery and degradation must mean something more than an event of fate, else there is no law of progress that bears men on through storm, tumult and tempest to the goal of peace. We are just crossing the bitter waters, and can scarcely see our landing; we are not safe over, yet we hope to escape the storms that are still beating upon us, and moor our bark on the shore of freedom. Dear friend, read this simple story carefully, and ponder its lessons. What if it had been your child, stolen from your home, borne to a foreign shore, doomed to such a life, and destined to become the progenitor of a race bound to toil and woe, would not your heart flow in sympathy with the weakest of that race who should come to you in sorrow? But, say you, the day of trial is over, the stream of sympathy may be dried up because of the nominal freedom that has been vouchsafed. I say to you nay; my whole race is yet in peril, and God only knows the end. The love of gain, the lust of power is still dominant, and ceases not to inflict their burdens and enforce their demands.

Sorrowing at the situation, pained at the necessity which yet drives our brethren from pillar to post, or binds them to the wicked caprices of their old masters, yet we appreciate the open hearts that welcome them to new homes, and the willing hands that minister to their dire necessities. We have yet much to ask of others; we have much more to accomplish for ourselves. What has been wrought in the past cannot be overcome at once. Gradually the work of demoralization does its work, and not much swifter must be the work of regeneration. We cannot save ourselves without aid and sympathy from others; without the protection of just laws and righteous judgment; others cannot save us without our aid—without the consecration of all our best faculties to the work before us. Let us, then, work mutually in unfolding the mysteries of that Providence which is not only bringing us up out of bondage, but which is to redeem the whole race of mankind from the gloom of darkness and the thralldom of sin.

With these thoughts I leave, asking you to give your hearts to wisdom, restraining yourselves from selfishness, and living for the good of others. There has been enough of pain, and sorrow, and despair. The whole current of life must be changed, and men be taught no longer to hedge the way of others, but to scatter sunbeams, solar sunbeams; the sunbeams of life in their path.

equals. His pen has carried light and comfort to many a h
people. He was one of the pioneers of the anti-slavery ι
earliest days, when agitation was at its height. Let his hι
held in grateful remembrance, to be handed down frι
posterity.

Dear reader, this simple story of my life is no record of b
with the multitude constitute the hero; no tell tale of fic
the imagination. It is a story that is real, that is earnest;
the simple heart that has power to sympathize with thι
times of adversity, and to mingle in the joys that come
giving peace and satisfaction to the soul, it will accompli
have hesitated in this work, feeling that ordinarily the eχ
individual life are sacred, and that the bitterest and thι
one's own self, and can never be felt by another. But theι
experiences the public have a right to know; lives wrι
interest of some great cause, or so linked to the progress ι
they modify and mould its destiny. The life that is buι
living perpetually in God's sunshine, realizing every thin
existence, has little in it that touches the chord of sy
necessity calls for its revealment. Yet there are those in tι
reap an experience that, when made known, unfold a lessι
and comfort to others. Life's ways, in this regard, are sι
we are dumb to the inquiry: "Why is it so?" Yet, flowiι
see the Guiding Hand preparing us for better things, n
better life. The slave-life of which this little volume sι
analogous to this.

No mystery was ever deeper than that which shrouds t
men were led into bondage, and no system was ever
intolerant than that which inflicted stripes and bur
without cause, and deprived them of liberty and the right
we look back upon God's dealings with his early people,
wrought in bondage and suffered in their wanderings froι
power of bringing good out of evil, light out of darkneş
school of wisdom to the world. So the first slave ship
ocean, with its stolen fruits of life and liberty, of boι
sinew and nerve, of flesh and spirit, bore tidings
wretchedness to generations, whom, yet through the da
of two centuries the Great Disposer of all events saw tı
unable to see it. The wail of the bondmen toiling in th

CHAPTER X.

COLORED MEN DURING THE WAR.

In battle—Kindness to Union men—Devotion to the Union—29th Conn.—Its departure—Return—The noble Kansas troops—54th Mass.—Obedience to orders.

IT is a fact to be lamented that the historians of our country speak so little about the heroic deeds of the colored troops; in fact, by some no mention is made of them at all; but, let it be as it may, the fact that they, after many petitions to be allowed to take their place in the ranks, fought bravely and well, lives in the heart of every true American citizen. Many were the commendations they received from their officers. Look at them at Fort Pillow, Miliken's Bend, Port Hudson, Fort Wagner, and Olustee! Where do we find them? In places of most imminent danger, where the battle raged hottest, closing up where their ranks were thinned out before a reeking fire of grape and canister.

> "Cannon to the right of them!
> Cannon to the left of them!
> Onward they went,
> 'Noble black regiment!' "

The black man went into the war with but one determination: that once learning the use of arms, he would never again be made a slave. Whether he ever enjoyed the blessed privileges of freedom himself it mattered little to him so that his race derived the benefits. Says one officer: "I never saw men more willing to sacrifice themselves on the 'altar of their country' than those in the 8th U. S., of which I have command." Says a captain of another colored company: "I never saw a more heroic company of men in my life." And thus it might be said of many other colored regiments that went into the field. None were ever known to flee when the hour of battle was nigh; nay, rather it was as much as the officers could do to restrain them till the order to fire should be given.

The slaves had it in their power, when their masters were away to the war, to kill their defenceless wives and children, many of whom had been left in their care. How often has the case been when the master, just before leaving his home, has called to him his most faithful servant and left in his charge those most dear to him; and I have known cases where silverware and other valuables have been stowed away in some old cabin till "mar's comes back." Ah! the slave-holder knew the slaves could be trusted—a fact which the North was not long in finding out, even before it tried the experiment of organizing them into troops.

A Union soldier being wounded, probably left in the woods to die, having wandered about under cover of night, at last falls upon the cabin of some old "aunty." A sense of safety and security steals over him, for he knows that no power on earth could make her betray him. I copy an extract of a letter, showing the kindness of the slaves towards the Union soldiers, to which many of them can testify:

"ADVENTURES OF TWO ESCAPED PRISONERS, AND THE HELP
THEY RECEIVED FROM THE SLAVES IN THE PERILOUS
VOYAGE THENCE TO KNOXVILLE, TENNESSEE.

"Two Union officers, Lieut. Col. Thomas J. Leigh, of the 71st New York, and Lieut. Tincker, of Indiana, had made their escape from the prison stockade at Columbia, S. C. They traveled two nights, and got within three miles of Lexington, when they met a couple of slaves, and asked them the direction to Ninety-Six Station. They pointed out to the officers the road, and asserted positively that 'they were their friends, and when they wanted assistance they must crawl up to the fields about dusk, and wait for a field hand to come along; that they would furnish them with provisions, and never betray them.' On the fifth night of their journey they were making north-west for Knoxville, Tenn. On the evening of the sixth day they ventured cautiously to a plantation where they saw a large number of hogs in a field running toward them as though they expected to be fed, and they judged from this that a slave would soon come and feed them. They were right in their conjecture, for in a few moments a slave came along with a basket on his head, with corn for the hogs. Col. Leigh called to him, and, as he came up to him, questioned him 'if he would betray him?' The slave replied: 'No; the negroes in that part of the country did not do that sort of thing.' He said: 'You must be hungry?' The officer replied: 'That was what I hailed you for.' The slave advised him 'to wait about an hour, and he'll have lots to eat.' He then started for the house, and in about an hour came back, along with several other slaves, all carrying eatables—chicken, possum, rice and shortcake—sufficient to last two days' journey. As it began to rain, the slaves advised them 'to lay still that night, and it would clear up before morning.' Both of the officers took their advice, and they kept them company all night.

"They were very anxious about the state of affairs. They asked the officers 'if they thought Jeff. Davis was going to give the slaves arms;' and then said that their 'masters had made propositions to them, that if they would take up arms and fight for the South, they would be free.' One of the officers asked them 'if they would fight against the North?' They promptly replied: 'Only let them give us arms, and we will show them which side we will fight for.' They said: 'We have now some arms hid;' and wanted to know 'if, when they were formed into companies and regiments, whether they could be together, and talk with one another.' He told them 'Certainly.' One slave remarked: 'My master offers me my freedom if I will take up arms, but I have a family—a wife and five children—and he does not offer to free them; and we have come to the conclusion that there is no use in fighting for our freedom when any one of our children we may have are to be made slaves.' He felt that he could not himself enjoy the blessings of freedom while his own wife and children toiled in hopeless bondage. Continued he: 'When we get the use of arms, and are permitted to be together in regiments, we can demand freedom for our families, and take it.' Another one remarked 'that their masters did not venture to whip them now; that they were fed on a little better food than before the war, and they believed this was only done to humor them and keep them quiet.'

"They departed the next morning, wishing the slaves 'good luck,' and they replying 'God bless you,' which is a very common expression in that portion of the country. They then pursued their journey, without anything worthy of note happening, until they arrived in the Pickens District, S. C., on a plantation of Dr. Earl, who was publicly known to be a secessionist. Here they were in the midst of a large number of slaves of his plantation, and others, discussing the arrival of Gen. Sherman, at Augusta, Ga.

"It appeared that they had in a secret manner sent one of their number in haste towards Hamburg, to get fresh information about Sherman, with the intention, on the arrival of the courier, to make a general stampede into the Union lines. They counted on between five and eight thousand slaves, who consented to go with them. All of these men treated the officers very kindly, and gave them a large supply of provisions. They told them 'to stop at the home of John W. Wilson, a strong Union man.' Accordingly, the next evening about half-past nine o'clock, Col. Leigh knocked at Wilson's door; he came, holding a revolver in his hand, and demanded to know who they were. They told him that 'they were escaped Union officers.' After hearing this, he invited them into his house, and treated them very cordially. He informed them of the re-election of President Lincoln, and as they were about leaving him, went kindly with them to the middle of the road, where they all gave three cheers for Abraham Lincoln.

"Being properly directed on their course, they reached Bumcomb County, in Western North Carolina. There they saw a woman in a field plowing; she informed them that in that County, and also in Henderson and Madison Counties, there were over five hundred men who had been conscripted—enrolled militia-men—her husband among the number, who, refusing to join the Confederate army, lay concealed in caves in the woods. The country is ransacked by Rebel details, who plunder the defenceless women and children, and shoot the men if found in the woods. In traveling over a distance of one hundred thirty miles, across the mountains, a scene of great destitution prevailed; women performed the duties of men; the children had no shoes, and the country seemed given up to entire lawlessness. The remainder of their journey was executed solely under the guidance of women, and on the evening of December 13th they reached Knoxville, having spent forty-four days in their perilous travels."

Many a soldier has been carefully nursed by slaves, and sent back to the army a well man. It will be seen, moreover, that the slave was no respecter of persons, as in this instance. A slave mother, who, in bidding her son "God speed," on his way to the war, exclaimed: "If you see Mar's, pick him out de fust one." The name "Yankee," to these poor, depressed people meant freedom, and they were never known to turn their hand against a blue-coat.

At the beginning of the war many black men went as servants, and at times of battle begged for a bayonet, and took their places in a company. How many brave souls perished this way will never be known till the judgment. History has made no note of them, though they died riddled with bullets, with the bayonet grasped firmly in the hand.

Some of the slave-holders offered their slaves freedom if they would join the Confederate army. Says one: "I have a wife and children in slavery; he don't say a word about freeing them. No, sir, I don't fight unless they can be free, too." Others, on being interrogated as "to what they'd do if arms were put in their hands, whether they would fight for the South," replied: "Let them give us arms, we'll show them which side we fight for." And so, at last, when the experiment was tried, whether the black man would run in battle, it was soon found out which side they were determined to fight for.

As soon as it was made known that colored volunteers would be accepted they came pouring in from all sections. In Norwich a regiment was soon formed, (29th Conn.,) which did good service in the field. Never did we feel prouder than when, after a few weeks' encampment in New Haven, they marched away with flying banners and martial music.

Some of the ladies of color instituted a Ladies' Aid Society, which met once a week at the houses of its different members to make up both fancy and useful articles, as they intended to hold a fair in one the largest halls in the place—the proceeds of which were to be devoted to getting up a box for the brave 29th. There was in it almost every conceivable delicacy that could be imagined, that would bring delight to any one far away from home and longing for its luxuries. There were also useful and needy articles, put up by loving hands, for the brave boys who had given their lives for their country. Some few of them lived to return. In the severe fighting before Petersburg many found an early grave.

The fair was held for one week, at Breed Hall, which was most handsomely decorated with flags and banners. The tables were arranged around the hall, and fairly crowded upon them were articles of every description. Many thanks are due to those who so well patronized us. Many influential families sent in contributions, both of money and articles to help the cause. Too much can not be said of the members of the society for their untiring zeal—how they met, through storm and rain—nothing deterred them from their work. If, at times, their spirits seemed to flag, thoughts of the brave 29th, at their dangerous post, stirred them up with renewed vigor. The fair netted a handsome profit. The box was quickly made ready, and sent on its way.

We have the surety that the box reached its destination, from the following extract of a letter written by E. C. Green, to an officer of the regiment. It reads thus:

*   *   *   "Before closing may I refer you to the pleasure you gave to the ladies of our Soldiers' Aid Society, a year since in allowing them to furnish your regiment with a box of hospital supplies, and say to you, if your supplies are at present insufficient, we would be glad to forward another box of similar articles, if your surgeon would have the pleasure of sending us a list of articles needed. With much esteem,

Yours, very truly,

E. C. GREEN."

DEPARTURE OF THE BRAVE TWENTY-NINTH CONN.

At two P. M. the regiment stood in waiting. A few moments after, a carriage containing Major General Russell, Major Tyler, Major Wayland, and Alderman Marble, drove up in front of the regiment; every man of which stood erect and manly as if conscious of what was before him. A handsome flag was presented by Miss Diantha Hodge, to whom Col. Wooster responded in a soldier like speech; after which the order was given, and they marched off by the right flank, amid the cheers of the assembled crowds, and the farewells of old friends. Cheer after cheer came from the lips of the men as they saw the stars and stripes floating to the breeze along the line of march. The regiment halted on the old Green for an hour, waiting for the tide to rise to enable the steamer Warrior to near the wharf, then the line of march was resumed down Chapel Street to State, down State to the wharf. At six o'clock, the regiment marched on board, with orders to report at the depot of the ninth army corps, at Annapolis, Md.

Reaching this place they found themselves anything but comfortable—a sharp, raw north-east wind prevailing. The tents did not arrive till nearly dark; these were hastily pitched and occupied. In the morning they awoke to find themselves covered with from one to three feet of snow. Crackling, blazing camp-fires were built, and around them cheerful blue coated dark skins gathered, full of wit and humor. On the 27th of April, 1864, the regiment left for the front. Its sufferings in the bloody struggle before Richmond were terrible and heart rending. It went into the fight of eleven hours with four hundred and fifty brave, armed and equipped men; it came out with one hundred and eighty men, all told—no field officers, and one wounded company officer.

THEIR RETURN.

On the morning of Oct. 14th, 1865, orders were received to prepare to be mustered out of the U. S. service. Oct. 16th the boys bade good-bye to hard-tack, salt horse, and other delicacies known nowhere but in the army. They embarked on board the steamer, singing "Homeward Bound." After reaching New York they embarked for Hartford, where they would be paid off, and receive their discharge papers. Here they were met by the Mayor and a committee, and marched up to Central Row, headed by Colt's Brass Band, where they stacked arms and unslung knapsacks; then the battalion formed in two ranks and marched to the City Hall, where a splendid feast awaited them.

On entering the hall the first thing to be seen was the "Star Spangled Banner," extended across the hall, and in the centre a banner bearing the following: "Welcome, 29th C. V.;" "Deep Bottom," "Strawberry Plains, Va.," "Siege of Petersburg," "New Market Heights," "Danberry Town Road," "Chapin's Farm," "Fair Oaks." At the head of the banner was an evergreen wreath, prepared by the ladies. On the stand were the busts of Lincoln, and others.

After feasting, they were ordered to march to Central Row, where they learned the 31st U. S. C. I. had just arrived. The 29th and 31st then formed in a square on State House Square, where they were addressed by Mayor Stillman; afterwards, by His Excellency, Gov. Buckingham. After a few remarks from Col. Wooster and Gen. Hawley, the 31st were escorted to the City Hall, where a breakfast awaited them. The 29th were then dismissed.

THE NOBLE KANSAS TROOPS.

On the 29th of Oct., 1862, twenty-four men of the 1st Regiment of Kansas, Colored Volunteers, having advanced beyond the limits prescribed, were charged upon by one hundred and twenty of the Rebel cavalry. There was a desperate hand-to-hand encounter. There was no flinching; no hesitating; no trembling of limb. Each man saw exactly how matters stood, and, with calm precision, made every stroke tell. Finally re-inforcements came up. Out of the twenty-four men, only six escaped unhurt. The Rebels were armed with shot-guns, revolvers and sabres; our men with Austrian rifles and sabre bayonets. This last is a fearful weapon, and did terrible execution. Six Killer, the leader of the Cherokee negroes, shot two men, bayoneted a third, and laid the fourth with the butt of his gun. Another was attacked by three men. He discharged his rifle and had no time to load again. When asked to surrender, he replied by a stunning blow from the butt of his rifle, which knocked the Rebel off his horse.

So ended the battle of Island Mounds, which resulted in a complete victory to the negro regiment. It has been found out that black men make splendid soldiers—that they are anxious to serve their country and their race. No one can point the finger of scorn at the Kansas troops and say they were cowards; yet four months passed and they were not mustered— still they adhered to their organization through every discouragement and disadvantage. Chances of recognition were slim. They demanded of the military authorities to be either accepted or disbanded.

The 1st North Carolina Regiment was commanded by Col. James C. Beecher, brother of the Rev. H. W. Beecher. Their camp was on the south side of the Neuse River. The ground had been enclosed by the men so that the locality presented quite a neat appearance. Col. Beecher thus writes to his friends:

*   *   *   "I wish doubtful people at home could see my three weeks' regiment. They would talk less nonsense about negro inferiority. Our discipline is to-day better than that of any regiment I know of; and I believe, by the blessing of God, our efficiency will be second to none."

A little later he says:

*   *   *   "My regiment is a 'buster,' improves every day; and such a line of battle as we form! It would make your eyes shine to see these six weeks' soldiers going through a dress parade. A month later the regiment is considered ready for a fair fight."

Towards the last of July they left Newbern for Charlestown, and were put to digging trenches, getting only a lull occasionally on the beach by moonlight. It was quite a romantic scene: the hard, white beach; the ocean waves splashing along the sand; the long line of black soldiers, their guns shining in the moonlight. They had a great desire to learn; and, although the digging went on, the officers would instruct them at night in the speller, so that before they went to Florida three hundred of them had learned to read and write.

Much has been said about the bravery of the 54th Mass. On one occasion it saved a whole brigade from being captured or annihilated. The lamented Col. Shaw was one of its commanders. At Fort Wagner, when the color sergeant fell, and our flag would have been trailing in the dust, one of its noble boys seized it, sprang upon the parapet, where he received three severe wounds. When the order was given to retire, the noble color bearer still held the flag in the air; and, with the assistance of his comrades, succeeded in reaching the hospital, where he fell exhausted, saying: "The old flag never touched the ground, boys."

There was a great deal of murmuring among the friends of the regiment in Boston, because of statements reaching them that it was called upon to perform more than its proportional part of dangerous duty; and this seems true, since, in the most perilous places there would be found the glorious 54th.

I mention a few facts to show that the slaves were so accustomed to obeying orders that they would follow out any instructions to the very letter. It is said that while Gen. Grant was walking along the dock, smoking, a colored guard came up to him and said: "No smoking on this dock, sir." The General looked at him and said: "Were those your orders?" "Yes, sir." "Very good orders," replied the General, smiling, and throwing his cigar into the water. Again, a Rebel picket offered a large piece of tobacco to a colored sentinel if he would give him one biscuit, or hard-tack as it is called. "Against orders to exchange with you Rebs.," he replied, and no entreaties would cause him to swerve one iota from his instructions.

A Reb. was found by two colored pickets skulking outside the Union lines. How he cursed and swore when he found that he must be brought into camp under the surveillance of two black soldiers. He refused to stir one step; "he'd die on the spot first." "Just as you please," replied the guard, "we take you, dead or alive." The Reb. raved the more, and said: "It was enough to make his father rise up out of his grave." When last seen he was marching into camp at the point of the bayonet.

In consequence of the breaking of the Weldon R. R. by Grant, much of the Rebel munitions of war and supplies had to be run over a distance of sixteen miles, and then transferred to the cars. Every thing that could be used for carrying purposes was pressed into their service. Horses and mules were scarce in the Confederacy, so, in many instances, negroes were hitched to the wagons, and it was said made better time than when horses were used. They would go on their way, singing and joking; and, after a half-hour's intermission at certain places, would push onward as fresh and lively as ever.

The slaves were of great assistance to the Union army on account of their thorough knowledge of the country: its ways and resources: its wood, water, fuel, game: and also of the habits of the enemy. Nothing escaped them. They'd tell to-day what happened yesterday thirty miles off; would risk their lives to give any information which was to be of advantage to the Union.

At Washington the contrabands, as they were termed during the war, knew every inch of ground between there and Richmond, and gave valuable information for maps, engineering parties and reconnoissances. Contraband pioneers, armed with sharp axes, would go on expeditions through the woods, under cover of the carbines of the cavalry, hewing away the heavy timber, and preparing the road for the advance. Every thing in the shape of a dog was killed. About the plantations could be seen the lifeless bodies of bloodhounds whose deep baying would no longer be heard about the swamps, indicating the close proximity of pursuers.

CHAPTER XI.

RECOLLECTIONS OF THE WAR.

The spirit of the South–Delaware–Kentucky–Meetings–Conventions–Gen. Wild's raid–Slave heroism–A reminiscence of 1863–Sherman's march through Georgia–Arming the slave.

THE spirit of the rebellion still shows itself in many of the States. Its influences are plainly manifested in the State of Delaware. In my escape from the South I passed through this State. How I ever succeeded, without being detected, I can not tell to this day. Nothing but the mercy of the Lord ever carried me through. Here, in the height of slavery, I went on board the boat at New Castle, and no white man questioned me as to my whereabouts, or asked for my pass. As for the town of New Castle, the very atmosphere seemed tainted with slavery.

The feeling was most bitter in Odessa, during 1865, against persons of color from the North giving lectures in the town. On one occasion a mob of white ruffians surrounded a colored church, showering stones and bricks at the doors and windows, swearing that the meeting should be dismissed. One of the local laws of the State says that: "Any negro or mulatto coming into the State, who is a non-resident of the locality he may visit, is liable to a fine of fifty dollars, six month's imprisonment, and twenty-five lashes." Learning of this, they concluded to dismiss the meeting.

March 4th, 1865, Maj. Gen. Palmer issued an order that: "All slave pens, and other private establishments for confining persons in Louisville, be suppressed; and all confined persons discharged, except such as have committed crimes." A colored police officer brought out many an innocent man and woman. Some had iron bars on their legs, reaching from the hip to the ankle and fastened on with iron straps.

There was a time in the history of Kentucky when colored men, women and children found upon the highways after dark were surrounded by the city guard, and flogged by them in the public streets. In Louisville the Rev. Mr. James called a meeting at which delegates were appointed to hold an interview with the President, calling his attention to a few of the laws which bore so heavily on our race: First, they had no oath; second, they had no right of domicile; third, no right of locomotion; fourth, no right of self-defense; fifth, a statute of Kentucky makes it a penal crime, with imprisonment in the penitentiary for one year, for any freeman of color, under any circumstances, to pass into a free State, even for a moment. Any freeman, not a native, found within her borders is subject to the same penalty; and for the second offense shall be a slave for life.

In 1865 the first delegation of colored men that ever left Kentucky, on a mission of liberty, started for Washington to accomplish the noble work entrusted to their hands. The interview was satisfactory, the President assuring them that the government would yield them every protection, and that the martial law would continue till the Kentuckians should learn more truly their position, and their duty to the nation.

The first free convention in the State of Virginia, during a period of two hundred and fifty-five years, was held in Alexandria, at the Lyceum Building. Fifty delegates were present. Addresses were made by Geo. W. Cook, of Norfolk; Peter R. Jones, of Petersburg; and Nicholas Richmond, of Charlottesville.

THE CELEBRATION OF THE FOURTH OF JULY IN LOUISVILLE, KENTUCKY.

For the first time the people celebrated this day as a free people. Extensive preparations were made. There was a great out-pouring of people. They came from the factories, the work-shops and the fields to enjoy themselves in the pure, fresh air of freedom. The procession was formed in the following manner:

123rd U. S. C. I.—eight hundred strong.
Band.
Fifth St. Sabbath School—Asbury Chapel S. S.—Quinn Chapel
S. S.—Jackson St. S. S.—Green St. S. S.—
York St. S. S.—Centre St. S. S.
Band.
Government Employees, one hundred and fifty—Sons of Union—
West Union Sons—Sons of Honor—United Brothers of
Friendship—United Fellows.
Car tastefully decorated, drawn by four horses, filled with misses,
representing the Fifth St. Baptist Aid Society.
Car representing the Original Aid Society in Kentucky.
The Colored Ladies' Soldier's and Freedman's Aid Society.
Car filled with working men, plying the saw, plane,
hammer and mallet.
125th U. S. C. I.—six hundred strong.
Band.

Fully ten thousand persons marched in the procession, and ten thousand more assembled on the ground. A sumptuous dinner was prepared for the soldiers after which the speaking began. Addresses were made by David Jenkins, J. M. Langston, Chaplain Collins and Lieut. Ward. When Gen. Palmer appeared such a shout as went up was enough to bring all the invisible sprites and spirits from their hiding places. As soon as it became quiet he began. His speech was continually applauded. He finished amid rounds of applause, banners waving, and the band playing the "Star Spangled Banner." That night the heavens were ablaze with rockets, fiery serpents and blue lights.

GEN. WILD'S RAID.

During a march, when our troops neared a plantation, the slaves would eagerly join them. In many instances in plundering the houses slaves were found locked up. Continually during this raiding expedition, slaves came pouring in from the country in every direction, with their household furniture, thronging the lately deserted streets. This expedition was to search out guerrillas, lurking about the neighborhood of Elizabeth City and firing on our pickets. A force of colored men fell on their camp. There was a hasty escapade, and the soldiers came in possession of fire-arms and horses. Leaving Elizabeth City, they passed by vast fields of corn a mile in extent, commodious looking buildings and magnificient plantations. Here the troops commenced to work in earnest, and became an army of liberation.

On the first plantation they found fourteen slaves, who gladly joined them. An old wagon was found, to which a horse was harnessed. Such furniture as the slaves needed was placed in it, and the women and children on top. And so they went from house to house, gathering together the slaves, and whatever teams and horses could be found. Meanwhile, foraging went on, as there was an abundance of geese, chickens and turkeys. All the planters were "Secesh," so no restrictions were placed on the troops. The line of march continued, the contraband train continually growing in length.

At Indian Town bridge Gen. Wild came upon a guerrilla camp. His men started upon the "double quick," and pursued them through woods, across corn fields, until they came to a swamp. Here no path whatever could be seen, and how the guerrillas succeeded in covering their flight was, at first, a mystery; but our men were in for it now, and did not intend to turn back before ferreting out the matter. They began a careful search, and soon found the trunk of a felled tree, well-worn with footsteps. Near by was another, then another till they made quite a zig-zag footpath across the swamp. This solved the mystery. This, without doubt, led to the guerrilla quarters. Going single file they came upon a small island, which had been hastily evacuated—every thing was lying about in great confusion. According to orders, the soldiers burned the huts and took possession of whatever was worth keeping. The slaves on the plantations, ahead of the line, were notified by scouts to be ready to join the train when it should pass. By the time it reached Currituck Court House it was a mile in length. After three weeks the entire expedition returned to Norfolk. The raid was considered a very important one.

The tables were now turned. Those proud-hearted planters, who claimed such strict obedience from their slaves, now actually fell down on their knees before these armed blacks and begged for their lives. The great cry among them was: "What shall I do to be saved?" Yes, now they were ready to take the oath of allegiance, give up their slaves; any thing "to be saved." Whole families ran to the swamps when they heard that the raiders were near.

This raid put at rest forever the question as to whether the negro troops were efficient in any part of the service. They performed all the duties of white soldiers—scouting, skirmishing, picket duty, guard duty; and, lastly, fighting. Gen. Wild had decided at one time to attack a guerrilla camp. With the exception of thirty-five men, who were too lame to march, every man wanted to go and fight the guerrillas, notwithstanding those could remain back who wished to do so. A hundred men, however, were needed to guard the camp. No persuasions could induce them to volunteer to remain; so at last Gen. Wild was obliged to detail the required number for this duty. Did any one ever think that the men who had been accustomed to hunt runaway slaves in the swamps of the South would now be hiding there themselves, be hunted by them? Mysterious are thy ways, Oh, Lord!

When the rebellion first broke out a great many people thought "now the slaves will make a grand rush for the Northern side." They had prayed so long for liberty. Here it was, right in their hand; but the slaves didn't do any such thing. Remaining quiet, and looking about to see how things on both sides were moving, was the very means that saved them. How were they to contend with their masters? They had no arms, nothing to fight with; their masters had been collecting implements of war for some time and the slaves knew it; knew where they were hid; knew all the lines of fortification which they had been compelled to construct. Ah, the slaves were too wise to run any risk, with nothing but hoes in their hands. They said nothing, saw every thing, and at the right time they would give the Union valuable information. The Rebels lost their cause, and why? Because the slaves were loyal to the government. If they had been disloyal, the Confederates would no doubt have won, or else some foreign power might have intervened and made trouble. As it is, the Rebs. owe an old grudge to the freedman, as much as to say: "Its your fault we didn't win."

HEROISM OF A CONTRABAND.

It was just after the victory of the Excelsior Brigade at Fair Oaks, when Gen. Sickels received word that the enemy were advancing. Orders for preparation for battle were given. At last all was in readiness for the advance; but only a few shots were to be heard in the distance, otherwise every thing was quiet. What did it mean? The General asked Lieutenant Palmer to take a squad of men with him and ride cautiously to the first bend in the road, but he, too impetuous, rushed daringly ahead till he was within range of the enemy. He fell, pierced with bullets. His soldiers hastily retreated to their camp and told their news. Among the listeners was a negro servant of Lieut. Palmer, who quietly withdrew and walked down that road—that road of death—for after passing our picket guard he was openly exposed to the Rebel sharpshooters. When our soldiers came up, the faithful servant was found by the side of his dead master. I regret that the name of this heroic soul remains unknown to the world—a name worthy to be emblazoned on the pages of history.

We used often to hear the question asked, can the negro take care of himself? If he is set free, to rely on his own resources, will he not die of starvation? Let us see. At Pine Bluffs there was a full black, known as Uncle Reuben. He was born in Georgia, and displayed such energy, tact, and devotion to his master's interest that he was left in full charge of every thing on the plantation. The slave raised his master from poverty to wealth. At last his master died, and his widow depended still more upon Uncle Reuben, placing all in his hands. He became more ambitious, and succeeded so well that the number of cotton bales increased every year. The children were sent North to school. The white overseers became jealous of him, and compelled his mistress to place a white, nominally, over him. However, he was not interfered with and his mistress treated him as kindly as she dared. Then the sons returned from the North, with no feelings of gratitude to one who by his industry and prudence had educated them, and amassed a fortune of one hundred and fifty thousand dollars. Thank God, he lived to see freedom's light, and after being assured that the Proclamation was a fact, he came over to us.

A REMINISCENCE OF 1863.

Probably no act—the Ku Klux system excepted—was more distressing than the ever to-be-remembered riot which occurred in New York city during the year of 1863. (The mob spirit first manifested itself at a meeting held in Boston, December 3d, 1860, in observance of the anniversary of the death of John Brown.) I can but look back and shudder at that great carnival of blood. The mob commenced on the 10th of July, and continued day and night for more than a week. My heart aches when memory recalls that awful day, when the whole city was in a state of insurrection. The full force of the infuriated mob fell upon the black man, the harmless, unpretending black man, whose only crime was that his skin was of a darker hue than his white brethren; that he came of a race which for more than two hundred years has felt the sting of slavery in its very soul. I know of no race that has undergone more sufferings than the black race in America.

Brought here from our mother country, we have bedewed the soil with our blood and tears. Unlike the Indian, we leave vengeance to the Lord. "He will repay." In this riot hundreds of colored people were driven from their homes, hunted and chased through the streets like wild beasts. A sweet babe was brained while holding up his little arms, and smiling upon his murderers. Many little children were killed in this manner. Strong men were dragged from their homes and left dangling from some lamp post or tree, or else slaughtered on the streets—their blood flowing in streams down the pavements. Able-bodied men, whose mangled bodies hung up to lamp posts, were in a great many instances burned to cinders. The colored people were panic stricken and sought shelter in out-of-the-way nooks and places; but even then some were discovered by the mob on their way to a retreat and quickly dispatched; hundreds flocked to the doors of police stations, prisons and jails, and begged admittance. No colored man, woman or child was spared if found. As a general thing, colored tenants occupy whole streets, so the mob knew pretty well what localities to plunder. Pistol shots were fired through the windows, murdering many at their homes and by their firesides. This accounts for the great loss of life, greater than if the people lived more scattered. The police were not able to cope with the murderers, though it is believed they did what they could, going in companies of two or three hundred to such parts of the city as needed their protection most. A most heartless transaction committed by these fiends, was the destruction of the colored Orphan Asylum, after first robbing the little children of their clothing. These helpless lambs were driven friendless upon the world from the burning Asylum, which had been their abode. The mob went on at a terrible rate.

My family were quietly seated at the table one bright July morning when we were startled by the sudden ringing of the door bell. Upon responding, we found that a family with whom we were well acquainted had succeeded in escaping from the city, and sought refuge in our quiet suburb until quietness and peace should reign, so as to enable them to return to their own home. Oh! ye people of the North, before you censure too strongly the actions of the South, rid your own soil of that fiendish element which makes it an opprobrium to call America "the land of the free and the home of the brave."

SHERMAN'S MARCH THROUGH GEORGIA.

During Sherman's march from Atlanta to Savannah, many thousands of slaves came into the ranks, all of whom appeared overjoyed that "de Yanks. had come." It would often happen that he would encamp on the plantations that planters had deserted. Here would be found an abundance of good things of this life, of which the soldiers would readily partake. At one place only the old, decrepit slaves were left. These were half naked, and nearly starved; they had been told frightful stories about the cruelties of the Yankee soldiers, and were as frightened as could be when the army arrived. Upon being reassured that no harm would be done them, they were overwhelming in their thanks to Gen. Sherman for clothing and feeding them.

And thus it was; all along the march the most pathetic scenes would occur. Thousands of women, carrying household goods, some with children in their arms, all anxious to join the column. When refused, some most heart-rending scenes would take place; such begging to be allowed to go on to Savannah, where, says one: "My chillens done been sold dese four years;" or to Macon to "see my boy." Gen. Sherman, with great tact, succeeded in quieting them, telling them they would return for them some day and they must be patient. An aged couple had been waiting sixty years for deliverance. No one to see them at work on the plantation would suppose that they were anything but satisfied with their condition. No murmur, no words of discontent ever passed their lips; they made no comments on the actions of runaway slaves; their master had no fears for them; yet, could he have seen the face of the woman when she heard that the Yankees had come, he would have seen that he had not read her heart aright. Such an expression as her countenance assumed was terrible to behold. "Bress de Lord," she exclaimed, "I expects to follow them till I drop in my tracks." As her husband did not see the situation of things as quickly as she did, she angrily said: "What are you sitting dar fur, don't yer see de door open? I'se not waited sixty years for nuttin'." It is said that no persuasions would prevail upon her to remain where she had suffered so much, and old as she was she would follow the army. This is only one of the many hundred cases which constantly occurred during the war. This poorly enlightened people all seemed to think that the Yankees would come some time or other, and that their freedom was the object of the war. This notion, I suppose, they got from hearing their masters talk.

The Rebel leaders had their attention completely absorbed by the vast preparations they were making for carrying on the war, by the increasing of State debts, etc. The question of arming the slaves, which had been warmly debated at Richmond, was overlooked. The governors of the several Southern States had also pondered this question as the only means to save the Confederacy, which under its various reverses, was slowly but surely dying. The South knew it could not hold out much longer. An intelligent mulatto in Macon, Ga., who used to attend his master's store would often make mention of such conversation as he overheard between his master and some of the first men of the city. They used to get together in the counting-room and say: "It was no use to fight the North any longer; the South would surely be whipped in the end, and the best thing that could be done, would be to fix up the old Union." When asked if these men talked so on the public street, he replied: "No sir," these very men would go out on the street and talk wild about "whipping the Yankees, the South never giving up, and a lot of other trash." It is said that the Rebels so frightened their slaves, telling them stories of the cruelties which would be practiced upon them if ever they put themselves in the power of the Yankees that the most ignorant knew scarcely which way to turn, when the question of arming the slaves was discussed. There was nothing said by the South about the reward for their services. It rather looked upon them in the same light as when they worked in the field; neither was it prepared to meet the various objections raised by the white soldiers, if compelled to fight with them, side by side. So, as all parties could not be satisfied, the matter was allowed to drop, though I have no doubt but that to save herself, a few would have been willing to have increased their forces, by accepting the assistance of the slave.

CHAPTER XII.

THE EXODUS.

Arrival of negroes in Washington—Hospitality of Washington people—Suffering and privation—Education of the freedmen—Causes of emigration—Cruelty at the South—Prejudice at the North—Hopes for the future.

THE Rebellion at length closed after a bloody carnage of about four years. The manacles of the slave had been burst asunder. Left in abject poverty, he is suddenly thrown upon his own resources for support. In many instances the ex-slave-holder employed his former slaves on his plantation, paying them certain wages; others hired their own ground, and being perfectly familiar with the raising of cotton, sugar, corn and other grain, succeeded in making quite a comfortable living and having something laid by "for a rainy day." But this was not to last long. The peace of the quiet villages and towns was soon disturbed by night-raiders. Law-abiding citizens were torn from their beds at midnight, hung, robbed and flogged. This was not alone confined to black men, but white men also suffered. The cruelties inflicted upon both races during this "reign of terror" are almost indescribable.

This, together with the unjust treatment by the planters in relation to paying wages, renting land, etc., forms the cause of the exodus. We read accounts of where hundreds are leaving their native soil and beginning life anew in another clime. Whether they will be able to withstand the rigorous winters of the West remains to be seen. Already many have perished from exhaustion and cold, not being sufficiently clad, and being wholly without means to procure articles necessary to their comfort. Yet when we look back and see the wrongs heaped upon a poor, down-trodden race we can not but cry: "On with the Exodus!"

I had read of hundreds of freedmen leaving their homes and starting for the West, but I never expected to be an eye witness of such a scene. In December, 1879, while visiting Washington, preparatory to going further South, there arrived at the depot from two to three hundred freed people, among which were a number of children. It seems their money gave out as they reached Washington, and here they must remain until means could be obtained to send them further on. Here they were strangers; no where to go, near the edge of evening, yet no where to lay their heads. At this crisis the Rev. Mr. Draper hearing of their situation kindly offered them his church, (St. Paul, 8th St., South Washington), till other arrangements could be made. Here they were made as comfortable as possible, and seemed pleased that they were under shelter. I was told that quite a number had gone on some weeks before, and that they were mostly men. This last party had a majority of women, many of them going on to meet their husbands. The people of Washington were very kind to the strangers, giving them food and clothing in abundance. On the Sunday following their arrival, the pavements were blockaded for squares, all anxious to get a peep at them. The church was not a large one, so to prevent confusion, visitors were requested to pass in one door and out of the other.

Within, a novel sight presented itself; the gallery in the rear of the church had the appearance of a nursery. Children, from a two months' babe upwards, were lying here and there upon the benches, or under them fast asleep. Others were busily engaged in satisfying the inner man. The day I was present there was a reporter gathering scraps of information for his paper. It was really interesting to hear some of them converse. Many appeared to be quite intelligent; says one: "Do you suppose I'd leave my little home, which I owned, and go to a place I know nothing of unless I was compelled to. 'Taint natur. We heard dey killed a man the day we left, dey was so mad, and in some places dey tore up de track to keep us from leaving." Says the reporter: "Suppose you get to Indiana and you find no work there?" Answered: "Den I keeps going till I finds it." They all seemed willing to work if they could only find it to do.

Visitors, as they passed around, on coming to the altar found two small baskets into which they could drop as much money as they felt disposed. This was to assist in defraying the expenses the rest of the journey. As often as a certain amount was made up, they would send away so many at a time.

There was among the company a white woman, whom at first I took to be a leader, as she seemed so energetic, going out and begging proper clothing for the most destitute, distributing food, among them, etc. But upon conversing with her I found I was mistaken. She assured me she was as much a part of the "Exodus," as the rest. That she received no better treatment at her home than the rest did, and she was glad to get away. Some of the prominent lady members of St. Paul's Chapel were most kind in their attentions to the wanderers, leaving their own duties at home to spend days in administering to their comfort; and often were the expressions, "God bless you, de Lord will pay you back, honey," heard on all sides. I did not have an opportunity to see them but once, for when I went again I found they had gone; and it is hoped they have all found good, comfortable homes, in that land towards which their hearts had turned with so much faith and hope.

TERRIBLE SUFFERING OF THE FREEDMEN AT WASHINGTON.

A host of miserable women with children, besides old, crippled and sick persons were driven out of Maryland and sought refuge here. Those who were able to work went out by the day to earn money with which to pay a rent of from five to six dollars for some old shanty, garret, cellar or stable. Hundreds of old persons and children were without shoes and stockings, and were badly frost-bitten. Infants, only a few days old, without a garment, perished with cold. Very few of the older persons had any under-garments, for they came from Maryland and Virginia clothed in rags; very few had comfortable beds and household utensils. The children died off rapidly. During the hot weather the quartermaster's department furnished about eighty coffins per week, mostly for children. "In slavery," the mothers say, "our children never dies; it 'pears like they all dies here." One family lost five out of ten children; another, three out of seven. Sleeping on the shanty and stable floors during the winter brought on colds and pulmonary diseases which terminated the lives of hundreds. The ladies of the District were indefatigable in their efforts to relieve them. Those in Springfield, Mass., kindly solicited aid for these distressed people, gathering clothing of every kind, and were quite successful in sending something to their afflicted brethren.

EDUCATING THE FREEDMEN.

This is a matter which absorbed the minds of the North: whether the negro would learn, and eagerly improve the facilities opened to him through his liberation. Almost immediately after the close of the war barracks used by the soldiers were turned into schoolhouses, and it was no rare sight to see a number of these freedmen crowded into them, over whom presided some noble-hearted lady engaged in her duties as school-marm. Would they learn? Let the record of the last fourteen or fifteen years testify.

I can not let this opportunity pass without paying a tribute of respect to the memory of Miss Stebbins, who died while devoting her life to this cause. When I last saw her she was in Washington, D. C., at the barracks on the corner of Seventh and O Streets. She lived in one portion of the building, and, although school hours were over, she was instructing two bright, interesting girls in the mysteries of the alphabet. In one corner of the room were boxes of clothing which she distributed among the most needy of her pupils, that they might look presentable day after day. Not only children, but adults attended school, and it was not unusual to see a father and son, a mother and daughter in the same class, eager and anxious to learn. Says one teacher, who kept a night school for the benefit of those who were not able, on account of their work, to attend during the day: "I had a boy present himself as wishing to become a member of the school. After examining him, I found he was pretty well up in all the first principles of arithmetic, except long division; of this he knew nothing. I was astonished to find, after going over a few examples, explaining carefully as I went along, that when the pencil was put in his hand he worked as well as I could." From that night he had no more trouble with long division. That boy was afterwards a hard student at Howard University, and learned to read Latin with ease.

What nation, after years of servitude, has made such rapid strides of improvement? All over the South we find schools with efficient teachers, many of whom were formerly pupils, now going over the same ground others had taken them. The barracks have given way to school buildings of the most modern design. The school are all graded, the scholars advancing step by step till they reach the topmost round. Perhaps no better examples can be furnished than the District of Columbia, where the school system is fixed upon a firmer and better basis than elsewhere.

THE BEGINNING OF THE END.

The emigration of my people from the Southern States has engaged my attention for some time. In Heathsville, Va., the place of my birth, the colored people are not treated with such severity as in the States further South, for in Heathsville, they have more privileges than they have in Western Virginia. I think the cause of this great emigration is owing to the fact of ill treatment, equal almost to slavery; because of cruelties heaped upon them in the South, and because of the hopelessness of obtaining an education for their children. It was the burden of their complaint; their political rights had been denied them, and every possible advantage had been taken from them, and feeling aggrieved they had looked around for relief, and the only solace offered was to emigrate. In some parts of the South our people labor without hardly wages enough to get them food, which places many of them in a starving condition, and without sufficient clothing. Twenty-five cents a day is considered great wages, taking part corn for pay. My heart has been drawn out for them in sympathy, knowing myself what is was to want, even in Virginia, a meal of victuals.

The emigrants adopted a plan of action to appeal to President Hayes, for him to enforce the laws to protect their rights. Then they appealed to Congress to set apart a territory, or aid them to emigrate to Liberia. Our people lost all hope of bettering their condition at that time. In 1877 they petitioned Congress and President Hayes. Not hearing from this petition, the colored emigrants became exasperated, saying, "let us go any where in God's world to get away from these men who once enslaved us." Many of the white republicans of the South are treated not much better than the colored people, because they are republicans. Since they have emigrated many children, fathers and mothers have died from starvation and exposure, for they were without shelter and nothing to wear, lying on the cold ground, exposed to the winter blasts with only the sky for a covering.

The number of those who poured in upon the State of Kansas, early in the spring of 1879, is known to have been four or five thousand. Steadily has been the flow of the small stream which attracted so little attention and by the opening of the spring of 1880 over ten thousand arrived, and probably since the spring of 1880 twice the number have emigrated. I think that something must be the cause for their great emigration more than common, for my people are a home-like people; they would never leave the Southern soil if properly treated, or had wages enough to make them comfortable; as a general thing they are home-loving and law abiding citizens. While living South they felt they had "no rights that the white man was bound to respect."

All praise is due to Mrs. Comstock, for her self-denying philanthropy exhibited towards my people, for they must have suffered more had it not been for her endeavors, in writing all over the United States to our most prominent citizens for help to relieve their sufferings. The people in many places have responded to her call. Here, in Norwich, the ladies have come up to the work as they always do where assistance is needed among my people. God bless them for what they have done; hoping that they will think of them in the future, as they are still leaving their land of slavery, as they expect the freedom which they have fought for and hoped for. In their going away their places can not be filled, for they were the bone and sinew of the South.

While I write, there are fifty thousand pounds of clothing, sent on in 1879 from England, held at the New York Custom House for duty to be paid on them. They were sent for my people in Kansas. It is wicked to deprive these poor, suffering people of comfortable clothing while so many are dying for the want of it. I trust that the hearts of the people everywhere will be so softened towards my injured people that they will be induced to send them on, even if obliged to pay the duty on them, and not wait for Congress to decide. Shall this people die, who have stood by us in sunshine and storm? Shall we let them suffer for the want of bread, for the want of corn, for the want of clothing? God forbid it! As they stood by the flag once, they stand by it still, because it bespeaks freedom to them and their posterity.

When the Rebel army was five miles from the Capital, and the skirmishers were three miles from Georgetown, when it was conjectured that the assault would take place the next morning, it was then our colored soldiers met the waves of conflict; it was then the bone and sinews of the South saved the Capital of the United States. Aye; my soul listens already to the glad prelude of the song of triumph, welling up from myriads of hearts, and swelling into a paean that fills the vast concave of heaven itself with the deep-toned melodies of an universal jubilee: "Washington is saved!" Then our colored soldiers came up to its rescue, which contradicts the saying, that colored men will not fight. Well did they do their duty, and proved their manhood at Fort Wagner, Fort Moultrie, Petersburg, Milliken's Bend, Fort Fisher, and other places, while their families were left starving at home. We all know that these things are so, although they are not recorded in history with other events of the war.

We hope the time will come when our children, attending white seminaries of learning, may receive medals the same as white students. In Connecticut, and elsewhere, prizes and medals have been, and are withheld from our most brilliant scholars of color. In one of our Eastern colleges a colored student was robbed of his essay, and had recourse to a law-suit to have justice done him; but was obliged to write another, and received the prize at his graduation, after the law-suit was ended. He was obliged to go another year in order to accomplish it. The wrongs of this system will go up before the Throne of Infinite Justice.

The United States ought to be strong enough in intellect, in moral sensibility and Christian feeling, to conquer her prejudices. Until she does, the poet's tribute to "Columbia" as "the land of the free and home of the brave," will be a satire that shall provoke a reproachful smile—attesting her fidelity to justice and liberty, God and man.

The leading question of to-day is, why do the colored people emigrate? Almost every day and week during the spring of 1880, it was discussed among the senators and representatives in Congress, the argument having taken up most of the time; the question also created quite a discussion in 1879; the Southern senators, who were the majority in the Senate, were loath to drop the question.

In conclusion, I must say that the more I contemplate the condition of my people the more I am convinced that this is only the beginning of the end; but the end is not yet.